THE
REST
OF THE
[TRUE CRIME]
STORY

A Critical Look at Canada's Criminal

and Correctional Systems

JOHN L. HILL

Foreword by Justin Ling

Author of Missing from the Village

With contributions by David Dorson and Michael Crowley

AOS Publishing, 2024

Copyright © 2024

John Lorne Hill

ISBN: 978-1-990496-38-7

Cover Design: Phoenix Slater

Visit AOS Publishing's website:

www.aospublishing.com

This book is dedicated to those who strive to make our prisons more humane: such groups as The John Howard Society, The Elizabeth Fry Society and the Canadian Prison Lawyers Association. Appreciation also goes out to the volunteer lawyers and staff at Innocence Canada who fight to correct the mistakes the system sometimes makes.

CONTENTS

FOREWORD

Justin Ling

The public knows far too little about what goes on in our prisons.

That is both by choice and design.

The average Canadian can only hope that our carceral system is doing what it is meant to do — sequestering those who present a threat to the public, at a minimum; and, ideally, rehabilitating any inmates it can. Governments have done all they can to assure the public that the system is running smoothly. Some governments have even gone so far as to tell their constituents that the system is working a little *too* well.

All the while, the machine runs in secret.

This book is a collection of stories that pull back the curtain and expose the machine for what it really is: An engine that runs on human suffering. Our prison system is simultaneously under-resourced and unbelievably expensive. It is full of people with intense mental health problems and offers virtually no support for them. It is filled with Black and Indigenous people, the by-product of a long and miserable series of failures and racist policies. It is a place for us to stick the people we don't want to think about: Just far enough away, into the shadows, so we may delude ourselves into thinking that all is well.

We can't begin to address these problems until we understand just how much the system fails the people we put into it.

From its very inception, our justice system is maladapted for the job we want it to do. It is built around the supposition that prison would be such a daunting prospect that would-be criminals would abide by the law to avoid this horrible fate. We know that this concept of deterrence is bunk. We've known it for a long time.

A 1999 review of 50 studies, covering 300,000 offenders, could not find a single bit of research that established a firm connection between imprisonment and a reduction in recidivism. In fact, longer sentences correlated to a higher rate of re-offending. The Canadian government knows this: They conducted the review.[1] Two decades on, a review published in the journal Crime and Justice, looking at another 116 studies, came to the exact same conclusion.[2]

These realities aren't talked about, of course. The government can't well admit that the very foundation of its criminal justice

---

[1] Gendreau, P. Goggin, C., & Cullen, F. T. (1999). The Effects of Prison Sentences on Recidivism. Ottawa: Solicitor General Canada.

[2] Petrich, Damon & Pratt, Travis & Jonson, Cheryl & Cullen, Francis. (2021). Custodial Sanctions and Reoffending: A Meta-Analytic Review. Crime and Justice. 50. 10.1086/715100.

system doesn't work, because we would ask them to fix it. The opposition parties, meanwhile, can't win votes promising to incarcerate fewer people. Indeed, if election campaigns touch the issue of criminal justice, it is often a race to the bottom to see which candidate can promise to lock up more people.

So we all operate on the mythical physics that powers the machine.

As Canadians, of course, we pride ourselves on being better than the eye-for-an-eye philosophy which governs justice south of the border. Successive governments like to feed that smug belief — Liberals, with constant promises to add more programming and supports; Conservatives, with a refrain that our prisons have become too cushy and coddling.

In reality, our institutions are places of mind-numbing boredom, where inmates couldn't substantially improve themselves if they wanted to.

Inmates receive schooling that amounts to a GED, at best. They have no access to the internet. Their libraries are outdated, ill-stocked, and understaffed. Their three meals are disgusting, salty, schlop. The costs at the commissary are nothing short of gouging, while further taxes on their stay amount to extortion. Healthcare, including mental health support, is woefully lacking or missing entirely. Work programs are more akin to slave labour than productive on-the-job experience. The environment is so rife with violence, sexual assault, and drug trafficking that should any innocent person find themselves incarcerated, they are liable to walk out as a well-trained criminal.

To some, all of these problems are features, not bugs. It is, to some degree, a defensible position. After all, most people still labour under the misconception that prisons serve a deterrent effect. The more prisons can elicit fear, the myth goes, the less likely someone is to risk going there — or, at least, to risk going back. Some, a minority, don't care: The punishment becomes an end unto itself.

After all, inmates are criminals. (Except for the few rare cases of the wrongfully convicted, of course.) If they didn't want to do the time, they should not have done the crime. We can slay the myths of deterrence and rehabilitation, but a head of the hydra remains: Punishment.

We can only understand how truly wrong-headed it is to operate a multi-billion-dollar state-run punishment machine if we start to look at whom we're punishing.

The populations of these prisons are reflective of our collective failures. There are people with severe mental health issues who are incarcerated because we were unwilling or unable to provide basic support to help them manage their illness. There are poor people who believed, rightly or wrongly, that their only way to economic independence was through crime. There are Black and Indigenous people, wildly over-represented in the prison system, who are a testament to the systemic racism and colonialism that has defined Canada as a nation to this point.

Yes, there are hardened criminals, gang leaders, serial killers, and psychopaths. I should know: I've covered their crimes, sat in on their trials, and talked to them from prison. But there are also people who made mistakes, young men who never received the mental health care they desperately need, women who struck back against abusive husbands, and people who truly want to do better. And then there is, of course, the 25% of federal offenders who are serving time for non-violent crimes.

Even for the most earnest and sympathetic inmate, some degree of punishment may still be warranted. But just how far should we go? We pride ourselves, as Canadians, in a belief that human rights abuses cannot be justified in the name of any policy objective — and certainly not in the name of retribution. We abolished the death penalty and corporal punishment in our prisons, and we were proud of ourselves for doing so. Unfortunately, some of that legacy remains.

Ottawa, for example, got away with a prolonged program of systemic torture by rebranding the unconstitutional practice of solitary confinement as "administrative segregation." After years of litigation, as the Supreme Court of Canada admonished the federal government for lying to cover up these abuses, the government pivoted once more: Today, inmates are locked in a windowless cell for all but a few hours a day in "structured intervention units." Sometimes as punishment, other times for their own protection, because they fell sick, or because they are severely mentally ill. Warnings from watchdogs that this practice — much like solitary confinement — could pose massive mental health risks to inmates have been ignored. Those inmates return, eventually, to general population even more maladjusted than when they went in.

That's not all, of course. The Office of the Correctional Investigator has repeatedly warned about a systemic use of force problem. Inmate-on-inmate violence is endemic. Self-harm is a constant problem.

Of course, not everyone does poorly. Well-affiliated gang members smuggle drugs and run criminal fiefdoms from inside their prison cells. Some incoming inmates affiliate for self-protection, perpetuating organized crime's stranglehold on these institutions. Sometimes the underpaid, overworked, under-appreciated, poorly-trained corrections officers are in on it.

So prisons do not deter, they do not rehabilitate, and their punishment can be totally decoupled from the crime. Even if we accept that segregating these people from society, the rule of law tells us that we must release nearly every offender eventually. Some, sooner than others. Survey the pervasive rot that afflicts this machine and it's clear that few people are walking out of a Canadian prison better off than when they walked in.

The government keeps these realities from the public because admitting any of this would reveal just how badly government after government has allowed things to get. And it would mean capitulation in a slew of lawsuits and constitutional challenges that could make the government liable for hundreds of millions of dollars of damages if not billions.

And it would require admitting to the public that Correctional Services Canada receives convicted individuals and sticks them in a violent, chaotic environment with no meaningful room for self-improvement, subjects them to malnourishment, and then tortures them for virtually any reason.

Then, in nearly every case, we throw them back into the community.

This machine may be broken, but it delivers predictable results. Look closely, and there's no justification for this. The best defence Correctional Services Canada and the federal government can mount is that they are doing their best given the crisis they face. In effect, this is an institution passing the buck onto someone else — the corrections system, onto communities and local police; and governments, onto their successors.

Much in the same way we warehouse the people we don't want to deal with in the darkness, we keep in the darkness the entire issue of our prison system. We would rather believe that the machine is running smoothly.

Some have worked diligently to try and wake us up to these problems. A lineage of occupants of the role of Correctional Investigator, and their staff, have tried to hold Correctional

Services Canada to account. Senator Kim Pate has worked throughout her entire career to call attention to these issues and demand better. Groups like the John Howard Society and the Elizabeth Fry Societies have done the tough advocacy work that few others do. Legal outlets like the B.C. Civil Liberties Association, the Canadian Civil Liberties Association, and Prisoners' Legal Services are making a real difference by exposing governments' individual and systemic failures. Journalists have done their best to tell the stories of what really happens in all of these institutions.

But every single one of these earnest efforts is frustrated by the systemic secrecy imposed by Correctional Services Canada. I learned this firsthand during the COVID-19 pandemic. I had given my phone number to a few lawyers and told them to hand it to any inmate facing difficulties because of the virus. My phone wouldn't stop ringing for months. Inmates rarely have the opportunity, or permission, to reach anyone in the outside world beyond their friends, family, and lawyer (if they even have one.) As one inmate passed my number onto the next, the floodgates burst open.

Correctional Services didn't like that. Inmates have lost their phone privileges for daring to speak with reporters. Others have been threatened by guards to keep their mouths shut.

But it was those stories that revealed the injustice and dysfunction taking place behind closed doors. And the stories in this book can help do the same.

Because, despite how desperately broken things may seem, they are not hopeless. We can do better. We can improve public safety, save money, keep corrections officers safe, and help those inmates get better instead of worse. We could run a corrections system that we are proud enough to show off.

Those solutions have been written about in great length, but they are not terribly complicated.

We need to incarcerate fewer people and operate fewer prisons. Thousands of non-violent criminals can be released to community supervision, parole, or conditional release without much of a threat to public safety. Convicts with severe mental health issues should be sent to dedicated facilities designed to provide treatment first and foremost. A smaller, more manageable, prison population should be given real-world, marketable skills training and productive things to do that would encourage social behaviour. Maximum-security facilities can, and should, be operated to isolate truly violent and dangerous offenders, but lower-security facilities should be geared toward preparing inmates for re-entry into society. Prisons do not need to be pleasant, but they should be rational.

None of this is a magic solution. Prisons will never end crime: We aren't even sure if they can reduce it. But we should constantly be striving to, at the very least, reduce harm.

As you read the stories contained in this book, think about how a more sensible, functional, purposeful corrections system could have changed things. A system that didn't weaponize boredom as a punishment. A corrections officer who opted for compassion over vindictiveness. A judge who investigated why the same offenders keep appearing before the court.

We have made more radical changes in the past. However bad our regime is today, it was once worse. Revolutions in our understanding of mental health, human behaviour, and human rights have fundamentally changed corrections for the better. We have, unfortunately, become complacent. There is more work to do, and it's time we get to it.

Justin Ling is an award-winning investigative journalist who specializes in stories that are under-reported or misunderstood. He is the author of Missing from the Village: The Story of Serial Killer Bruce McArthur, the Search for Justice, and the System That Failed Toronto's Queer Community.

PREFACE

There is a quotation often attributed to Andy Warhol, "In the future, everyone will be world-famous for fifteen minutes." We have all read about horrendous acts of violence and perhaps followed court cases where the perpetrators are tried and convicted. Then our attention moves on. These criminals in a metaphorical sense had their fifteen minutes of fame, or more accurately, their fifteen minutes of shame. The next news cycle has new atrocities to stir our outrage. Yet a person's life comprises more than fifteen minutes. Sometimes what these infamous people experience after their names are dropped from the headlines is as stirring as the crimes reported. The aim of this book is to look at several individuals who shocked their communities for a brief time and then faded from public view.

Let's face it; sometimes we don't really want to know how the sausages are made or just don't have the time to research it to find out what could be easily discovered. It's easier just to continue to believe in a world we imagine and not in a world where we have to confront our own misconceptions.

For the bulk of my career, I practiced criminal and prison law. I was astounded by how much misinformation the public sees as truth. Why do people become involved in crime? How are they treated once they are convicted? Are there mechanisms allowing us to learn from people who die untimely deaths while incarcerated? Part of the problem in discovering how our criminal and correctional systems work is that our focus is concentrated on the publicity surrounding high-profile crimes. Often, the immediate attention that the media attracts is short-lived leaving the rest of the story untold.

I have worked for decades in the criminal and prison law field. I have dealt with some of Canada's most notorious criminals. When I began my legal practice, I accepted the general notion that our system operates effectively and efficiently. Over the years, I have found that this is not always the case. Indeed, there is almost a predisposition to manufacture myths that explain away the incongruities we see cropping up in our criminal courts and prisons. This book is an anthology of stories about how easy it is to create myths unless we understand the whole truth and nothing but the truth.

I see so many people who are eager to believe there is a simple solution for why crime occurs. One of the most virulent myths is that criminals suffer from mental illness. We see this explanation when we turn on our televisions and hear a newscast about another mass shooting in which far too many innocent victims are murdered. "The shooter must be mentally ill," we often hear as though there was a simple explanation for the causes of crime. Such an explanation, besides being facile, does a disservice to people who truly suffer from one of many forms of mental illness and who are anything but dangerous to others. Furthermore, the stigma attached to this explanation for crime prevents us from looking further to find that the root cause of societal disruption (which is the essence of crime) is not always the mental state of the shooter but of laws that enabled the slaughter to occur in the first place.

On the other hand, we often hear it said that we do not do enough to alleviate the pain and anxiety experienced by victims of crime. Rather than having victims' rights groups lobby for enhanced compensation for individuals and families that have been victimized, we hear a call for tougher penalties. Of course, the unstated premise that tougher penalties will deter crime rests on the acceptance of the notion that people consider what will happen if they get caught. Lawyers and judges refer to granting harsher sentences on this basis as "general deterrence."

General deterrence is a myth, albeit one that is often exploited by our courts in handing down excessive sentences. I have found that premeditation of the penalty associated with an illegal act seldom arises at or before the instant in which the crime is committed.

A reliance on general deterrence also assumes that it is somehow magically ordained that when one takes on the position of a judge, that person is imbued with the ability to ascertain what period of incarceration is needed to reform the person convicted of a crime. In some jurisdictions, there are "sentencing guidelines" to assist a judge in determining what sentence is considered appropriate while other jurisdictions have enacted minimum sentence laws. My experience tells me that these are simply myths to persuade an unthinking public that justice is being done. Every individual is different. Some convicted criminals can be rehabilitated simply by having to endure the criminal law process and will never again involve themselves in criminal activity. Other individuals can never be rehabilitated. Imprisonment for these people keeps them from interacting with society (other than those working inside or confined within our prisons). Yet our laws also provide us with a system wherein experienced professionals working with inmates become adept at understanding when a prisoner is or is not "street ready." As well, parole board members become highly qualified to assess when an individual is a manageable risk in society and what conditions need to be in place to ensure public safety is ensured to the maximum degree possible.

Our justice system also requires that we not become complacent in the enforcement of our laws. A Toronto man's conviction for impaired driving was recently stayed when the court found that the legal requirements of processing were not completed in a timely manner. The man spent excessive hours in custody before determining if he should be granted bail. Such events happen when police and others required to carry out the law become complacent. Yet we can expect victims' rights groups to protest that the law is being perverted so that a drunk driver can walk free while untold victims of impaired drivers are left to suffer.

No one can discount the agony experienced by those who are left behind in the wake of criminal activity. Yet to demand that our laws be altered to appease those demanding harsh treatment be satisfied is a call for laws equivalent to vigilante treatment.

My hope is that the reader will ask how our treatment of what society would acknowledge as our undesirables are treated. What myths are being exploited to justify unusual situations where justice suffers so that society, as we want it to be, can rest in comfort?

Besides the stories of criminals with whom I have dealt directly, I have included a chapter written by a man calling himself David Dorson. Unlike many growing up in poverty, Dorson was a business executive who late in life found himself in violation of the law and was sentenced to imprisonment. He can tell us what it is like to suddenly go from an executive office to a barred cubicle. There is also a chapter written by Michael Crowley. Now retired, Crowley served for over two decades as a senior member of Canada's parole board. Yet he has experienced arrest and separation from family and friends under different circumstances. How has his life experience transformed the way he did his job in our correctional system?

This is not a treatise arguing that our legal system is a farce. In fact, it is just the opposite. It is a call to reform our institutions so that real justice can prevail. If you are with me in this fight, let's work for a system that respects the Rule of Law. What we want is public safety, effective policing, and humane treatment for those who are convicted. Rather than focusing on the evils involved in a criminal act and not looking at what happens once the deed is out of the spotlight, let's look at specific examples of crimes. Instead of looking just at the horrors involved in their commission, let's look at what led up to a crime's commission and what happened after conviction. It's our way of getting the rest of the story.

John L. Hill

CHAPTER 1

READY FOR PRIME TIME

Selva Subbiah: Canada's Most Notorious Rapist

> *They're gonna put me in the movies*
> *They're gonna make a big star out of me*
> *Writers: Johnny Russell, Vonnie Morrison*
> *Performer: Buck Owens, Act Naturally*

Mara [1] had just arrived in the big city eager to shed her rural insecurities and to live life to the fullest. It was the fall of 1990. She was twenty-four, full of self-confidence and open to trying any new challenge that came her way. Mara wasn't looking forward to cooler fall and winter weather. Last summer, she had her picture taken while spending a leisurely Saturday on a sandy beach on the shores of Lake Ontario. The picture was published in one of Toronto's daily newspapers. She had friends call her up remarking that she looked very beautiful in her swimwear.

---

[1] Not her real name

The most intriguing call had been left as a voicemail while she was at work. The call was from the Wild Talent Agency on Keele Street. She was asked to call Richard Wild, the owner of the agency directly to set up a time to meet. Mara was thrilled. A talent agency! Visions of modelling and maybe even appearing on TV excited her as she fantasized about what might ensue after the meeting.

She made the call. She spoke with Richard Wild directly. He sounded charming on the call. Did she detect a British accent? Even though Wild mentioned his agency, he said he, himself, had been in Toronto sporadically over the summer. He was, at the time of the phone call, busy working on the set of a movie being shot in Toronto and the surrounding area. Nonetheless, Richard was keen on meeting Mara as soon as possible.

Mara and Richard checked their respective diaries while on the phone and it was agreed to schedule an interview at a coffee shop close to where Mara lived two days hence. Mara couldn't wait. Was this the opportunity of a lifetime?

Finally, the day arrived. Mara was a few minutes early. She looked around to see if Richard had arrived. He hadn't. She took a seat at a table and ordered a coffee. It was only a few minutes after the scheduled arrival time when Richard showed up. Mara was the only young woman seated. Richard looked her way, smiled, and gave her a wave, silently indicating that he would join her once he had ordered a coffee as well.

Mara, for the first time, felt some disappointment. Richard wasn't the tall, dark, handsome man she had assumed from speaking with him. Instead, he was average, even short, in height. He was casually dressed with a dark blue windbreaker, but not wearing the suit and tie that Mara expected of a senior executive. Once he placed his coffee on the table, Richard sat down. The two re-introduced themselves. They exchanged some small talk, all the while Mara's desire to talk business raged in her mind.

Finally, Richard honed in on the subject matter that Mara was excited to talk about. Richard told her he had seen her picture in the newspaper and was immediately impressed. They talked briefly about Mara's job as a secretary and her desire to leave the corporate environment and participate in the world of fashion and glamour.

"You have what it takes," Richard said. "You could well be a model. Did you bring a portfolio?"

Mara was not accustomed to questions of what it took to land a modelling career. "I'm sorry, I didn't," Mara answered with a dejected feeling apparent in her voice.

"It's not a problem," Richard responded. Mara's sense of excitement was immediately restored. "We'll just go over to the studio and we can get the necessary photos taken. Do you have the time to do that right now?"

"Of course!" Mara responded, with a full smile on her face. Richard returned the smile. The two rose simultaneously from their seats to head off to Richard's office.

The home-office wasn't what Mara expected either. In one room was a small but neatly furnished workspace with a desk, two chairs that did not match, and an oversized couch. Against one wall was a small waist-high cupboard with several bottles of rum, whiskey, and vodka. In the bottom were a dozen or so glasses. Mara eyed the selection as Richard began the interview by offering Mara a drink. She asked for Scotch whiskey.

"Good choice," Richard said as he poured two ounces into each glass. "I have a commercial I'm ready to cast for this manufacturer. You'd be a perfect choice for one of the roles."

Mara sipped away as she recounted her previous work history and hopes for the future. "I thought you were going to take some pictures," Mara asked.

"We'll get to that in due course," Richard replied. "Let me freshen your drink."

Without any response from Mara, Richard took Mara's glass and stood with his back to the wall as he fixed another drink and handed the glass back to Mara. The routine conversation continued as Mara sipped at her drink. The second drink went down easier and faster than the first.

As Mara was speaking to Richard, she became uncomfortable. Her eyes lost focus - she was having difficulty pronouncing her words.

Richard took Mara to the couch and pulled a 35 mm. camera from his desk drawer and started taking pictures. Suddenly she passed out.

When Mara came to, she sensed that her clothes had been tampered with. More alarmingly, she realized she had been sexually assaulted. She felt anger but she also felt shame. She blamed herself for letting her own vanity get the better of her. The words "How could I be so stupid?" raced through her brain. "Nobody can ever know," was her most fervent wish.

Richard was not around. She had no idea of the time. Would he kill her if she attempted to leave? Mara was thoroughly embarrassed with herself for ever thinking she should accompany Richard to his office.

It took several minutes for Mara to wallow in self-pity. Then it came to her. She could not let this happen to anyone else. She had to make a report to the police.

Police Report

Police investigated and discovered that the talent agency was merely a ruse for the commission of sexual assaults.

Detective Sergeant Lou Villani of the Metropolitan Toronto Police Force told the *Toronto Star* newspaper that the agency was established "so a man could meet young attractive women, ply them with liquor and drugs, photograph them and assault them." It had not taken much time for police to look into the scam. Mara was assaulted on November twenty-first, 1990 and the newspaper account was published on December fifth. In addition, it was reported that two seventeen-year-old girls had also been lured to the same office and assaulted. Police feared there would be additional victims. Moreover, police also discovered that the man calling himself Richard Wild sometimes used a young woman to assist him in his con.

Police arrested thirty-year-old Selva Subbiah, alias Richard Wild, and charged him with three counts of sexual assault and one count of theft.

By November first, 1991, Subbiah's charges had risen to seventy. Police were reported as disclosing that Subbiah's *modus operandi* was to approach women on the street and offer them the opportunity to be cast in various roles in an upcoming motion picture or an alcoholic beverage commercial. In a search conducted on the suspect's home, police found Subbiah's "little black book" containing one hundred- and seventy women's names with ratings on a zero to ten scale. They also found identification and credit cards with various different names. Police retrieved hundreds of photos of women and reels of film depicting the indignities performed on seemingly unconscious women. Most disturbing, police found large quantities of powerful sedatives indicating his abductions were meant to continue.

The Rapist

Selva Kumar Subbiah arrived in Canada from Malaysia in January 1980 on a student visa. He enrolled in Toronto's George Brown College. His visa expired one year later but Subbiah did not return to his homeland choosing to stay illegally in Canada. He was a thin man and appeared quite agile. When he spoke, he exuded a natural charm. He often sported blue or green-tinted contact lenses. With dark hair and a clean-cut appearance, he had a youthful look that was attractive to the opposite sex. He could mimic a passable English accent, which could convey intelligence and nobility. His biggest passion was for sex. It was even more arousing when the act was forced on his partner. He was a sex addict.

But it was not only women to whom Subbiah held an abnormal fascination. Barry Kent MacKay, a previous director of the Toronto Humane Society was a noted conservationist. MacKay came to be acquainted with the name Richard Wild when complaints at the Humane Society were made about a man going by the name of Richard Wild who was selling exotic animals as pets. Not only was MacKay concerned with the manner in which these wild animals were being treated, he was equally concerned that his staff at the animal shelter could be exposed to unnecessary danger if such animals were seized. The staff were used to dealing with household pets but they lacked training when having to deal with wild animals. MacKay's hands were tied in dealing with the exploitation of exotic animals because there really was no legislation in place outlawing the practice. He tried to set up "sting" operations to halt Subbiah's attempts to sell wild animals, but his efforts came to naught. The best he could achieve was writing complaints to the *Toronto Sun* that ran ads for the sale of these animals, but those complaints were ignored.

December twenty-first, 1992 was a red-letter day for Barry Kent MacKay. Three events, MacKay wrote in the *Toronto Star*, became his "best Christmas present". On that day, royal assent was given to the *Wild Animal and Plant Protection Act*. The new legislation allowed Canada to enforce obligations under the Convention on International Trade in Endangered Species as well as encourage increased enforcement of national wildlife protection regulations. That same day, MacKay was awarded a medal in recognition of his animal protection work. Perhaps best of all, that was the day Selva Subbiah, a.k.a. Richard Wild, an exotic animal trafficker and rapist was sentenced for his crimes.

The Sentence

Selva Subbiah was thirty-two years old when he pleaded guilty to twenty charges, including sexual assault and administering a noxious substance. The sentence imposed was sixteen years imprisonment with eight years of parole ineligibility.

Originally Subbiah was charged with sixty counts involving assaults and drugs. Halfway through his preliminary hearing, after twenty-five women had testified against him, Subbiah knew the jig was up. He changed his plea to guilty.

"Women need protection from you, Mr. Subbiah," provincial court judge Joseph Bovard warned in handing down the sentence. Some of the victims were as young as fourteen. He raped six women and molested others. Some of his offences were committed while out on bail.

Twenty-four hours after that conviction, sixteen other women came forward saying they had been drugged and assaulted.

By February twenty-eighth, 1994, Subbiah was facing two hundred and seventy-four charges relating to assaults on seventy-two women. Charges included fifty-three counts of sexual assault, ninety-four charges of administering a noxious substance, and ninety-four charges of administering a stupefying drug. Other charges included uttering death threats, forcible confinement, choking, assault with a weapon, assault causing bodily harm and attempted buggery. Toronto Star reporter Dale Brazao quoted Metro police Detective Terry Wark as saying that complainants ranged in age from thirteen to thirty-seven. Some were married; others were single. Some of the charges went back to 1983.

On January twenty-eighth, 1997, Subbiah came up for trial on the new charges for which he once again pleaded guilty. Court heard that he had told his victims, many of whom were in their teens and were impressed with Subbiah's story of being the son of a respected diplomat, a dancer in rock videos, or a Broadway performer. Some visited his home to see the cougars and bear cub he kept caged in his basement.

Once the women were thoroughly impressed, he attacked them. Crown prosecutor Paul Normandeau emphasized to the court that some of his twenty-one victims felt paralyzed and lost consciousness. The effects of the drugs were such that they could not "move, talk, or scream, but could only sit and watch the act take place."

Many of the victims in court, cried as they relived their exploitation. One sixteen-year-old victim, Normandeau told the court, refused to tell her parents about the abuse she suffered because "at that age, she believed it was her fault."

By the time matters came on for sentencing, Subbiah, now thirty-seven, pleaded guilty to fifty-six criminal charges, twenty-three of which were for administering stupefying drugs. Even though the maximum penalty would have been life imprisonment, Justice David Humphrey of the Ontario Court of Justice (General Division) [now called the Ontario Superior Court], imposed these sentences:

- Administering a stupefying drug, twenty-three counts – twenty years on each concurrent;
- Sexual Assault, twenty-one counts – eight years on each concurrent;
- Assault with a weapon, four counts – four years on each concurrent;
- Common assaults and/or threatening, eight counts – two years on each concurrent.

Furthermore, the judge recommended that Subbiah be deported immediately upon being paroled or upon statutory release when he had served two-thirds of his sentence or in the event the Parole Board sought his detention, at his warrant expiry date. The judge also recommended that, given how dangerous Subbiah was, his return to Malaysia should be escorted.

Although some press coverage suggested Subbiah would be serving a sentence over six hundred years long, the meaning of the term "concurrent" meant that all these sentences ran together. Subbiah was sentenced to a total of twenty years, not six hundred and sixty years. Moreover, the trial judge opted to have the twenty years run concurrently with the unexpired portion of the sixteen-year sentence imposed in 1992.

Given the merged sentence, it was expected that the sentence administrator at Kingston Penitentiary, where Subbiah was headed, would conclude that he would be eligible for parole in about eight years. Nonetheless, he would be entering prison labelled as "arguably the most pernicious and persistent serial rapist in Canadian history."

Date Rape Drugs

As the media coverage of Selva Subbiah's crimes shocked the public, there was growing consternation over the threat that what once seemed a harmless activity to many (going to the bar and accepting a drink) could be a life-altering experience. Coverage of the use of date rape drugs was reaching epic proportions in the

United States, but by the mid-'90s, Canada was also bracing itself for an onslaught of such cases. Although evidence that the use of such drugs was anecdotal, rape crisis centres were suggesting that more and more women were being victimized by the use of pharmaceuticals.

The Subbiah case was cited as a prime example of their use. He had administered the knockout drug Halcion to his many victims. Halcion was a sleeping pill available through prescription at a pharmacy. Even easier to obtain was a street drug, gamma hydroxybutyrate, known popularly as GHB, which could be legally purchased at some health food stores. It was a central nervous system depressant with legitimate uses in the treatment of cataplexy, narcolepsy, and alcoholism. But it became known as a "club drug" or "date rape" drug. A third drug was another sedative called Rohypnol, a colourless, odorless substance manufactured by Hoffman-LaRoche often nicknamed "roofies". Smugglers brought it into Canada and the United States from Mexico, one of eighty countries where it was legally available.

The public mind made no distinction on the nature of the substance. Slipping a substance into the drink of someone unsuspecting to disinhibit behaviour or make one oblivious to one's surroundings was considered an ultimate betrayal of trust. It may be on that account, that when Subbiah was sentenced, the harshest penalty was meted out for administering a stupefying substance.

In the public mind, Subbiah was a pariah and no sympathy could be expected whatever treatment or punishment he might endure in the future. Moreover, the extensive publicity given to his trials and ultimate guilty pleas drew the attention not only of the general public but, quite probably, also of inmate populations where he would be imprisoned.

Kingston Penitentiary (K.P.)

Many were disappointed that the prosecution had not sought a dangerous offender application. That could have caused Subbiah to spend the rest of his natural life in prison or until such time as the Parole Board determined he was a manageable risk to re-enter society, widely interpreted to mean "never."

Selva Subbiah would now be known by his birth name. He could not hide behind the aliases he used while committing his atrocities on unsuspecting women: Richard Wild or Ryan Hunter, names that bore an uncanny connection with his other illegal compulsion, exotic animals.

The nature of the crimes for which Subbiah was convicted required that he be "pen placed" in a protective custody institution. The Correctional Service of Canada knew that it must protect this inmate's life no matter the nature of the crimes he committed.

The physical structure of the aging Kingston Penitentiary meant that Subbiah would not be treated with any luxury, even by prison standards. The massive limestone building lying on the western outskirts of the City of Kingston was an ominous structure despite its setting on Kingston Harbour. The prison was constructed in 1833 and 1834 under the reign of King William IV while Canada was still a colony under English rule. Its first inmates arrived on June first, 1835.

At the centre of the prison was the dome. The dome served as an entrance to a series of cell blocks that radiated from the central core like spokes on a wheel. The dome served as a major location for the brutal events of the 1971 Kingston Penitentiary riot. On that occasion, several inmates who were suspected of being convicted of sex offences, or "skin beefs" as inmates called them, were clustered together and physically tortured. It was deemed a part of the "con code" that "skinners" were the lowest form of life and liable to be severely beaten or killed simply because of the crimes for which they were convicted.

Being a rapist or a child molester was the equivalent, or even worse, than being called a "rat" or police informer. One's life was in constant danger if one fits into one of these categories. No trial; no questions asked. It didn't matter that every inmate in K.P. was in protective custody. Part of the code was that every inmate in this "p.c. joint" must keep his head down and not become too arrogant or brag about one's criminal past.

There would be consequences that Subbiah should have realized if he continued his sexual obsession once behind bars. The legal consequences could indeed be less severe than the perhaps lethal consequences other inmates might bestow. And certainly, the last thing Subbiah should want would be more publicity.

Police and the Media

Yet more publicity is what he got. In 1998, the CTV investigative TV show, *W Five*, aired an expose of what Subbiah had been up to while imprisoned. On the show, Christine Neilsen introduced the segment as follows:

"Well, police call him 'the most notorious serial rapist in Canada'. He's had hundreds of victims. and they thought when they put him away for twenty years that he wouldn't be able to victimize women anymore. But he has been, from jail.... Subbiah's been in prison since 1992 – a twenty-year sentence. But even maximum security hasn't stopped this predator. Police told *W Five* that even while in jail Subbiah has been stalking women – by telephone, by mail, and via willing female accomplices on the outside. So far twenty-five victims have come forward. Police believe there are many more.... Subbiah is currently in Kingston Penitentiary. He's eligible for day parole in two years. Police say they might be able to stop that from happening if enough women come forward."

Neilsen was interrupted by host Valerie Pringle:

"So what he's doing now is not against the law, I guess, eh? Phoning people and [finding out if] they want to have phone sex with him, I guess?"

Neilsen responded:

"Well, the problem is that it's not against the law. So, what the police are hoping is that by talking to the media about it, talking to us about it, people will watch this story and say, 'This guy's been calling me.' The more women that come forward the more women that say 'This guy has invaded my space' the less chance there is of him getting paroled."

Much of the public is unfamiliar with Canada's parole system. There is a general confusion about what is meant by saying that an inmate is eligible for parole or eligible for day parole. There is even confusion about what the terms mean. Parole is discretionary. Even though *the Corrections and Conditional Release Act* makes provision for parole eligibility at the one-third mark in the sentence, the Parole Board of Canada is highly unlikely to grant parole unless there is evidence presented to it at a hearing that the offender is a manageable risk to re-enter society. Day parole may be granted six months before full parole eligibility. A grant of day parole allows an offender to be housed in a halfway house (provided the inmate could find a halfway house willing to accept him) under strict conditions if again, the Board finds that in such placement, public safety is well protected.

While the *W Five* story may have been accurate that Subbiah was continuing his predatory behaviour, it became unduly alarmist for police to use the press to incite the public that women in the community might soon be at risk. Even if the Board were to consider granting parole or day parole (which was highly unlikely) it was an improper use of police power to rile the public and even more improper to put an additional burden on the administration and staff of a federal penitentiary to have to contain the risk of violence that such a story could incite.

At one time, prison administration could block the flow of news that could cause disruption and in some cases that could instigate violent outbursts. However, even the antiquated Kingston Penitentiary provided its inhabitants with a television cable. Even though inmates had to buy a television from their modest allowance, most inmates considered having a television a necessity to mitigate the daily boredom of prison life. When a TV story featured one of their own, prison inmates sat up and took notice. Subbiah's peaceful stay at KP was severely threatened.

The *Toronto Star* also ran a story of Subbiah's continued luring of women. On December twenty-sixth, 1998, under the byline 'Ashante Infantry', the *Star* recounted the story of a Toronto woman who had placed an ad for companionship in March 1996. At the time, Subbiah would have been at a Toronto detention centre awaiting sentence. Toronto police sexual assault squad confirmed with the *Star* that the woman knew things about Selva Subbiah that were not public knowledge. Even though an alias was used, police had no doubt the woman had been in contact with Subbiah. Even while in a provincial jail awaiting sentence, he posed as a modelling agent and talent scout. The woman was stricken with the man she would later learn to be a jailed Malaysian prisoner. The *Toronto Star* quoted the woman's reaction to her telephone meeting with Subbiah. Even though she had received over a hundred responses to her ad, it was Subbiah's that had the most impact: "It was an amazing interesting message with a wonderful British accent to die for…. He had verve in his voice. He sounded so alive."

The woman completely believed the assumed name the prisoner was using was legitimate: "Richard said he was currently working in Collingwood on a production starring Geena Davis and Samuel L. Jackson." There had been press coverage of the filming of *The Long Kiss Goodnight* in the media so "Richard's" story seemed credible.

Subbiah used female assistance to continue his aggression. Ordinarily, a telephone call emanating from a provincial jail or a federal penitentiary would be identifiable because a recorded message at the outset would begin: "You have a collect call from…" However, some inmates learned that this distinctive feature could be bypassed. Subbiah also worked around the system by calling the number of a female accomplice who would answer the collect call and then dial the number of the person the inmate really wanted to reach. It was called "three-waying."

Sometimes the accomplice would act as "Richard's" assistant. This "assistant" the *Star* was told would sometimes answer the phone with the greeting "Alliance Films," the company supposedly employing "Richard." Sometimes, during calls, requests were made for pictures including nude photos. Surprisingly, no red flags were raised, suggesting the call might be a scam.

It would be a case of blaming the victim to suggest that women who responded to Subbiah's requests bore the blame for their own naivety. Rather questions should be directed to the Ministry of Correctional Services or to the Visits and Correspondence Officer at the various institutions. In both the provincial and federal prison systems, checks are in place to monitor calls. Three-way calls, if detected could lead to loss of phone privileges. Mail is also opened and inspected to ensure the continuation of deceit and criminal activity is not continued. Of course, the root of all blame rests with Subbiah himself for failing to take the opportunity for rehabilitation that his incarceration afforded him.

The Prison and the Media

Following sentencing in Toronto, Subbiah was returned to Kingston Penitentiary to continue his now-extended sentence. *Kingston Whig-Standard* reporter Rob Tripp had a tip that Subbiah was continuing his stalking behaviour on Kingston women. In a January sixteenth, 1999 story, Tripp tells of his response from Kingston Penitentiary assistant warden John Odie when asked about what K.P. was doing to keep tabs on Subbiah. "We'll comment on that once we talk with the police department," Odie told Tripp. But the reporter pressed on by posing the same question three times over the course of two days.

The answer Tripp received was as though the assistant warden was a deer caught in headlights. "We have not been able to contact [the police] at all," Odie responded. The Toronto police had no difficulty meeting with a TV crew and newspaper reporters but the

Kingston police, if Odie is to be believed, had a problem dealing with an agency that kept Subbiah restrained and supposedly charged with the responsibility of safeguarding the public from Subbiah's predatory activities.

By 2008, the National Parole Board [now called the Parole Board of Canada], was due to meet with Subbiah to determine if he should be released on statutory release. Ordinarily, once an inmate has served two-thirds of the court-imposed sentence, the inmate is entitled to be released to continue serving the balance of the court-imposed sentence on the street subject to supervision by a community parole officer. In cases such as Subbiah's, the Correctional Service of Canada can refer the case to the Parole Board asking the Board to detain the offender in prison until warrant expiry date - the date the sentence imposed by the sentencing court ends.

Selva Subbiah elected not to attend a hearing called to make this determination. Instead, he opted to have the Board decide his fate based on the files that had been made on his behaviour while in prison, the sentence imposed, the judge's recommendation, and the case analysis made by the case management team as a result of rehabilitative steps taken and psychological and psychiatric profiles.

In effect, by choosing not to contest the hearing, Subbiah was signalling he knew the outcome would not be in his favour and he had to content himself with the notion that he would be serving every day of the sentence that had been imposed on him.

Subbiah assessed his situation correctly. On December ninth, 2008, the Parole Board determined the risk to the public was too great to release the prisoner. Even though he was to be deported to Malaysia, the Parole Board took it upon itself to consider Subbiah was too great a risk to be exposed to the public.

Shortly after the decision was filed, Rob Tripp made an application as a "person who demonstrates an interest in a case" to obtain a copy of the Board's reasons for detention. A copy was forwarded to Rob Tripp on February twelfth, 2009. This time, Tripp posted the Board's reasons to his website, CanCrime.com.

Subbiah learned of the posting when his wife notified him that this information was publicly available online. The posting of the document containing details of Subbiah's crimes could well reawaken concerns for his safety. The prison has a legislated responsibility to look out for the health and safety of those in its custody. How would the prison respond?

Life on the Range

The Correctional Service has various ways it can protect vulnerable inmates. One method is for an inmate who fears for his safety to "check-in." This requires the inmate to make a declaration that he feels his life is threatened and that to prevent violence he voluntarily accepts time in a segregation cell, often called "the hole". Segregation is not pleasant; it is the same as punishment meted out for breach of the prison rules. Whether it is called administrative segregation or punitive dissociation, it's the same bed.

Although Subbiah had spent several stints in "admin seg," he preferred to keep his peace in the prison's general population. He was able to earn a small wage as the dome cleaner. That required working afternoons and evenings in the dome clearing garbage, washing floors, and cleaning.

Shortly after Rob Tripp had posted the Board's decision on Subbiah, on May fourteenth, 2009, Subbiah was assaulted by two inmates who had cells on Upper B range. Upper B was a special range for inmates preferring not to be part of the general population.

On this date, a correctional officer ordered Subbiah to deliver some cleaning materials to Upper B. As he was doing so, an inmate from Upper B blocked the door from closing. Two inmates from Upper B sprung forward and assaulted Subbiah stabbing him with a homemade knife or "shiv." Subbiah was cut and bruised but he survived. He was transported to Kingston General Hospital where he received CAT scans, other tests, and was sutured. Instead of returning to his cell, he was placed in the institution's health centre and was under observation for 24 hours. The institutional healthcare team provided him with Tylenol 2 and 3 for pain and he was instructed to eat only soft food for a few days.

Subbiah wanted compensation for his physical injuries and mental distress. He contacted my office requesting that I commence a lawsuit to recover damages. At first glance, he appeared to have a good cause of action. Although he was of questionable character and the Department of Justice would surely seize on his past wrongdoings, there was no doubt that the Correctional Service is responsible for the safety of those in its custody. Subbiah was willing to sign an affidavit that he had alerted the Correctional Service that the release of sensitive information such as that which the Rob Tripp data displayed could lead to his becoming a marked man in the prison. Although he did not request a transfer to segregation, he was confident that a transfer to another institution would have helped ensure his safety. It was a Correctional Service employee who directed him to attend on Upper B range and the Service should be held to account when it gives a direct order to remove an inmate from a place of safety to a situation where his well-being is compromised. Furthermore, Subbiah could count on the sworn evidence of another inmate who stated he had seen a printout of the Tripp posting being passed around.

The Lawsuit

The injuries Subbiah sustained were minor and his recovery had been swift. It was agreed that an action would be commenced in the Federal Court using simplified procedure. The special rules that apply to a simplified claim limit damages to fifty thousand dollars but the proceedings are much faster than if conducted under the ordinary rules. It is the Federal Court's version of Small Claims Court. Even with a speedier trial, it was not until 2013 that the matter came on for a hearing. The judgment was handed down on November twenty-seventh, 2013.

However, when one goes to Court, nothing is ever a "sure thing." A decision to award damages is only as good as the evidence that is elicited in chief and in cross-examination. In the Subbiah trial, what could go wrong did go wrong.

The Prothonotary that heard the case, found Subbiah's evidence to be "evasive" when he testified about disclosing his fear of being attacked to prison authorities. Worse yet, the answers he gave at trial varied from the statements he had sworn in an affidavit filed at the beginning of the lawsuit.

Even worse still was the testimony of Subbiah's corroborating witness. This was the man who had written to me establishing he had recalled the Tripp document being passed around. Two paragraphs from the judgment sum up the problem:

"[The witness] frankly stated that he had no independent recollection of any of these events as he had 'fried his brain.' He said he did this by virtue of having consumed copious quantities of LSD Twenty-Five when he was young to stave off suicidal depression. While he says the LSD helped him avoid the suicidal depression, it had a significant adverse impact on his brain and he now could not remember anything that happened more than eight months ago. All of his recollections for the evidence he gave flow from a letter he wrote in 2010 to counsel for Mr. Subbiah. He frankly admitted that all of his current evidence is based on what he wrote in that letter.

"[The witness] has no independent recollection of the events he described in his testimony. He cannot independently recall the specific document he supposedly saw being passed between inmates, or which inmates were involved. He does not remember which range he was in when he saw the document exchanged, and he does not remember the names of those inmates he worked with at that time. He could not give evidence concerning relationships between inmates, specifically the relationship between [the attacker] and Mr. Subbiah."

Even though compensation was denied, the Correctional Service eventually did the right thing and transferred Subbiah from Kingston Penitentiary to Warkworth Institution, a medium security institution that has a well-regarded sex offender treatment facility.

Warrant Expiry and Deportation

With every last day of his sentence served, it was now time for the Immigration and Refugee Board of Canada to decide what was to become of Selva Subbiah. Once released from prison on a Saturday, he was immediately arrested and held in custody so his status in Canada could be reviewed two days later.

A hearing was held on Monday, January twenty-ninth, 2017 in which Subbiah was ordered deported from Canada to his home country accompanied by three guards from the Canada Border

Services Agency. The *Toronto Star's* Peter Edwards covered the hearing and quoted Andrew Laut, who chaired the review: "You are the worst offender and the highest risk that has ever come before me in my career."

Although Subbiah had not returned to his homeland after leaving it in 1980, he addressed Chairperson Laut saying, "I'm ready to leave, sir." Subbiah had entered the hearing without legal representation.

The Border Service Agency spared no time in seeing to Subbiah's removal from Canada. By the first week in February following the deportation order, Subbiah was back in Malaysia and permanently exiled from returning to Canada. Although he claimed to have strong family support in his homeland, one must be skeptical. Newspaper headlines there contained bold letters stating "The Beast Returns".

"Good riddance" would be the sentiments of most of the women he manipulated. Some to this day bear the emotional baggage their experience with Selva Kumar Subbiah left behind.

Many had come into his grasp unwittingly with the lure of a career in movies or television extinguishing any sense of danger. None of Subbiah's victims made it to the big screen. Of all those Subbiah that were promised movie or TV exposure, Kingston Penitentiary became the only beneficiary of the movie and television industry. It was the backdrop for the American television series, *The Mayor of Kingstown.* The penitentiary is now closed and offers itself as a rather pricey tourist attraction and film set.

CHAPTER 2

REFORMER OR MANIPULATOR?

Clifford David Maltby – Hostage Taker

> *Vision without integrity is not mission – it's manipulation*
> **– Howard G. Hendricks**

Ordinarily, a lawyer meets an incarcerated client in an interview room. It was, therefore, odd, that on one day in the mid-1980s, I met with my client and conducted my interview while he remained behind the bars of his cell at Kingston Penitentiary. Just as odd was the head pressed up against the bars of the cell to my left of my client, wanting to contribute to the conversation.

"It's all right. David knows all about my situation," said my client, Timothy Engen. Engen was hoping to overturn the wrongful conviction in disciplinary court for an alleged breach of prison rules. It was not a major wrong that needed correction, but with the intensity with which Tim and David became involved in the discussion, one would feel it was an issue that would generate international headlines. It was obvious that the two men behind bars cared deeply for one another's well-being and both had a burning desire to ensure prison justice would prevail.

I agreed to represent Tim on this minor issue, I was unaware at the time that in years to come I would also represent David in a case that did indeed draw international headlines.

Tim was a tall fellow with sandy hair. His most noticeable feature was his badly chapped lips. They looked painful but Tim gave them little notice. Timothy Engen was the product of a broken home. His troubled youth led to a series of criminal convictions that resulted in his landing in a federal penitentiary at age sixteen according to the Correctional Service of Canada. According to David, Tim wound up in penitentiary three years earlier than records state. Either way, he was one of the youngest inmates sentenced to federal custody in modern times. Nobody spoke up on Engen's behalf with concern for what might happen to a teenager being incarcerated in a penitentiary populated by hardened adult convicts.

Timothy Engen, born in 1964 was in his early twenties when I first spoke with him. He was serving a nine-year sentence on a variety of robbery charges. Most people would agree that putting a fourteen-year-old into federal custody is wrong. But does incarcerating a sixteen-year-old seem acceptable? Jacques Belanger, spokesman for the federal correctional services department told a news outlet that Engen entered the federal penal system in 1978 at age sixteen when he was convicted of two theft charges.

"We have a few sixteen-year-olds. They get caught up when the juvenile system is overloaded or if there is a serious offence," Belanger was quoted as saying. He made no distinction between a penitentiary and a training school.

Tim Engen tried not to stand out from his fellow inmates even though his size could have been intimidating. Engen's pal, David, also kept a low profile. Like Engen, David spent considerable time in solitary confinement. Maltby, a native of Nova Scotia, was also a big man. He was 6 foot 1, about one hundred and eighty pounds, with long brown hair and brown eyes. When not caged in a solitary cell, the two kept close contact with one another, rarely interacting with other prisoners or staff. It would be David that would become my primary concern.

I hadn't asked for David's full name. Few people knew much about him. There were no mentions of his crime that could be found in press clippings and no judgments that could be accessed to give a complete picture of David. All that anyone knew about David was what he would later reveal about his childhood and upbringing. His full name was Clifford David Maltby.

David's Background

A search for a record of his criminal past draws a blank except for a few paragraphs in the *Saskatoon Star Phoenix* published in 2002 that tells the tale of a Saskatchewan man, twenty years prior, going by the name Robert Courvoisier. Courvoisier claimed to be related to the cognac-making Courvoisier family and was promoting a plan to use zeppelins to export loads of water-retaining rare earth from the prairie province to Saudi Arabia. Clifford Maltby, alias Robert Courvoisier, was able to induce several investors to buy into his scam before he disappeared. Maltby had defrauded fourteen people out of one hundred and sixty-four thousand five hundred dollars.

When Maltby was arrested in 1982 he was held without bail at the Provincial Correctional Centre in Saskatoon to await trial. Maltby was astounded by his treatment in custody. He had not been convicted and yet he objected to being treated "like a criminal" when Canadians have a constitutional right to be deemed innocent until proven guilty by a court of competent jurisdiction. His concerns drew immediate support from other inmates of the Saskatchewan Correctional Centre. By August twenty-first, 1982 an inmate hunger strike increased to 29 participants after inmate Basil Bellegarde had been on twelve-day liquids-only fast protesting rules at the facility and its disciplinary procedures. This hunger strike was in support of the manner detainees were treated while in remand. The hunger strike was a tactic Maltby would not forget.

Maltby encouraged three of his fellow captives to bring suit against the Saskatchewan provincial government claiming a declaration that his citizen's rights had been violated. The four applicants lost in the trial court and appealed to the Saskatchewan

Court of Appeal. Once there, the appellate court on its own motion questioned whether the application was now moot since each of the four bringing the challenge were out of the system. The Saskatchewan Chief Justice took only eleven paragraphs in his written reasons to address why the appeal was declined. The court took it upon itself to try to establish the motive for the prisoners' discontent. The written judgment states:

" Perhaps the more compelling reason for refusing to hear the appeal lies in the applicants' real purpose of pursuing the appeal and the material available to the court for this purpose. As noted, the purpose at this stage of the proceeding has changed to one of obtaining judicial declaration of censure having as its aim a sweeping condemnation of the practices followed by the correctional authorities in the treatment of remand inmates. [Based solely on the affidavit material filed] the application would be an unjudicial exercise of this court's discretion."

The experience set Maltby up as a prisoner rights advocate at a time when any advocacy for the more humane treatment of prisoners was in its infancy.

Maltby was sentenced in 1984 to five and a half years in federal penitentiary and an appeal of that sentence was also dismissed. But Maltby did not give up his new-found zeal for criticizing the harsh treatment of inmates. Maltby's obstinance led him to serving several lengthy stints in solitary confinement.

On one instance when Maltby was segregated, another inmate, Gordon Henry Taylor was severely beaten by guards. Taylor had a mental age of twelve and was punched and kicked until he died.

Inmate Greg Frenz testified at a later inquest that Taylor had been punched or kicked by at least two correctional officers and dragged past his cell where Frenz could hear Taylor taking another thirty to forty blows. Maltby also witnessed the fatal attack on the inmate, although he testified that Frenz may have exaggerated, presumably in the number of blows administered. It is ordinarily a breach of the "con code" to cooperate with authorities by giving evidence. Yet this attack was so brutal against another inmate that there would be no retribution for helping identify Taylor's attackers.

Like Maltby, his younger sidekick also experienced solitary confinement. "He's experienced every conceivable prison horror, yet he's retained his sanity," Maltby said.

"I'm the only friend he's ever had [and] he's the only friend I've ever had."

Release from Imprisonment

In prison, credit was given for "good time". Days of "earned remission" were calculated monthly, such that an inmate could leave prison after serving two-thirds of the court-imposed sentence. After serving a little over two-thirds of his five-year sentence, Clifford Maltby, then thirty-nine years old, was awarded statutory release on March sixteenth, 1986. Prison had afforded him no opportunity to reintegrate successfully into open society. He was alone and without a job. Without his only friend Tim by his side, he focused on his passion for the suffering of those around him, from the homeless to the impoverished. His heart went out to the homeless he could see around him. Instead of just accepting the things he could not change, he decided it was time to change the things he could not accept. Who would listen to an ex-con ranting about prison and social reform? He needed assistance.

Clifford Maltby was not greatly knowledgeable about Canadian politics. He did know that John Turner had been Prime Minister briefly after Pierre Trudeau stepped down until Turner's Liberal Party was routed by Brian Mulroney's Progressive Conservatives in September 1984. Maltby expected that an opposition leader would not have the security details that a Prime Minister would enjoy. Perhaps Maltby could encourage a man with the stature of a former Prime Minister to negotiate on behalf of oppressed prisoners and the poor. People would sit up and take note. The problem was that Maltby was unable to make contact with Turner.

The Hostage Taking

Maltby shifted his plan. He donned the clothes of a Catholic priest with a pastoral collar and a crucifix hanging from his neck. He then attended the Bahamian high commission office on the third floor of a downtown Ottawa office tower. There were three embassies in the building and security at the Bahamian embassy appeared the weakest.

Maltby entered the embassy and conveyed the message that he was carrying a confidential message for the high commissioner and, if she wasn't available, vice-consul Janet Rahming was the only other person to whom the message could be delivered.

"He was all dressed in his priestly garb and everything, and he played the part very, very well," Rahming later told CBC Radio's *As It Happens.*

The thirty-three-year-old vice-consul was unaware until Maltby entered her office that he was carrying what appeared to be a pistol.

Once inside, Maltby closed the office door. He appeared nervous but Rahming remained stoic.

"I had no fear that he would kill. I never thought that I would die in that incident. Something told me that man was not really a murderer." Rahming continued, "I guess it was just a matter of convenience. He told me that he had been stalking the building for a week [with] two other embassies in the building [that] he'd checked those out as well."

Outside the embassy, emergency measures were activated. More than one hundred policemen as well as fire and ambulance personnel were standing by. The neighborhood was cordoned off and people were evacuated from the building. Maltby kept communications open between himself, police, and the press.

The bravery of Janet Rahming cannot be underestimated. "He had his gun ready constantly" during the fifteen-hour ordeal Rahming said. The hostage-taking began at about five p.m. on Tuesday, April first, 1986, and ended at seven a.m. the next morning.

During the standoff, Maltby was in telephone communication with police and listing his demands for the surrender of the hostage. He also was in telephone contact with the *Ottawa Citizen* and with the television station CJOH. In calling CJOH, he was able to carry on extensive conversations with veteran TV journalist Charlie Greenwell. That reporter was later granted access to the interior of the building while the stand-off was ongoing. He acted as an intermediary between the police and Maltby. It was a tough job. Greenwell considered it his task to keep Maltby calm and oversee a shouting match between the RCMP and the Ottawa Police force as to who had jurisdiction over the situation. As the police shouting intensified in the stairwell and the jurisdictional dispute carried on, Maltby began banging on the door wanting to know what the commotion was all about. Greenwell kept Maltby calm. Through Greenwell, the public became aware of Maltby's demands.

He wanted an unused firehall in Ottawa to be converted to a shelter for the homeless and further demanded authorities release Engen and transport the two of them by helicopter to "the northern wilderness."

The authorities were unwilling to consider any terms suggested by Maltby. Rahming remained brave and what seemed like the

Stockholm Syndrome in reverse; she kept Maltby quiet and gained his respect. He even encouraged Rahming to call him David – that's what his friends called him. When Maltby surrendered himself to the police he took the crucifix from his neck and gifted it to Rahming. The two parted exchanging God's blessing for one another. Her only injury was a loss of a night's sleep.

Maltby was returned to custody. He knew he would have to serve out the remainder of the original court-imposed sentence now that he breached his statutory release. He just wanted to return to the penitentiary as quickly as possible.

Return to Prison

Before the week was out, he opted not to have a lawyer and pleaded guilty before Provincial Court judge Patrick White to eleven charges including threatening and attacking an internationally protected person, four weapons offences, and two charges involving explosives. The hostage-taking began on April 1st and he appeared in Court on April 4th.

Immediately after Maltby's surrender, the RCMP announced they had beefed up security around ninety-seven foreign missions in Ottawa and elsewhere in Canada. Police also discovered after the arrest that the handgun Maltby was carrying was an improperly altered target pistol that would have blown up had the trigger been pulled. The two containers that police originally suspected as being explosives were not explosive at all. One was a mixture of hydrochloric acid and lye; the other was acetic acid mixed with aquarega, a substance used to engrave metal.

The fact that some of the charges were incapable of being proven in court did not dissuade the prosecuting Crown attorney, James Stewart from asking for an "exemplary" sentence. He argued that such a sentence would act as a deterrent to "nip this sort of thing in the bud." He was unimpressed with the social conscience Maltby was expressing in his demands. "Ottawa is full of embassies," Stewart told the court, and "we must try to discourage so-called copy-cat incidents. We certainly don't want this repeated weekly or monthly, as sincere as the individual may be." Even though the hostage-taking lasted overnight, the court should recognize that Rahming was fearful for the first hour and a half, the prosecutor pointed out.

Maltby acting without a lawyer had surrendered himself, pleaded guilty at the first opportunity, and was dealt with in what seemed to criminal lawyers as unprecedented haste later in the week after his surrender.

Maltby spoke in his own defence. He claimed to have "a good deal of remorse." He added, "It's not a good way to solve a problem. It will only add to a good deal of anguish" Nonetheless he reaffirmed his strong feelings for the plight of the homeless and for the horrors that Tim Engen had suffered in Kingston Penitentiary.

Maltby's statement in court echoed his comments to the *Ottawa Citizen*. He told a reporter while detained at the Ottawa-Carleton Detention Centre awaiting a court appearance that what he did "was terribly wrong" yet, in Maltby's view, was necessary to make society listen to the needs of children and the poor. "What I did was not right in Canadian society. It's not right to take a gun and point it to get what you want."

Some would argue that Maltby's so-called remorse and admission of wrongdoing was simply a ploy to mitigate what was expected to be a harsh sentence. Others would state that it was a true expression of a man with a social conscience doing the only thing in his power to sway public opinion to a pressing social concern. Some would see Maltby as a prisoner seeking social justice; others would see a convicted fraudster using the media and "all the right words" to justify his wrongdoing.

Provincial Court judge Patrick White took the early guilty plea into account and found that Maltby deserved some leniency. "A substantial factor is that you did not indulge in gratuitous terror tactics," the judge held. He continued, "However misguided, your motives were not greed or self-service."

The judge then passed sentence. He imposed a five-year prison term to be served consecutive to the term of imprisonment Maltby was serving at the time of his statutory release.

The Appeal

The office of the Attorney General was shocked by what it considered a ridiculously low number of years of imprisonment. It appealed the sentence. It also chose David Fairgrieve, a very experienced and knowledgeable, Crown Attorney to argue its case. Maltby asked me to represent him on the sentence appeal. I agreed knowing full well that the state wanted a maximum sentence of 14 years to be imposed,

The three-judge panel consisting of Justices Grange, Lacourciere, and Thorson, were all very experienced highly regarded jurists. My appearance before Justice Grange was the first time, I had encountered him since my call to the bar. I had served with him on a Bar Admission Course committee before his appointment to the bench. He was well-respected for his knowledge of the law and for his hard work. Now appointed to the bench, he was thorough and thoughtful in the questioning of both prosecution and defence counsel. So were the other judges. I was able to report to Maltby that we had a very fair hearing before a very good panel.

David Fairgrieve had made an impressive presentation urging the court to accept that Maltby had committed an act of terrorism. He urged the court to impose a double-digit term of imprisonment as the appropriate penalty to ensure terrorism would not become an accepted means of achieving a political goal. More than that, visitors to our country, especially an officer of a diplomatic mission, are owed a duty of protection. Canada had signed a Convention of the United Nations specifically making murder, kidnapping, attacking, or threatening an internationally-protected person a crime.

I was left to argue that, although inappropriate, the motivation for Maltby was sincere and well-meaning. The commission of his crime was just a few weeks after his release and the remanet of his sentence in 1982 would have to be served. It would not be until November of 1987 that the five years imposed for the hostage-taking would take effect.

On October 29, 1986, the appeal court published its decision. Justice Sam Grange wrote on behalf of the panel. I was eager to read the Court's decision. A charge of harming an internationally protected person had not been tested before. Would this case be a precedent for handing down extremely long sentences of imprisonment?

After the Court of Appeal listed the factors that David Fairgrieve had so eloquently enumerated in argument, the written reasons contained a sentence that is music to a defence counsel's ears: "Having said that, however, I must also recognize that there are many mitigating features about both this crime and this criminal."

The Court of Appeal decision allowed both sides to claim partial victory. The five-year consecutive sentence was replaced with an eight-year consecutive term.

Clifford David Maltby was returned to Kingston Penitentiary and regained his cell beside Tim Engen. Except for one incident, he kept a low profile until he was again released on mandatory supervision [the updated term is now statutory release] in 1993.

Going UAL

By 1991, Maltby had been transferred to medium-security Warkworth Institution located in a rural area east of Toronto. He was making progress in anticipation of an upcoming parole hearing. The Parole Board would want to see that an inmate was ready for release and would satisfy itself if the inmate could show progress by first experiencing a brief visit to the community with an escort. Such visits to the community with escorts would be repeated to gain the confidence of the escort and the institution. If successful, the next step would be an unescorted pass, usually to a halfway house to gain support before a grant of day parole. Day parole was being allowed in the community during specified daytime hours but spending the remainder of the time at the halfway house. Only then could an inmate be granted full parole to reside in the community under supervision for the duration of the sentence.

In April of 1991, Maltby indicated that he wanted to be assessed by the Portsmouth Centre in Kingston for possibly serving his day parole there. The pass was granted. It was the second unescorted pass Maltby had received. Prison authorities seemed assured the risk was manageable. But this time, Maltby failed to return. The pass had required Maltby to return to Warkworth Institution by two p.m. on April seventeenth. He failed to show. The pass was cancelled and Maltby was declared unlawfully at large. Maltby remained unlawfully at large for three days. The manhunt was extensive using helicopters and tracking dogs. Once apprehended, he would return to prison but this time his credibility before another parole hearing would be negligible.

On April 18, Durham Regional police found a red 1986 Honda Prelude abandoned in a swamp north of the town of Port Perry. It was the car Maltby had driven while on the unescorted pass. The same day Global TV news reported it had received a copy of a letter sent to Prime Minister Brian Mulroney. The letter contained demands for action on the homeless and for prisoner rights. The letter threatened that if the demands were ignored unspecified action would be taken against unnamed public officials.

The Next Release

Sooner or later all inmates are released. Maltby's sentence expired in 1992. Maltby's name was recorded once again in a March 4, 1993 edition of the *Ottawa Citizen*. This time it was about the February fifteenth death of a Stratford Festival employee Douglas Grass. Grass was a props maker at the Stratford theatre. Stratford Police Chief Lewis Lawson announced that Maltby, now forty-five, and his accomplice, twenty-two-year-old Robert Leroy Gaunt, who like Engen had been taken under Maltby's wing, were wanted in connection with the murder. As well, the two were also wanted in Hawkesbury and Sarnia with the robberies of two real estate agents. It was alleged the two posed as potential buyers and when shown an available property, the two beat and robbed the agents.

Maltby was once again apprehended in Quebec in March of 1993 and charged with a string of robberies and abductions in Quebec and Ontario after killing Grass. Maltby was returned to Ontario where he pleaded guilty in November of 1993 to the first-degree murder of the Stratford Festival employee. Gaunt pleaded guilty to manslaughter in connection with the death.

Maltby acting on his own behalf entered his guilty plea before Justice John F. McGarry of the Ontario Court (General Division) [now renamed the Superior Court of Ontario]. The guilty pleas related to robbery, theft, unlawful confinement, and possession of dangerous weapons – twenty-four in all – including homicide.

The statement of facts read into the record was that Maltby attacked the forty-year-old Grass with a hammer. He hit the prop maker fifteen times on the head until he collapsed and died. The judge was shocked at the description of the attack calling it a "shocking, terrible death."

Before the passing of the sentence, Maltby rose in the prisoner's box and delivered an eight-minute statement.

Flanked by four uniformed police officers, Maltby started by addressing the parents of the victim:

"Please forgive me for causing you so much pain," Maltby called out emphasizing the "please forgive" words hoping to draw sympathy.

Maltby told the court that he and Gaunt had arrived in Stratford the day before killing Grass. The two attended a bar and asked about renting a room. They were told that Grass had a room that he might rent out. Grass was described as a homosexual who preferred younger men.

It was at that point that Maltby decided he would kill Grass. Maltby said he saw Grass as resembling those who had preyed on him in his years as a child prostitute.

Maltby then asked the judge to allow voluntary euthanasia. He stated that Parliament had erred in rejecting capital punishment.

"I want to die. Eighty percent of people [in prison] can be rehabilitated. The other twenty percent are better off dead. There's no point in keeping them alive." There was no statistical study verifying Maltby's assertion. He simply made the numbers up.

Justice McGarry said he could not reinstate the death penalty from the bench. He was bound by law to impose the sentence required by law for premeditated murder – life imprisonment without eligibility for parole for at least twenty-five years.

Gaunt was sentenced to fifteen years for his part in the tragedies. Additional charges for the abduction and robbery of the Sarnia real estate agents and the robbery of an elderly couple in Prescott would ensue but having received the maximum sentence, those charges would only result in concurrent sentences for Maltby.

Euthanasia

Once back in penitentiary, Maltby made it known that he wanted prison officials to let him commit suicide. It was an unusual request; most inmates of that mind just do it. Instead, Maltby sought out press attention by going on a hunger strike. He told reporters that he would hire a lawyer to apply under Canada's *Charter of Rights and Freedoms* to get judicial authorization that would allow prisoners to kill themselves. Suicide, he was convinced, was a better option than spending his remaining days (he was forty-six in 1993) in a penitentiary.

He did not bring a test case for judicial approval of euthanasia; he did not kill himself. Maltby lives on.

The desire to escape prison by way of a pine box parole also lives on. APTN News reported in April 2023 that nine inmates have made use of medical assistance in dying (often referred to as MAiD) between November 1, 2016, when the law in Canada came into effect, and March 31, 2022. The Correctional Service of Canada reports that none have occurred since.

When lawyers and judges consider a case, very often they examine the factual scenario that has led to a court appearance. Seldom do counsel or the courts have the opportunity to look for patterns that can be crucial in effective decision-making. Those of us in the criminal justice system seldom look beyond the who, what, where, and when questions to try to answer the why.

Maltby's story contains patterns that would have been helpful to explore in dealing with his criminal behaviour. Maybe his statement that he was abused by pedophiles is true; maybe it wasn't. But had that scenario been true and had it been explored, perhaps a lot of the trauma experienced by victims and accused could have been avoided. Courts are overburdened and an early guilty plea, especially where no defence counsel is involved allows for matters to be completed expeditiously. Maybe we should expect more from our criminal justice system than doling out punishment. Maybe we should consider using the system to ask why crimes happen and what are the best means to avoid their reoccurrence.

CHAPTER 3

INCORRIGIBLE

Patrick Pirozzi – Dangerous Offender

> *April is the cruelest month*
>
> **– T.S. Eliot**

Criminal defence lawyers regularly deal with perpetrators of vicious crimes. Some of that behaviour can lead to the wrongdoer spending years in prison. Yet seldom do these lawyers actually witness the tragic events in person. I had the dubious honour of witnessing a crime that landed the perpetrator in prison for decades until he died. The man who committed the crime was not my client. What I witnessed was highly unusual but it did not cause me any upset.

The April Incident

On April ninth, 1985, federal penitentiary inmate, Patrick Jerome Pirozzi, was escorted into a Napanee courtroom by officers on the Tactical Response Unit of the Ontario Provincial Police. The thirty-four-year-old had been transported separately from other inmates of nearby Millhaven Institution, a federal maximum-security penitentiary located not far from Napanee. Ordinarily, correctional service officers would be responsible for transporting inmates to court. But Pirozzi was a special case. He was considered highly dangerous and having a specialized team bring the prisoner into court would be a silent signal to observers that prison staff were fearful of this individual.

Pirozzi had been brought to court because he had been charged with assaulting Kreg Frederick on March thirtieth, 1984. On that day, Pirozzi was an inmate of the special handling unit (SHU) at the Millhaven prison. He was kept in isolation for misbehaviour. Solitary confinement was nothing new to Pirozzi. He had been kept segregated for much of the prison sentence he had been serving since first coming to prison in his early twenties.

If there was one word to sum up Pat Pirozzi's character it would be "anti-authoritarian". He resented anyone or any organization that tried to enforce their will over his. Additionally, he had the strength to do so. He had a short compact torso of pure muscle. He bragged that he could bench press five hundred pounds. He probably did not have to prove it but conditions had taken their toll on his body and his mind. He had been confined in solitary without access to the prison weight pit almost continuously since 1982. This Sault Ste Marie native, born November twenty-third, 1950, had been sentenced to imprisonment as the result of assaults he inflicted during a bar brawl. Then, once inside prison, he stood up physically to whoever was seen as an attacker – guards and inmates alike. These assaults led to more convictions.

By the time he was led into the courtroom in 1985, he had rung up fifteen convictions for assaulting peace officers plus another three counts of assault causing bodily harm.

Of course, injuring a guard or an inmate can, and in Pirozzi's case did, lead to transfer to Special Handling Units in Saskatchewan and most recently at Millhaven. Isolating a trouble-making inmate was seen as a means to protect the officers assigned the task of controlling difficult prisoners. What did not enter into the calculation was that lengthy periods of solitary confinement did not reform the troublemaker. Indeed, it often worsened the problem of attitude.

To make matters worse, Pirozzi was pitted against a culture dominant in the prison custodial staff that saw nothing wrong in treating inmates violently. One retired correctional officer described the attitude in these terms: *"We occasionally were told to "tune-up" cons that were acting up in the hole. We would hog tie inmates with shackles and handcuffs and leave them, put hockey helmets on them backward sometimes so they could not see. If they were good, we would unchain them so they could use the cell toilet. I would have to say probably all of my incidents in the hole were caused by the environment and guards who thought they were tough. I was a social worker working with young offenders prior to becoming a guard so it was difficult at times to make adjustments to my skills when dealing with the inmates. I was taught by old, experienced guards with military backgrounds and farm experience. Good people but pretty rough and would take no shit! There was good and bad to this but I still think CSC has not found the "happy medium" yet! I often thought if I was in the hole, I would turn really bad and welcome the opportunity to hook an asshole guard. Sad but true."*

Even when there was an apparent shift in the culture, the antiauthoritarian streak in Pirozzi interpreted a darker intent to rehabilitation programming. He told an interviewer in 1995 while confined at the Prince Albert Saskatchewan SHU:

> "Rather than tie the prisoners down physically to get them to stop doing things, they just tangle them up in programs like a dolphin in a tuna fish net."

Pat Pirozzi compared SHU programming to a ball and chain in which the SHU was the psychological version of the old physical apparatus of control. The programs that prisoners were required to complete for release from the SHU were the modern versions of the metal ball. His interviewer interpreted Pirozzi's comment to mean "The prisoner would take one program and then be told that there was another program which he must now take. The programs became links in a chain and over time the prisoner would be weighted down with programs just as surely as in the past he had been weighted down by steel and iron. Once a prisoner admitted the need to take programs, he was on a path from which he could never escape and he would be forever bound by his ball and chain. This was a path that Pirozzi was not prepared to begin to embark upon."

While an inmate at Saskatchewan Penitentiary, Pirozzi told his interviewer about how he saw himself: "I'm afraid that if they succeed in breaking me, I won't be me anymore. I'm like a centaur in chains. I have the sensitivities of a horse. I've got the stubbornness of a mule and they're asking me to pull a cart that's much too big to get through a small opening."

Like a horse on that April day back in 1985, Pirozzi reared up and lashed out at the TRU team while they were adjusting his chains in the prisoner box in the Napanee courtroom. Pirozzi mustered all his strength to rip the anchor to which he was chained from the prisoner's box. He used the chain and the broken piece of wood and lock assembly ripped from the box in lashing out at the four police officers. He threw a bible at Crown Attorney Rhys Morgan. I recall the judge scurrying quickly to his chambers. But within minutes, Pirozzi was brought under control. He was led out of the courtroom to face five more counts of assault with a weapon. Except for some damaged courtroom décor, judicial matters proceeded shortly after this outburst as though nothing had happened. I had no idea that this event would keep the man confined for the duration of his natural life.

It should not have come as a surprise for the Correctional Service of Canada (CSC) to learn that keeping men in isolation for prolonged periods could have unintended repercussions. After all, in considering the case of an inmate named McCann back in the 1970s, a British Columbia judge said this in his judgment: "Isolation as a preventative technique serves only to exacerbate problems of aggression and resentment and, since in such cases it is obviously counter-productive, it should be abolished." But it would be many more years before the concept of solitary confinement would be declared unconstitutional in Canada. Pirozzi's problems with aggression and resentment were punished by more brutal treatment and isolation. They continued to escalate. The most intense punishment was confinement in a Special Handling Unit, a super-maximum facility.

But why was Pirozzi in court on that April day? Not surprisingly, he was attending a court hearing for aggravated assault on a correctional officer. The background is this: Pirozzi was exercising his right to an hour outdoors, alone, before going back to his locked cell in solitary confinement. He was wearing what was known in prisons as a "body belt." It was a double chain link belt encircling the inmate's waist to which handcuffs were attached on each side. The guards obviously wanted to restrain hand movement while the prisoner was mobile.

At about a quarter past three in the afternoon on March thirtieth, 1984, Officer Kreg Frederick ordered Pirozzi back to his cell. Pirozzi knew he had not spent an hour in the yard and resented that his time of relative freedom was being abruptly curtailed. He was able to shed the body belt. Now armed and able to swing the chains, he responded to the guards, "Come and get me you pig bastards and see how tough you really are."

Even though he was armed with the chain, Pirozzi returned to the prison building. He never attempted to take a swipe with the swinging chain at any guard. However, he acknowledged his ability to do damage.

"If I hit you with this, I could kill you," he shouted as he hit the fence and a wall with the chain. Once inside, Pirozzi approached a barrier where he was required to place his hands through a square opening allowing for the removal of the handcuffs.

Officer Frederick unlocked the cuffs from one hand and was in the process of unlocking the cuffs from the second wrist. Suddenly and without warning, Officer Frederick felt a blow to his head. Pirozzi had landed a punch in Frederick's face just below the left eye. It was not a heavy punch but the act was unexpected and shocked the guard. Frederick ordered Pirozzi to return to his cell. Pirozzi replied, "Come and get me you fucking cowards."

When Pirozzi was halfway between the barrier where the handcuffs were removed and his cell door, the barrier was opened and six or seven correctional officers, including Frederick, charged toward Pirozzi. Pirozzi appeared as though he was about to comply with the order to return to his cell. As he was almost at the door to his cell, he stopped abruptly. By this time Frederick was at his side. Pirozzi grabbed Frederick around the waist with both arms and buried his face into Frederick's chest. Frederick was somewhat puzzled but suddenly Pirozzi lifted his head crashing it into the left side of Frederick's face just below the eye. A scuffle ensued in which Pirozzi bit Frederick's left arm.

When the guards were successful in controlling Pirozzi and returning him to his cell, it was realized that Frederick had sustained a depressed fracture of the left cheekbone requiring surgery to lift the bone into position. The bite caused some bruising but there was no deep penetration.

Yet Another Conviction

In June of 1985, a jury convicted Pirozzi of the assaults on Frederick. Sentencing was adjourned until July. But before passing sentence, Pirozzi advised the court that he had fired his defence counsel. He had become dissatisfied with the way his lawyer, Terry O'Hara (later appointed as a Provincial Court Judge) had handled his case. Pirozzi was upset that more was not done to challenge the correctional officers who had testified against him at trial and had committed perjury. By minimizing their aggressive behaviour that led to the incident in the corridor where Frederick was injured Pirozzi would be unable to persuade a jury that the supposed punch to Frederick's face at the barrier was just a reflex action. He claimed Frederick unintentionally irritated a nerve in Pirozzi's hand while removing the cuffs. Nonetheless, the jury had spoken and the judge was bound to accept the verdict. The trial judge, Bernard W. Hurley agreed to the adjournment and set a new date of August thirtieth for the sentencing. Pirozzi scrambled but obtained representation from a prison rights lawyer, Fergus J. "Chip" O'Connor. It caused O'Connor some difficulty to ensure that the Ontario Legal Aid Plan would cover his fees but O'Connor worked tirelessly within the court-imposed time restraints to ensure that Pirozzi would have proper representation on sentencing.

It was not a simple matter of speaking to the sentence that O'Connor may have been expecting. Crown Attorney Brian Gilkinson saw Pirozzi's actions as a flagrant attack on correctional officers and as a pattern of behaviour that had been established throughout Pirozzi's prison term. Gilkinson wanted to move to have Pirozzi declared a dangerous offender which would see Pirozzi locked away indefinitely.

O'Connor disputed the attempt to see his client declared a dangerous offender. He urged clemency. The trial judge agreed. Instead of declaring Pirozzi a dangerous offender, Judge Hurley proceeded with sentencing and imposed a sentence of three months for the assault and nine months for the assault causing bodily harm. Of course, this sentence would be added to the prison term that Pirozzi was already serving. There were still the charges relating to the April courtroom outburst in which the prisoner's box was destroyed and a bible was thrown at the Crown Attorney. But until he was convicted on those charges, he remained technically innocent. He returned to the penitentiary to serve out his time and expecting trial on the latest rampage. He was expected to go before another jury the following November. However, when the November date arrived for a jury to be selected, Crown Attorney Brian Gilkinson objected to the panel and was successful in rescheduling the jury trial to the following spring.

Gilkinson had had his hopes of obtaining a dangerous offender designation dashed after the conviction on Frederick's situation. With a jury trial set to begin on the charge of assaulting Crown Attorney Rhys Morgan by throwing a bible at him, assaulting four members of the OPP TRU team and damaging the prisoner's box, Gilkinson announced a renewed attempt to have Pirozzi locked away for good.

Gilkinson pulled out all the stops. He announced his intention to call one hundred and fifty witnesses and that the jury could expect to be sitting for two months. In January of 1987, Pirozzi had pleaded guilty to throwing a bible at Crown Attorney Morgan.

When the trial on the assault of the police officers commenced in February, Judge Burke Smith of Toronto was assigned to hear the case.

Gilkinson's first witness was Cpl. Albert Edwin Sherwin, an OPP TRU team member. He testified that when he attempted to secure Pirozzi's leg restraints to the prisoner's box, Pirozzi kicked him. Later, as Pirozzi was exiting the prisoner's box, he was head-butted causing cuts to his mouth and lips and when he fell to the floor, he suffered bruising to his back and neck. He called Pirozzi "very unpredictable" and "prone to fits of violence."

As the trial was entering its second month, Gilkinson's plan was to paint a picture for the jury of the violent deeds in which Pirozzi was involved in his prison experience. To that end, Gilkinson called former correctional officer Paul William Bell about an incident that occurred at Kingston Penitentiary. Bell recalled an attack on inmate Norman Skedden, who had been pushed down a stairway onto a landing. The unconscious inmate was then repeatedly struck on the head with a Melmac cup and then kicked. The correctional officer said he observed Sneddon to be in "very bad shape" and bleeding from the ears.

The court also heard that Pirozzi had been charged by the Kingston Police Department for the serious attack on a fellow inmate in this 1976 incident. At the trial, Pirozi had unsuccessfully argued self-defence claiming Skedden had threatened to throw gasoline on Pirozzi and set him afire. Pirozzi claimed his actions were in retribution for this attack. After being found guilty, a sentence of eighteen months was imposed, one of the multitude of convictions Pirozzi had rung up during his penitentiary term.

As the trial entered its fifth week, Gilkinson pressed on dredging up the past history of violence attributable to Pirozzi. George Whitehead said that in the ten years, he was governor and later superintendent of Toronto's notorious Don Jail, he had experience dealing with half a million inmates. Pirozzi was the most dangerous inmate he had encountered. William Zodiapas, the assistant superintendent of the Ottawa detention centre testified he remembered Pirozzi when he had been jailed in Sault Ste. Marie back in 1974. He described Pirozzi as an inmate there as aggressive, continually in fights, prone to shouting and screaming and refusing staff-issued orders. He was not a cooperative prisoner.

Then there was the evidence of Allan Dunbar, the superintendent of the provincial jail at Burwash. He detailed an occasion when Pirozzi had struck a guard on the head with a scrub brush. Dunbar had personally experienced the man's violence when he suffered a cut above his eye after Pirozzi grabbed and broke a specimen bottle. It was also learned that while an inmate in Sault Ste. Marie, Pirozzi smashed toilets and had frequent placements in solitary confinement because of his unruly behaviour.

After the lengthy case adjourned to allow Judge Smith to decide Pirozzi's fate, he was returned to Millhaven maximum security penitentiary. But while awaiting the time to return to court, the sentence administrator concluded that for all the penalties Pirozzi had accumulated, he had reached the two-thirds level of the time imposed. By law, Pirozzi was entitled to be released from prison to serve the remaining third of his sentence under supervision in the community.

But Pirozzi was still under charge for the assault on the TRU team and breaking up the prisoner's box. He had also thrown a bible at a Crown Attorney. Therefore, instead of remaining in federal custody, he was transferred to the Quinte Detention Centre, a provincial institution that could hold accused persons who had not made bail.

There Must Be A Better Way

While at Quinte, Pirozzi's lawyer, Chip O'Connor, devised an ingenious solution. He proposed that Pirozzi be released on statutory release but ordered to reside at the Help Freedom Farm, a halfway house in Napanee capable of accommodating former inmates. In support of the move, O'Connor called Tom French who was able to describe life in prison and the pressures that exist to suggest that Pirozzi's life behind bars was not necessarily reflective of how he would act in the community. French was the Director of the Help Freedom Farm and could identify with problems newly released offenders deal with as French himself had served time in prison.

French described to the court the major difference between the culture that exists in prison and how it differs from life on the outside. French described the culture within penitentiaries as an "us" and "them" world. Inmates felt picked upon and abused by custodial staff. The guards felt the need to display no tolerance for unruly inmates. Between the two camps was a steel barrier to demarcate the boundaries between the camps. Sometimes custodial staff would feel threatened or intimidated by looks or comments that in the outside world would have gone unnoticed.

Sometimes inmates could not sympathize with guards who experienced personal difficulties in a job where alcoholism and divorce were rampant. It would be erroneous to attribute all unruly behavior to inmates; sometimes guards were often as responsible as the inmates for disturbances. French swore that he was aware of Pirozzi's reputation as a troublemaker. French attributed Pirozzi's misdeeds to being a product of solitary confinement. "Remember," he said," Pirozzi has lived in the toilet for years. You eat and sleep next to your crapper. At the farm, there are two hundred acres to roam."

It was not brought to the court's attention that the Correctional Service was unconvinced that Pirozzi would be a threat to public safety. There were provisions in the law that a referral could be made to the National Parole Board (now called the Parole Board of Canada) to secure an order that dangerous inmates be detained to serve the final third of their sentences. The Board would have to find a likelihood that the inmate posed a threat to public safety and would likely re-offend. Such a referral was never made and Pirozzi was never called to a detention hearing.

It did not take a lengthy trial to prove Pirozzi was dangerous. After all, dangerousness is a symptom of underlying social problems. Would the time and expense have not been better spent discerning the nature and remedy that misguided Pirozzi's actions?

Judge Smith was impressed with Tom French's solution but it required Pirozzi to be released from the Quinte Detention Centre on bail to serve his time on mandatory supervision at the halfway farm. The judge expressed his respect and admiration for the work French and his co-workers were doing "But I must put your offer on hold because we must assure the credibility of the justice system is preserved, even if it is imperfect." The judge worried that Pirozzi might

"fly the coop" if allowed to be released from custody before his trial was concluded.

After months of testimony and a litany of offences recalling incidents from all over Ontario recounting Pirozzi's intimidating words and actions, the jury returned its verdict. The May fifth, 1987 edition of the *Globe and Mail* declared, "A former Millhaven Penitentiary inmate was declared a dangerous offender yesterday and returned to the maximum-security prison to serve an indefinite sentence." The finding of guilt that triggered the application was for his assault on a peace officer and throwing a bible at a Crown attorney. The injuries sustained by the TRU team member were certainly not as serious as the damage done to the Millhaven correctional officer for which Judge Hurley imposed a one-year sentence. The Bible did not make contact with Crown attorney Rhys Morgan. But the dangerous offender designation would keep Pirozzi incarcerated indefinitely because it was the accumulation of past misdeeds – offences for which he had been sentenced and served time – that outraged the public as found by the Court.

Parliamentary Oversight

In November of 1987, a seven-member committee of parliamentarians visited Kingston-area penitentiaries. The committee included five members from the governing Progressive Conservative Party as well as members from opposition parties, John Nunziata of the Liberals and Svend Robinson of the NDP. The committee was to study prison and parole conditions to improve the "imperfect" justice system. The opposition members felt their work was being muzzled by the Correctional Service of Canada.

Svend Robinson charged that the inmates who made up the inmate committee at Millhaven Institution had been transferred to another prison the day before they were scheduled to speak to the Members of Parliament. Robinson also reported that Pirozzi had been beaten by guards and left bleeding the day before the committee arrived. Correctional Services spokesman Dennis Curtis admitted that Pirozzi was injured during resistance to a proposed transfer to Prince Albert prison in Saskatchewan. Nunziata also claimed the parliamentary committee's work was in vain because he was "concerned we were only being shown certain things."

Final Days

This appeared to be the last time Pirozzi came to public attention. Or, more accurately, this was the last time Corrections allowed Pirozzi's name to come before the public. By 2015 he had served about thirty-five years in segregation, perhaps the longest period of time an inmate has served in solitary confinement in Canada. Since the issue of the constitutionality of solitary confinement was coming before the courts, Global News sought to interview Patrick Pirozzi. Global News went through the proper procedures for making an interview request. Pirozzi was in agreement to do the interview. However, the request was denied because the Correctional Service thought bringing cameras and microphones into a prison would be disruptive. The interview never took place.

On November second, 2020 the Government of Canada issued a press release that read as follows:

"On October thirtieth, 2020, Patrick Pirozzi, an inmate from Millhaven Institution, Regional Treatment Centre, died while in our custody of apparent natural causes following an illness. At the time of his death, Mr. Pirozzi had been serving an indeterminate sentence for Assault (times nine), Assault with a weapon, Assault Cause Bodily Harm (times three), Cause Disturbance, Indecent Assault Female, and Theft over $200, since his sentence commenced May fourth, 1987."

Even in death, the CSC could not refrain from adding inaccurate descriptors to inflame public resentment against the man. There had been no conviction for an indecent assault on a woman or theft charges. He had been in prison long before 1987.

What cannot be denied is that Patrick Jerome Pirozzi lived a wasted life. His character flaw – his antiauthoritarianism – had pitted him against adversaries that made every day of his life a living hell. What if, at an early stage there had been an intervention to curtail, or at least allow Pirozzi to control, his anti-social attitude? Could he have lived a productive and meaningful existence? Would society have been safer? Without that intervention, several people were injured. We will never know because our approach to dealing with crime is to use the stick and not the carrot - beat it down and eventually incapacitate it – an approach similar to that taken by Patrick Pirozzi on his victims.

CHAPTER 4

MOMMY, MOMMY: WHEN THE SYSTEM MAKES A MISTAKE

Tammy Marquardt and her Wrongful Conviction

> It is unwise to be too sure of one's own wisdom. It is healthy to be reminded that the strongest might weaken and the wisest might err.
>
> **– Mahatma Gandhi**

With tears in her eyes, a polite soft-spoken woman with short brown hair sat on the other side of a desk in the interview room of Kitchener's Grand Valley Institution, a prison for women.

"I'm sorry," she said, rubbing her eyes with her fists to stop the flow of tears.

She explained she had been involved with the prison's "kitten project." A local veterinarian had placed a litter of day-old motherless kittens with inmate volunteers. The volunteers took it upon themselves to attempt to nurse the felines to the point that they could manage on their own, without constant bottle-feeding. This woman's kitten did not make it, and she was grieving.

The woman was Tammy Lynn Marquardt. Tammy was serving a sentence of life imprisonment without parole eligibility for at least ten years. She wanted to apply for parole, and the preparation for a future hearing was the reason for my visit.

Tammy's Background

Born in Toronto and raised by her mother, Tammy was sexually assaulted by her mother's boyfriend as a teenager. She left home at seventeen and continued to bear the scars of her mistreatment. Feeling alone in the world and lacking a sense of self-worth, Tammy turned to alcohol and drugs.

She was only nineteen when she gave birth to her firstborn son, Kenneth Wynne, on May eighteenth, 1991. It was discovered that Kenneth had severe health issues including asthma, pneumonia, and epilepsy.

By 1993, Tammy was no longer living with the child's father and had begun a relationship with Rick Marquardt. Together they had another child, Keith, and Tammy moved in with Rick in September 1993. Tammy was now twenty-one and had to manage herself and her two children with little support from her partner. Rick was abusive towards Tammy, and they had severe fights. During one absence from home, Rick hooked up with his former girlfriend and she became pregnant. Tammy though, did not see this as cheating, as she and Rick had been separated when the girlfriend announced her pregnancy. The two reconciled and Rick came back to live with Tammy.

Kenneth suffered from epilepsy and experienced seizures from time to time. He required medical intervention. This involved a trip to the Emergency Department. Any time Kenneth experienced a seizure it greatly upset his mother.

On Saturday, October 9, 1993, Tammy was home with Kenneth and Rick Marquardt. Around eight o'clock in the morning, Rick received a call from his former girlfriend. She was about to give birth and wanted him to be with her. Rick felt it was right for him to be present, and he convinced Tammy too. Rick was out of cash, so Tammy gave Rick her ATM card. Tammy was alone with her kids and expected to be alone the rest of the day. Both mother and children took an afternoon nap.

Around four in the afternoon, Tammy woke up and went to the bathroom. She heard

Kenneth calling her. It was muffled, but it sounded like "Mommy mommy." When she got to the bedroom, Kenneth was rolled up in the bedding, his head was at the foot of the bed and his body twisted up in the sheets down to his chest. He was tangled up and it was hard to get the sheets off him. Tammy panicked. His pleas soon faded from "Mommy" to simply "Mom," and Tammy realized that there was something seriously wrong. She finally managed to untangle him from the bedding.

In Tammy's Own Words

Tammy was able to describe the time period of events in her own words:

> When the police later asked me how long this all took, I said about 20 minutes; that is how long it seemed to me. For some reason, I noticed the clock in the bedroom said 4:33. I later came to know that the 911 call was made at 4:38 so my time estimate was off; I can only say it seemed like an eternity as I tried to extricate Kenneth from the sheets.

(Yes, she used the word "extricate." Tammy did not see herself as others viewing someone in her situation might generalize. She may have dropped out of school and lacked formal education, but she saw herself as more than a "baby-maker." She read books and had hopes of one day returning to school and beginning a fulfilling career.)

Tammy found the boy gasping for breath. When she called for emergency assistance, the 911 operator instructed Tammy to perform CPR, but she was so distressed she couldn't take instructions.

Emergency workers arrived at the apartment at 4:42 p.m., within five minutes of the call.

Tammy was visibly distraught, but directed them to Kenneth, who was lying motionless on a couch Tammy had moved him to. His face was a grey-ashen colour and he was not breathing.

Tammy told the workers that he had a history of epilepsy. When efforts of resuscitation at the apartment failed, Kenneth was transported to Oshawa General Hospital immediately, and later the same day, to the Hospital for Sick Children in Toronto (commonly called "SickKids"). The emergency physician who saw Kenneth was not satisfied with Tammy's explanation for the child's condition, and he asked that the Suspected Child Abuse and Neglect Unit become involved.

Kenneth died in hospital three days later after being removed from life-support. Tammy felt that it was appropriate to spare another family the pain of losing a child, so she signed consent to donate viable organs for transplantation to other children. Kenneth's liver, kidneys, and heart valves were harvested for organ donation.

The Autopsy and Trial

After the organs were removed, Kenneth's body was taken for autopsy by Dr. Charles Smith, Director of the Ontario Pediatric Forensic Pathology Unit at SickKids.

Smith's autopsy report concluded that Kenneth had not died of natural causes but had likely been smothered. Three weeks after her son's death, Tammy Marquardt was arrested for murder.

At age twenty-one, Tammy had no "real world" experience. She retained a lawyer and a trial was held in Whitby, Ontario before a judge and jury. Dr. Smith provided expert opinion, having performed the autopsy. He testified that the absence of the harvested organs was a "minor inconvenience," and that the cause of death was "asphyxia" (which caused irreversible brain damage). He defined asphyxia as "a condition affecting the organs of the body or the body wherein there is impaired delivery or utilization of oxygen. An injury occurs because either there is inadequate supply of oxygen, or the oxygen which is present cannot be properly used."

Dr. Smith relied on scattered petechial hemorrhages (tiny red blood spots) over the surfaces of the boy's heart, lungs and thymus as evidence of asphyxia. He also testified that he found microscopic hemorrhages in the small skeletal muscles of the neck, which he deemed consistent with a non-accidental injury to the neck. He further testified that the child's brain was extremely swollen, which was part of the asphyxia and he put these findings together to provide this opinion to the jury:

"So what I'm left with in Kenneth is this: He has evidence of asphyxia. I have no natural disease that explains the asphyxia. I have some microscopic evidence of hemorrhage in his neck that would be consistent with neck injury, but I can't say whether that neck injury was accidental or non-accidental. It would appear to be not a severe or prolonged neck injury if it was real such that we see the petechial changes in or around his eyes or in the region of his face.

So, what I'm saying is that he died of asphyxia. The asphyxia could be environmental, could be an environmental lack of oxygen, could be something like a plastic bag or a gentle suffocation. It could be a neck compression, I can't rule that out, though I don't have incontrovertible evidence of that. I have no evidence that he died of things like hotdogs, but then I wasn't there, so I can't make that statement.

Dr. Smith went on to testify that his findings were consistent with suffocation, whether it be from a soft object, a pillow, a plastic bag or if someone held his nose and mouth closed. He discounted seizure as a cause of death, claiming to have no evidence "at all" of that possibility. In particular, he testified that "you don't have evidence of asphyxia" from sudden and unexpected death in epilepsy (SUDEP). However, he allowed that he was not an expert on this condition and that the opinion of a pediatric neurologist would be better than his own on that issue. But he concluded, if he were a "bettin' man" he would put his chips on a non-accidental death.

The prosecution led with evidence that Tammy lacked financial resources, parenting and coping skills, and that she was involved in an unstable relationship with Rick Marquardt, Kenneth's stepfather. There was also evidence that Tammy had abused alcohol and drugs as a teenager. It was noted that the Children's Aid Society had visited the home, although the child was not taken into protection.

The defence was that the child died in the throes of an epileptic seizure. No expert evidence was called on the point, and the defence did not seriously cross-examine Dr. Smith to highlight conclusions that one might deem speculative. After all, the trial judge had qualified Dr. Smith as an expert entitled to give opinion evidence, and a competent defence lawyer never asks a question without knowing full well what the answer will be.

With the substantial expert opinion of Dr. Smith, the jury quickly returned a verdict of "guilty" and the life sentence was imposed.

The Appeal

An appeal of the conviction and sentence was made to the Ontario Court of Appeal. That appeal was unanimously dismissed by a three-judge panel consisting of Justices Findlayson, Rosenberg and Goudge on January 22, 1998. This would not be the only involvement by Justice Goudge in the life of Tammy Marquardt.

* * *

Tammy Goes to Prison

Once convicted, Tammy was taken to the Prison for Women in Kingston. She also found out she was pregnant, an experience that would be heart-rending for a woman who had never been convicted for any criminal violations in her past. She knew nothing of prison culture and had to become a quick learner. There is a major sensory difference between entering a women's prison and a men's prison. In a male lock-up men want to convey toughness and showing any emotion could undermine that façade. Women, by contrast, tended to be very expressive with their feelings. One could hear women crying or screaming; it was bedlam.

Even though a prison is composed of inmates serving their time, there are definite hierarchies of offenders. In male prisons, the lowest of the low are those serving sentences for child molestation - or being a snitch (or a "rat.") Murderers are relatively high up the chain of respect, depending on the nature of their victims. In a female prison, those on the bottom rung in the chain are child killers, especially if the victim was one's own child. People on the bottom rungs of prison society are in constant fear of beatings or death.

Tammy asked what she should say if another inmate should ask about her crime. She was told just to say that she was doing life for killing her husband. That would be the safest way to go.

Kingston's Prison for Women, commonly referred to as P4W, was at one time Canada's only female prison. It was also a multi-level security institution, meaning that it housed inmates who were considered to require high, medium and low security demands.

Tammy was first placed in a "double-bunked" cell, wherein two inmates occupied a single cell measuring nine by six feet. There is barely room for *one* person to move, let alone two. To make matters even more uncomfortable, her cellmate was also pregnant. After about a month with the help of the Lifers' Group (a group of inmates all serving life sentences), Tammy was reassigned to a single cell.

But this was not the end of her problems. News stories about Tammy's conviction had seeped into the fortress that was the prison. Tammy and her unborn child were in peril, and for that reason Tammy opted to be placed in protective custody. It couldn't happen soon enough; inmates in the general population started calling Tammy a "baby killer," and threatened retribution should she walk again outside the protective custody range.

Tammy went into labour while in the penitentiary. She was strapped to a prison gurney for a day and a half until the baby was delivered. The newborn, named Eric, was immediately taken into protection by the Children's Aid Society. Following the birth, Tammy was handcuffed to a wheelchair, though in an act of kindness, a guard released the shackles from one of Tammy's hands so she could hold her newborn for a few minutes before a social worker showed up and seized the child.

Like her other son, who was taken by CAS when Tammy was arrested, the boys became Crown Wards and were eventually adopted. Tammy was made aware that they were adopted together and resided somewhere in Canada. Tammy was not provided the names or locations of the adoptive parents, but she was allowed to write her children a letter to be presented to them when they reached the age of 18 should they opt to make contact in the future.

P4W was a dreadful place to do time. Opened in 1934, the limestone multi-story building was dark, dingy, and without elevators. It has been described as "labyrinthine." Just four years after it opened, a federal government report called for its closure, and a 1977 government report called it "unfit for bears, much less women." Nonetheless, it was the only prison for women in Canada. Tammy Marquardt was forced to endure her fate within its walls until a newly constructed facility was opened in Kitchener, the Grand Valley Institution (GVI).

The new prison was one of six opened to house women inmates across Canada and replaced the P4W, which finally closed in 2000. Despite the clean and modern atmosphere, it was still a penitentiary. Yet Tammy was able to prepare herself for eventual release in much less oppressive conditions than had existed in the Kingston prison.

Tammy on Parole

The life sentence that Tammy was serving also included a provision that she could not apply for parole for at least 10 years. In those years, Tammy had made substantial progress in being able to convince her case management team inside the prison - and ultimately, the Parole Board - that she had obtained the maximum benefit of incarceration. She had reduced her security level to minimum, and there were no institutional charges on her record indicating she was obedient to prison rules and procedures. She was employed within the institution and had upgraded her computer skills.

Of particular importance - because of her past history of substance abuse - she had forty-three consecutive clean urinalysis tests. She had been accompanied by staff on seven occasions for brief community outings known as Escorted Temporary Absences. She had the support of a halfway house in another city, should she be released. All these indicators pointed the way to a positive decision of release by the Board. The one obstacle standing in Tammy's way was her ongoing denial that she had murdered her son. Usually, the Board liked to see inmates taking responsibility for their actions, but Tammy's refusal to lie to gain what would be a sure release remained impressive.

On May 25, 2005, Tammy went before the National Parole Board to ask for a series of Unescorted Temporary Absences and, ultimately, a grant of day parole.

Unescorted absences, or UTAs, give further assurance to the Board that an inmate can follow instructions. A UTA is used to introduce oneself to a halfway house and to make arrangements for banking, employment, or schooling once one re-enters the community.

The Board, despite Tammy's unwillingness to admit to the crime, concluded that Tammy was a manageable risk not to re-offend if placed in the community, and granted the day parole application conditional upon completion of three successful UTAs. Day parole would last for six months, with full parole to follow if reports of good conduct on day parole were presented to the Board.

In some respects, release on parole was more challenging than full-time residence in a penitentiary. While rules in prison were strictly enforced, the prison was also a place to stay with clothing and meals provided. In a halfway house, one was also expected to abide by strict rules - including a curfew, and abstinence from alcohol and drugs. One continues to reside with offenders, but during the day one was allowed to go into the community and pretend to be an ordinary citizen. Strict supervision was constant and lapses in expected behaviour could result in an offender's suspension on parole - and unless the suspension was cancelled – a return to imprisonment.

The Halfway House

Things did not go well at the halfway house. In years past, Tammy had taken to alcohol and drugs to cover the toxic shame and humiliation of sexual abuse. While on day parole there was even more stifling daily embarrassment of being regarded as a baby killer.

Day parole was extended throughout 2006 and most of 2007. Full parole was denied; however, the Board was very concerned with breaches of the alcohol and drug conditions it had originally imposed. It also noted that Tammy had broken off her longtime friendship with a female friend and had become romantically involved with that friend's boyfriend. The Board saw this as a re-enactment of the problems that landed her in prison. By November 30, 2007, the Board had heard enough and revoked her day parole, sending Tammy back to prison. It could take years before she would be able to convince another Board to grant a release.

Referral to AIDWYC (Innocence Canada)

When I lived in Toronto, I had been asked to join the Board of Directors of a relatively new organization called the Association in Defence of the Wrongly Convicted, or AIDWYC (now called Innocence Canada). I found myself in the company of a group of dedicated and knowledgeable lawyers and staff who were committed to righting the wrongs of a system that imprisoned innocent people. The workloads of the volunteers who made up the organization were crushing. There were simply not enough hours in a day to take on or "adopt" every case.

After seeing Tammy's reaction when telling me of her experience with the kitten program, I was able to see her as a person legitimately denying the offence of which she had been convicted. How could someone exhibit such grief for a dead kitten and still be able to kill her own child? I also knew there were rumblings that Dr. Smith was not the reliable expert he had been portrayed as by the prosecution, (one judge openly criticizing his evidence.) I was convinced Tammy was no killer, and in 2004, I wrote to AIDWYC staff urging its adoption of Tammy's case.

Fortunately, the AIDWYC Board decided to take up the cause. In April 2005, the organization wrote to Dr. Barry McLellan - at the time was Ontario's Chief Coroner – and to Attorney General Michael Bryant, asking for a full public inquiry into the work of Dr.

Charles Smith. Two months later, the Chief Coroner issued a press release announcing a full review would be made of the suspicious child deaths where Dr. Smith had conducted the autopsy. That review asked Dr. Pekka Saukko, a Professor of Forensic Medicine at the University of Turku in Finland, to examine Kenneth's case.

That review concluded with a report to the Chief Coroner in which Dr. Saukko found that Dr. Smith's findings - that Kenneth had died of asphyxia - were "illogical and completely against scientific evidence-based reasoning."

A second review was conducted by Dr. Simon Avis, the Chief Medical Examiner for Newfoundland. He concurred with the Saukko analysis and concluded that death was likely attributable to an epileptic seizure or other natural causes. Both Saukko and Avis said that the harvesting of organs was not a mere "inconvenience" (as Dr. Smith had testified) but represented a loss of critical information.

With these findings shared, AIDWYC counsel then applied to review the dismissal of the Ontario Court of Appeal decision in the Supreme Court of Canada. Since the time for an appeal had lapsed, it was necessary to have the Supreme Court of Canada allow an extension, which was granted the day following the February 10, 2009 leave application filing.

On March 12, 2009, Tammy Marquardt was granted appeal bail and released from Grand Valley Institution. By that time, she had served fourteen years.

Rather than ruling on the matter itself, the Supreme Court remanded the case to the Ontario Court of Appeal so that the fresh evidence of Drs. Saukko and Avis could be examined.

All the while, the Attorney General of Ontario had appointed Justice Goudge to head up and present a report, entitled *Inquiry into Pediatric Forensic Pathology in Ontario*. Goudge looked into numerous cases where Dr. Smith's evidence was questionable. Justice Goudge was also critical of Dr. Smith's testimony, and the confusing way Smith used terms such as "asphyxia" and other imprecise terminology before a jury, such as making a conclusion prefaced with the hypothetical situation of Smith being a "betting man."

Although the findings of Dr. Smith were critical for the Ontario Court of Appeal's decision in the Marquardt case, the Goudge inquiry cast a large shadow over not just the evidence presented by Dr. Smith, but also the manner coroners were instructed to view child deaths in Ontario at the time. The office of the Chief Coroner was vexed by the notion that many homicides were not being caught. A major embarrassment came when it was later found that Karla Homolka, along with her serial killer boyfriend Paul Bernardo, had murdered Karla's sister and that the cause of death was not recognized as a homicide. To avoid future criticism, the Chief Coroner issued what has become known as "Memo 631", an instruction for examiners to "think dirty" when encountering suspicious cases. This instruction imposed a presumption of guilt in lieu of the constitutionally recognized presumption of innocence to which Canadians are entitled.

Exoneration

On April 8, 2011, Justice Marc Rosenberg, writing on behalf of Justices Robert Sharpe and David Watt, allowed the appeal, set aside the murder conviction, and ordered a new trial.

In early June 2011, the new trial began before Ontario Superior Court Judge Michael Brown in an Oshawa courtroom. The Crown Attorney announced that rather than proceeding with a trial, the charge was to be withdrawn.

The judge commented that it was tragic that it had taken so long to uncover Dr. Smith's mistakes." You're free to go, ma'am," the judge said to Tammy Marquardt.

Tammy placed her hand on her chest and hugged her lawyer. Outside, holding a photo of Kenneth, she told reporters, "Honestly, I never thought I would see this day. I thought there is no justice. They're going to believe him and they're not going to believe someone like me."

Dr. Charles Smith was eventually stripped of his medical licence for professional misconduct and incompetence. Tammy Marquardt was awarded two hundred and fifty thousand dollars as compensation for her fourteen years of imprisonment. In actual fact, there were no winners. The system of justice and the reputation of the Coroner's Office had been dealt a severe blow.

No amount of compensation could ever repay Tammy for her ordeal.

Tammy wants to find her sons put up for adoption. However, after her exoneration in 2011, she made strides to rebuild her life. She moved into a small house in Toronto with her fiancée, his mother, and his teenage daughter and gave birth to a baby girl.

CHAPTER 5

PICKING BAD FRIENDS

Gary Harris: A Toronto Cabbie Murdered

> *Be wary of the company you keep for they are a reflection of*
> *who you are, or who you want to be...*
>
> **– Kenneth G. Ortiz**

Drugs and alcohol are factors that can disrupt an individual's life in society. Many explain the reason for the use or abuse of substances as stemming from social pressures. One pressure that is often overlooked comes from one's choice of friends and associates. It continually surprises me in exploring a client accused or incarcerated for a criminal offence, and how that person's life would have taken a different trajectory had it not been for an unfortunate choice of friends.

The man taking his seat in the interview room at medium-security Warkworth Institution was the most unlikely face for a murderer I had ever seen. He was not bulked up, as so many inmates are from hours spent lifting heavy weights in the penitentiary gym. If anything, he appeared slightly overweight. But his brown eyes were shining, and he wore a broad smile.

Gary Harris was ordered by Ontario's Court of Appeal to retain counsel to argue his conviction for second-degree murder. He had spent years at maximum-security Kingston Penitentiary, and through hard work and good behaviour had reduced his classification to medium. Perhaps there was an end in sight.

"That's a good sign?" he asked as he took his seat. I nodded affirmatively.

The indictment that landed him in prison was simple: "That on or about the 26th day of August in the year 1983, at the Municipality of Metropolitan Toronto in the Judicial District of York, did murder one Philip Davidson and did thereby commit first-degree murder, contrary to the Criminal Code." Almost a year later, on May 31, 1984, Harris was found guilty of second-degree murder, and his co-accused, Lance Timothy Woods, was convicted of first-degree murder in the venture.

Gary Harris' Background

Gary had endured a difficult upbringing. He had been raised in foster homes and got into his share of juvenile mischief. "Easily led," "manipulable," and "gullible" were common descriptors of teenage Gary Harris. At age sixteen, he dropped out of school having completed grade 9 in a special class for slow learners. By age twenty-one, he was married without children. He never spoke much of his family. It was obvious that Gary never had any significant male role model as he transitioned between foster homes. His friendships were few, and male friends tended to be self-styled "macho men." It was then that he met a new pal.

Harris met Tim Woods in early August 1983, and the two would soon be hanging out frequently. Tim posed as an extremely self-confident individual who liked aggressive sports and hunting. He too was unemployed and did not have a car, so Gary and Tim spent considerable time on their bikes – usually hanging out in shopping malls. A common meeting point was the Square One shopping mall in Mississauga, just west of Toronto.

Harris accompanied Woods to Square One in the late afternoon of August 26th. Woods had been bragging that he was an avid hunter and purchased a Kodiak hunting knife. He told Harris that he planned to use the knife for sport. To pay for it, Woods had secured some cash from a bank ATM and became frustrated that the bank machine had "eaten" his access card.

Upon leaving the shopping centre, Woods and Harris bicycled first to Woods' home and from there to the Harris apartment. Woods then divulged that he wanted to rob a taxi driver to get the money necessary for his hunting trip up north. Part of the plan was to "dummy" the taxicab driver.

Harris asked Woods what he meant by the term "dummy."

"I will kill him or wipe him out," Woods responded.

"You're crazy!" Harris exclaimed in disbelief. But Woods kept coming back to his murderous plan over the course of the evening.

Harris was in further disbelief by Woods' lack of reaction to being called "crazy." Woods saying that it was "nothing, totally nothing" both amazed and shocked Harris.

Harris loaned Woods an old white long-sleeved shirt, as it seemed inappropriate to head out in the evening with Woods wearing just a T-shirt. It also served as a useful cover for the hunting knife that Woods carried on his belt.

If they were indeed going to find a cab, they wouldn't need to take their bikes. The two ventured on foot to the Long Branch Loop - the westernmost stop on the longest Toronto Transit Commission (TTC) streetcar route, the 501 Queen Line, where the men knew there would be taxis for hire.

Discussions continued about the planned robbery. Woods gave Harris forty dollars in cash, with the understanding that Harris was to pay the cab fare and Woods would then rob the cabbie at knifepoint.

As expected, the men found taxis at the Long Branch Loop cab stand, hailing a cab driven by thirty-seven-year-old Philip Davidson. Woods took the back seat behind the driver while Harris climbed into the front seat. Woods directed Davidson to drive to the Transpo factory in an isolated Etobicoke industrial park.

"You can let us out here," Woods ordered the driver as he pulled into a driveway. Davidson stopped the car with the motor running. Harris, seemingly forgetting to hand the driver the forty dollars as planned, exited the vehicle. Instead, Woods tendered a twenty-dollar bill and stabbed the cabbie in the neck as he reached for the cash.

Davidson had only been cab driving for about four months. He tried to call for help on his radio, but he was too weak to be able to make himself heard. The taxi rolled ahead, crashing into a pole.

Harris claimed he was unaware that the stabbing had taken place. He admitted to having heard a shuffling noise, but it was not until Woods said "Gary, I stabbed him" that Harris understood the deed had been done.

The duo headed from the taxi around the side of the factory and cut through residential backyards. Harris was upset that Woods used the white shirt he had loaned Tim to wipe the blood from the knife blade. "

I've got to get rid of the shirt," Woods said as he continued cleaning the knife blade.

Woods then remembered that he had left the knife sheath in the backseat of the taxi and that his fingerprints were on it.

Once onto a main street, the two men split up to go their separate ways. The horrible nature of what they'd just done was an act that weighed heavily on Gary's conscience.

Harris Calls Police

Approximately an hour later, near ten p.m., Harris telephoned the police to report that he had "witnessed a stabbing." Later he met with the police and told them that he had been with a "guy" whose name he could not recall and who had stabbed the taxi driver. Harris told the police that this person resided with a lady in Apt. 508, 1300 Mississauga Valley Blvd. As a result of this information received from Harris four police officers arrived at Apt. 508 around a half hour before midnight to stake out the residence. They were admitted by a woman named Mrs. Button - but no man was present.

At a quarter after one in the morning, the police officers heard a sound at the front door and instructed Mrs. Button and her daughter to move to the kitchen area. Woods entered the apartment. As he bent over to take off his shoes, one of the officers - Detective Price – announced his team's presence and demanded the man to identify himself.

He immediately answered: "Tim Woods."

Detective Price then said: "You are under arrest, put your hands against the wall," as handcuffs were drawn from the officer's belt. Woods was quick to comply with all police instructions. One police officer, Constable Telfer, had drawn his service revolver. Woods later testified that he saw the gun pointed in his direction after he had entered the apartment. Constable Telfer testified that his revolver was pointed at the floor and that he holstered the weapon when the appellant put his hands on the wall.

After Tim Woods had put his hands on the wall, Detective Price went to Woods' left while Constable Telfer went to his right.

"You are under arrest for murder," Constable Telfer clarified. "Do you understand that?" Woods confirmed that he understood.

At some point, Constable Telfer took out his caution card from his wallet and read Woods the familiar primary caution: "You are charged with murder. Do you wish to say anything in answer to the charge? You are not obliged to say anything unless you wish to do so, but whatever you say may be given in evidence." Constable Telfer again informed Woods of his right to counsel in the following terms: "It is my duty to inform you that you have the right to retain and instruct counsel without delay. Do you understand?" Woods confirmed, "Yep".

The Woods' Confession

Constable Telfer testified that after Woods had indicated that he had understood both the caution and his right to counsel, he asked Woods: "Did you stab a guy in Toronto tonight?" Woods confirmed that as well.

"Were you wearing a white shirt today?" Price asked, and Woods replied that he hadn't. The time which passed between his indication that he understood his right to counsel and Constable Telfer's next question ("Did you stab a guy in Toronto tonight?")

was very short. Constable Telfer testified that one of the reasons he asked the question concerning the stabbing so quickly was that he was not sure that the police had the right person. There was a telephone in the apartment that Detective Price then used to make some calls. It was the police officer's evidence that Woods never asked for an opportunity to call a lawyer at any time while at the apartment building.

Woods was transported to 31 Division, Metropolitan Toronto Police, where he was taken before the officer in charge and asked certain routine questions concerning his name, address, date of birth, and whether he had any medical or health problems. He answered these questions, yet still made no request to telephone a lawyer. At a quarter to two in the morning, he was placed in one of the interview rooms and was left alone with the door closed for some two hours, during which time Sergeants Stewart and Cziraky spoke to the co-accused Harris.

Two and a half hours later, Woods was taken into another interview room where he was introduced to Sergeant Stewart and Sergeant Cziraky. According to the testimony of these police officers, they again advised Woods that he was under arrest for murder and further advised him of his right to counsel.

The police also read the secondary caution to him, warning that he was not obliged to say anything unless he wished to do so, and that whatever he did say may be given in evidence.

A Conflict in the Evidence

There was a conflict in evidence between the testimony of Woods and that of the police officers as to what occurred next. According to the police, the two officers proceeded to question Woods but, according to Woods, within approximately one minute of questioning, Woods asked if he could speak to a lawyer. Woods felt it would be necessary to speak to a lawyer before he made a statement. Woods testified that he was advised by the officers that he would be able to contact his lawyer later on, and they then continued to question him. Woods further testified that, when the police told him this, he decided to go ahead and speak to them but would not sign any statement. Sergeants Stewart and Cziraky denied that Woods asked to call his lawyer and denied ever telling Woods that he could have his lawyer's call only after they had completed their investigation. Access to counsel was crucial if the incriminating statements made by Woods were to be admitted as evidence at trial.

The two police officers interviewed Woods at length and, beginning at about a quarter after four in the morning, took from him a thorough and very incriminating oral statement which they recorded in their notebooks. At about five o'clock, the officers left the office and drove Woods to the scene of the crime, where he was further questioned. Eventually, on Woods' direction, the officers drove to the place where the hunting knife was said to have been hidden. The murder weapon was discovered, and the officers asked Woods whether that was the knife he had stabbed the driver with, to which he replied, "Yes."

The police then transported Woods back to 31 Division and returned him to the same interview room. Shortly after six a.m., Woods was again cautioned and advised of his right to counsel. Following his acknowledgment again that he understood the charge and his rights, the police officers proceeded to take from him a two-and-a-half-page typewritten statement. At the completion of the statement, Woods added a paragraph in his own handwriting that concerned an injury to his finger. It is unclear if Woods was alleging police brutality but made a few corrections to the statement and initialed them. He was then asked by the police to sign the statement, later testifying that he again asked to call his lawyer.

The Harris Interrogation

Gary Harris was also at the same police station undergoing interrogation.

After the crime scene was visited, police took Harris to the police station and questioned him further.

Q. Do you know Tim Woods?

A. Yes, I met him two or three weeks ago at Patty Button's place. Patty is a born-again Christian.

Q. I understand you phoned the police tonight from a pay phone and reported a stabbing.

A. That's right. I called from the pay phone. I waited for them to come and see me.

Q. Tell us what happened.

A. I was with Tim Woods when he stabbed a taxi driver tonight. I didn't know he was going to do it.

Q. How did it happen?

A. We went to the Long Branch Loop and I flagged down an Arrow Taxi. Tim got in the back and I sat in the front. I saw the taxi coming along the Lakeshore from Port Credit. The Loop was empty. Tim asked the driver to take us to Transpo on Milvan. When we got there, the driver asked if we wanted to be let out at the front or back of the factory.

Q. Where were you parked?

A. In the driveway.

Q. What happened next?

A. I opened my door. Tim handed the driver a twenty-dollar bill. As the cabbie was fooling around with the money, I heard a thud and a lot of shuffling. I was standing outside the cab, and then Tim jumped out the door behind the driver and said, "I stabbed him, come on, let's get out of here." We ran through the factories and over the fence. He was wiping blood on my shirt from the knife.

Q. I don't see any blood on your shirt.

A. No, no, I lent him a shirt earlier at my place.

Q. What did the shirt look like?

A. It is white. I don't remember if it is long-sleeved or short-sleeved.

Q. Why did you lend him the shirt?

A. To hide the knife. Tim was very pissed off. He said he left the sheath of the knife there in the car.

Q. Where did Tim get the knife?

A. We were at Square One in Mississauga today in a small store there, and Tim bought the knife from a lady.

Q. Can you describe the knife?

A. It was a Kodiak knife with a five-and-a-half-inch blade in a sheath. The handle of the knife was bone with a gold cap. He asked to see three: A Bowie, the Kodiak, and another little knife. Tim paid a hundred and seven plus seven dollars tax for the knife.

Q. What did you do then?

A. We went to the Toronto-Dominion Bank to see if we could get his green card back. The bank at King and Highway 10. We went on our ten-speeds. I saw Tim talk to a woman in the bank. He generally asked if there was a way he could get his green card back and she said, "Yes - in seven days." He had pushed the wrong keys, and the machine ate his card. We left the bank and rode to my place. I was supposed to meet my wife there at seven p.m. We waited until seven-fourteen, and during this time I lent him the shirt. We then left our bikes there and walked to the Long Branch Loop. My wife did not come home.

Q. What was the knife for?

A. Tim told me he wanted to travel up north and needed some money. He said he would like to dummy a cab driver and get some money.

Q. What does "dummy" mean to you?

A. He told me "wipe out or kill." On the way to the Loop, he talked about it. The Loop is about a mile-and-a-half from my place.

Q. Why did you walk to the Loop?

A. It was my idea to walk to the Loop as I knew there were cabs there. I didn't want a cab to come to my place.

Q. Why?

A. Because there would be a record.

Q. Gary, there seems to be more to this than you said.

A. I'll level with you. I knew. I knew at Square One. He told me he was going to kill a cab driver and take the money. I knew what he wanted to do, and I went with him. He gave me forty dollars and I was supposed to pay the driver when we got to the boonies and distract him, and Tim would knife him and kill him, and we would take his money. Tim gave the driver a twenty-dollar bill before I had a chance to pay him. I started to get out of the car, and he stabbed him, and we ran away, then he was wiping the blood on the shirt. He was mad that he left the sheath in the car because his fingerprints were on it.

Harris' Written Statement

Gary Harris then provided the police with a written statement, signed by him, which read as follows:

Question: On Friday, August 26, 1983, at approximately nine-thirty p.m., a cab driver by the name of Philip Davidson was stabbed to death on Milvan Dr., Toronto. What, if anything, can you tell us about this?

Answer: I was with Tim Woods. We met today at the Central Parkway Mall. We went to Square One to a little store there that had a lot of knives. He bought a Kodiak knife with a five-and-a-half-inch blade from the East Indian girl. He paid a hundred and fourteen dollars for the knife; it was in a sheath. After we left the store, we went to the TD Bank at King and Highway 10 and then we went to my place. At Square One he talked about dummying a cab driver and taking the money as he wanted to travel up north. I asked him what he meant by dummying and he said wipe out, kill. He asked for a shirt at my place to conceal the knife. I gave him a white shirt of mine and he put it on over his T-shirt. We waited for my wife to come home and when she didn't arrive, we left our bikes at my place and walked to the Long Branch Loop. On the way there we talked about robbing a cab driver, any cab driver. He said he would do everything. I saw a cab coming from Port Credit and I flagged it down and that was it. Before the cab stopped, he told me he had a place lined up in a factory area. I didn't know where the place was, but he did. From what he said I understood that he was going to knife the cab driver. I went with him because I had nothing better to do this evening, I should have stayed home with my wife. When the cab stopped, I got in the front and Tim got in the back. Tim told the driver to go to Transpo factory. He said it was 121 Milvan Dr. The cab driver said he would get us to the area and Tim could point out the area where we wanted to go. We went up the 400 to Finch and along Finch and over to Milvan whatever. He pulled into the factory after Tim told him that that was the place. I got out of the car; I knew what was going to happen. The driver said the fare was eighteen something. Tim handed him a twenty-dollar bill and as the driver was shuffling with the money, I heard a thud and some shuffling.

Then Tim got out of the car and said: "I stabbed him, let's run" or something along that line. We ran away. I saw the cab pull out forwards, it was coasting forwards. We ran through the factories and over fences. He was mad about leaving the sheath in the car. He wiped the blood from the knife on the shirt that I gave him. We split up. I became scared because the whole situation was out of proportion. I went immediately to the phone and called the police and gave my name and told them about the stabbing. After forty-five minutes the police came. I also called my wife and Patti Button from the phone, the phone booth at Satterley and Islington.

Question: Did you know he was going to kill the cab driver before you got in the cab?

Answer: Yes, I knew. After it happened, I felt sorry and guilty and that is why I called. I was very concerned about the cab driver's life.

Question: Is there anything further that you wish to tell us about this matter?

Answer: I am really sorry, but that doesn't help now.

The Matter Goes to Trial

This was essentially the evidence a jury considered when the matter went to trial. When Woods was examined by police, he was asked to sign a voluntary statement before talking with a lawyer. The trial judge refused to declare the confession inadmissible, declaring that the statement had not been coerced and that, given the substantial weight of other evidence, the violations of the killer's civil rights were not so substantial as to block a conviction. Woods was sentenced to life imprisonment with no parole eligibility for twenty-five years.

The jury had more trouble with the evidence as it pertained to Harris. The trial judge in his charge told the jury that a person may be convicted of murder if that person is a party to the offence. Being a "party to the offence" means that if Harris knew or ought to have known that a killing would take place, he could be convicted despite not having actually stabbed the victim.

It became obvious that the jury was having difficulty. During its deliberations, they came back into court with a question:

"If I [we] have a reasonable doubt that Harris did not believe at the time of the offence that there was going to be a killing, how do I [we] interpret sections 21 and 213 [the sections dealing with being

THE REST OF THE STORY | 115

a party to an offence and murder]?" The section giving trouble to the jury was subsection 213(d), which provided that a person who uses a weapon while committing a robbery can be convicted of murder regardless if the death was intended - or if the accused person had knowledge that death was likely to occur.

The trial judge explained that the reading of these sections meant that a person could be convicted of murder if the accused person was party to an offence in which the actual killer knew or ought to have known that death would result. Accordingly, the jury returned a verdict that Harris was guilty of second-degree murder. Harris was sentenced to life imprisonment without parole eligibility for 10 years.

A Reinterpretation of the Law

This was presumably the law as it was understood until the Supreme Court of Canada handed down a decision that would alter our understanding of the mental requirement necessary for a murder conviction. At the time Harris was convicted, being a party to an offence where someone else did the killing during a robbery meant that the party who did not do the killing could be convicted of murder. This was known as "constructive murder."

The Supreme Court decided, in a case referred to as *R. v. Vaillancourt*, that the constructive murder provisions as they had been applied were unconstitutional. Section 7 of the *Canadian Charter of Rights and Freedoms* guaranteeing a Canadian's rights to life, liberty and security of the person demanded that one must intend the killing in order to be convicted of murder. Death must be subjectively foreseeable and not objectively foreseeable. In a subsequent case called *Logan*, the "ought to have known" provision in the party to an offence statute was also struck down.

The application of this new jurisprudence opened an avenue where Harris could appeal his conviction. I was hired by Harris to argue his appeal.

I was clad in my Barrister's robes and seated in the Appeal Courtroom at Toronto's Osgoode Hall when a very distinguished panel of three judges entered: Chief Justice Howland, and Associate Justices Morden and Griffiths. The Court was anxious that I get to the point of setting out how the *Vaillancourt* and *Logan* judgments should be applied. The Ministry of the Attorney General was represented by W.J. Blacklock, a highly experienced and knowledgeable Crown.

Of course, I argued that there must be subjective foreseeability on Harris' part and that the question by the jury showed that there had been doubt on that point. Blacklock went to the words of the confession: when Harris was asked by the police if he knew Woods was going to kill the cabbie before he got into the cab, Harris replied that he knew.

The Appeal Court Decision

The Court reserved its decision, which I knew could go either way. Then, on April 10, 1989, Justice Griffith handed down the unanimous decision of the Court.

Once I received a faxed copy of the judgment, I did what most lawyers do and jumped to the last page where I found these words: "I would allow the appeal, set aside the conviction, and order a new trial." On a more fulsome reading of the judgment, I found the Court held that there was doubt that the subjective mental element of the offence was made out.

I was ecstatic as I delivered the news to Gary Harris.

Woods had also appealed to the Court of Appeal with the assistance of highly experienced counsel. The same panel of judges heard the Woods appeal. However, although it was possible that there had been a breach of Woods' right to counsel, his admissions were such that it would not throw the administration of justice into disrepute by allowing the confessions to be entered as evidence.

Woods lost his appeal, but Harris won. The Appeal Court ordered a new trial. I was overjoyed.

Gary Harris was brought before the Superior Court in May 1989, and a new trial date of October 2nd was set. Very soon afterward, my jubilation was terminated by the news that the Crown had decided to appeal the Court of Appeal Decision to the Supreme Court of Canada which would involve a delay. The Supreme Court only hears a fraction of cases decided annually. Only in those cases where a decision would have a significant impact on the administration of justice - or where a significant wrong must be righted – will the Court interfere with a unanimous criminal appellate court decision.

No Longer a Federal Penitentiary Inmate

Since his conviction had been set aside, Harris was no longer eligible to reside in the penitentiary. He was back in his pretrial situation of being held in custody pending trial. He did not have sureties acceptable to the Crown or the Court to ask for a bail review.

Harris was taken from the penitentiary and maintained at the provincial Metro West Detention Centre in Toronto. His life immediately changed. Despite the stigma of federal prison, he at least had enjoyed the advantages of participating in rehabilitative programming, having books to read, and having the company of less transient friends than is the case in a remand centre. Further, Harris wanted a constant connection to my office, which was more than an hour away in Cobourg. Warkworth Institution was just a short drive northeast of Cobourg and despite being a federal penitentiary, access to the client was much easier than visiting a provincially-operated prison in Toronto.

I could tell by our frequent telephone conversations that Harris was becoming antsy in his new location. I suggested, and he immediately agreed, that I would request the Minister of Correctional Services in the Ontario provincial government to transfer Harris from Metro West to the Cobourg Jail. It would be a smaller and less hectic environment that I could visit regularly. Fortunately, the Ministry of Correctional Services was willing to accommodate the request.

During the summer, Harris and I visited and communicated often. He would call me at the office or at home several times a week. That was, until the beginning of October.

We had been expecting the Supreme Court to decide if it would grant leave to appeal so that the new trial could begin on October 2, 1989. That did not happen. By mid-September, the Court advised that a decision would be delayed, and no new date was established.

More Bad News

I conveyed the bad news to Harris as soon as I learned of it. It wasn't the only bad news to come Harris' way, either. While at the Cobourg jail, he had initiated a relationship with a fellow inmate's sister who said she did not see him in her future, would have no further contact, and broke off the relationship. On October 1, Harris called me at home to tell me that he had been depressed with the girlfriend situation and that he was disappointed with the news from Ottawa, and yet, he sounded unusually happy.

"I want you to know how much I appreciated what you have done for me," he said before ending the call. He had never said anything like that before.

The next day I received a call from the jail. Gary Harris was found in his cell having attempted to hang himself with a bed sheet. He had not died but was immediately transported to the Cobourg Hospital and placed on life support.

The Final Visit

My next and ultimately final visit to Gary Harris would come when I visited him in the hospital. He lay motionless on a hospital bed. Staff told me that while his heart and internal organs were functional, my client was "brain-dead". I was asked by hospital staff to contact family members to authorize organ donations.

I had no need to make the call to family, which I was dreading to make, as Gary's mother introduced herself to me in the hospital waiting room. She was crying, and her voice was shaky.

"They want me to let them pull the plug," she said. "I don't think I can do it."

I tried to remain calm, telling her that I had quizzed medical staff and that they had told me there was absolutely no chance of Gary recovering. The question that remained was whether she thought it would be Gary's preference to assist someone struggling to be alive through an organ donation. For reasons unknown to me, the mother seemed consoled. She agreed that that was exactly what Gary would want.

"He was such a good boy," she said. "At least he died an innocent man." His conviction had been quashed but he had not been exonerated. This was not the time to quibble. She headed off to give the final instruction. Gary was twenty-seven.

I was left wondering what would have happened if Gary had lost his earlier appeal. He would be serving his sentence, but he'd still be alive. What if I had picked up on his thank-you call the night before? He had been telling me, in so many words, of his plan to kill himself. Could an early morning visit to the jail have prevented his death?

The front page of the *Cobourg Daily Star* on October 5 reported Gary's demise. It also linked it with the story that recounted a death in that jail 18 months prior. On March 17, 1988, a thirty-two-year-old from nearby Gores Landing, having been denied bail and facing a number of charges had hung himself with a bedsheet. A coroner's inquest had recommended that Ontario jails look more diligently for signs of depression and suicide – a recommendation that had obviously not been taken.

The Aftermath

Things did not go well for Lance Timothy Woods either, with the Court of Appeal upholding his conviction and Woods beginning his prison stay. In July 1989, Woods was transferred from maximum-security Millhaven Institution to medium-security Collins Bay Institution, both located in the Kingston, Ontario vicinity. Woods learned that his brother was getting married, and he applied for an escorted pass to attend the wedding ceremony. He was refused.

Not taking no for an answer, Woods cooked up an escape scheme with a fellow inmate who was being released on an unescorted temporary absence.

Woods fashioned a grappling hook from a pole he found in a prison shop. On December 13, 1990, he used the hook to scale the twenty-five-foot wall surrounding Collins Bay Institution. Guards spotted the inmate as he was in progress and fired warning shots – to no avail. Woods jumped from the wall to the street and was picked up by his fellow inmate in a stolen car.

The two broke into a Kingston house and hid out in the attic. The homeowner discovered the break-in and called the police. The house was searched, including the attic, but the two convicts had hidden under insulation batts in the attic and were not noticed.

The following day, the homeowner heard noises and ran to a neighbouring house to call the police once again. Police arrived and subsequently located the escapees in a nearby backyard.

The Harris Inquest

An inquest into the death of Gary Harris was held at the Court House in Cobourg on December 6, 1989, with a verdict returned on December 21st. Inquests are mandatory when a prisoner dies by suicide or other means while in custody. The rationale is for "the dead to speak for the living," i.e., that government officials can learn from the mistakes of one prisoner's demise so that steps can be taken to prevent such tragedies from reoccurring.

Once a coroner's jury reaches a verdict, that verdict (along with any recommendations) is kept in writing and shared with the government agency controlling the operations of the place of death. There is no legal requirement for recommendations to be implemented; rather, the government office is asked to provide a response indicating any actions taken within six months of receiving the recommendations. The jury found that Harris had died on October 4, 1989, at ten minutes before noon at the Cobourg District General Hospital, with the cause of death listed as "asphyxia and brain damage as the result of hanging." Three factors were recognized by the jury as having significance in Harris' suicide attempt. The first and probably most significant was the postponement of his court case. The second factor was the ending of his relationship with his girlfriend. And third, was the length of his incarceration in a provincially run maximum-security facility.

The Regional Coroner who conducted the inquest, Dr. P.A. Clark, was required by law to forward a copy of the verdict to the Chief Coroner for Ontario, then Dr. R.C. Bennett, and to the local Crown Attorney. This was done by letter dated January 5, 1990. The Chief Coroner reviewed and commented on each of the twelve recommendations the jury presented to stop such tragedies in the future. One of the most novel ideas was the suggestion to introduce a solid or meshed barrier to block a suicidal inmate from attaching a sheet or a cord from the cell bars. This recommendation, however, was given short shrift.

The Chief Coroner wrote: "I disagree. The idea has merit, but suicides by hanging have occurred from lower bars than what occurred here. Further study is required. The cost implications of this recommendation may be unreasonable." To date, nothing has been done. A 20-year study by the National Institute of Corrections in the United States found that 98% of suicides in prison were caused by hanging

Gary Harris was not a natural-born killer. He chanced upon a short-lived friendship with a man intent on robbing and killing a cabbie. By the publication of Supreme Court of Canada decisions that were handed down after his conviction but before his appeal, he was able to have his second-degree murder convictions overturned. Maybe more could have been done to deal with the depression that sets in when an inmate is confined with little mental stimulation for extended periods and suffers a breakdown in family or emotional support networks. How can we prevent people, especially easily-influenced people, from making bad friends? Of all the inquests held since his death, little has been done to foil attempted suicides. Inmate suicides and drug overdoses continue to be a problem for correctional systems. They frequently become the subject matter of inquests but little seems to be done to address the issues.

CHAPTER 6
FENTANYL

The Jeffrey Woodman Inquest

> *The evil that men do lives after them; The good is oft interred with their bones.*
>
> **– William Shakespeare, Julius Caesar**

A young man dies. A family grieves. That would be the standard takeaway for a reader of this obituary that appeared in the September 12, 2017 edition of the *Cambridge Times:*

WOODMAN, Jeffrey Bruce August 27, 1985 - September 4, 2017 It is with great sadness that we announce the sudden passing of our loving son. Survived by his parents Linda and Dennis of Kitchener and Jeff and Amanda of Goderich, Spouse Heather of Kitchener. He will be greatly missed by his adoring children; Anthony, Jayden, JJ and Curtis, Siblings; Kyle, Candace and Ryan of Cambridge, Alexandra, Noah, Mia and Ashley, grandparents Otto and Doreen of Cambridge, grandfather Robert of Nova Scotia and many aunts, uncles, cousins, nieces and nephews. He will be greeted at Heavens gates by his loving grandparent Betty, God and Francis. He was a devoted father who gave selflessly of himself to family and friends. His smile and laughter instantly warmed the hearts of those he met. He will be dearly missed by all who knew him. A celebration of life will be held at a later date. Cremation has taken place. A public graveside service will be conducted at the Williamsburg Cemetery, Kitchener on Thursday, September 14, 2017 at 11:00 a.m. Mark Jutzi Funeral Home assisted with the arrangements. Online condolences available at www.markjutzifuneralhomes.ca

That brief summary of a young man's life gave more details than a coroner's inquest heard in a three-day hearing that began on December 10, 2019, at the Court House in Cobourg.

The reason for an inquest is that Jeffrey Bruce Woodman died of a fentanyl overdose while he was a prisoner at Warkworth Institution, a medium-security federal penitentiary located northeast of Cobourg. We will never know if he intended to use a drug spiked with fentanyl or if he was simply accepting the use of whatever substance he could get smuggled in. We will never know if he overdosed, meaning too much use of a substance, or whether the amount of fentanyl mixed with the intended substance (likely cocaine) was just too overpowering. In any event, he died. Inquests are mandatory when a prisoner dies in custody of unusual causes.

Just Months Before Release

The inquest was a no-nonsense affair. A three-woman, two-man jury returned a verdict that Jeffrey Bruce Woodman had died on September 4, 2017, at 7:33 a.m. The cause of death was determined to be accidental due to fentanyl toxicity. The verdict was delivered on December 12, 2019.

Jeffrey Woodman was convicted in Kitchener on April 7, 2015, and was serving a sentence of four years and eight months after being convicted of Aggravated Assault on a Police Officer, Dangerous Operation of a Motor Vehicle Causing Bodily Harm, Flight from Police, Fail to Comply with a Recognizance and Theft Under $5000. He was scheduled to be released in June 2018.

Counsel for the Coroner, Jai Dhar, presented the jury with an Agreed Statement of Facts. The agreed facts recounted that

Woodman was locked in his cell at 10:30 p.m. on September 3, 2017, in Unit 2 of Warkworth Institution. At approximately 7:10 in the morning of September 4, 2017, Correctional Officer Gord Currell was conducting a morning security patrol of Unit 2. He observed Woodman through a small window in a solid steel door, though he could not verify if Woodman was alive. Currell immediately summoned assistance, and Woodman's cell was unlocked and entered. The officers observed Woodman lying on his back in his cot, with his left hand resting on his stomach and clutching a TV remote control. Foam was observed on the inmate's mouth; he was unresponsive.

Correctional and nursing staff moved Woodman onto the floor, where CPR and defibrillation were applied. Woodman was also administered naloxone, an antidote for opioid overdose, three times intranasally and once by injection. But he could not be revived.

Paramedics arrived at the prison and pronounced Woodman dead at 7:33 a.m. Three months later, a post-mortem examination was performed on December 6, 2017, by forensic pathologist Ingo von Both, who determined that Woodman had died as the result of ingesting over three times the level that was considered toxic.

Only two parties sought standing at the inquest: The Correctional Service of Canada, and the Union of Canadian Correctional Officers. Coroner Counsel Jai Dhar advised the jury that Woodman's family would have been granted standing to examine witnesses and advance recommendations but could not attend to do so for health reasons.

Both the Coroner's Counsel and counsel for the two parties with standing offered recommendations, but the jury accepted only three:

To the Correctional Service of Canada

1. Incorporate information about the specific clues and signs of an opioid overdose into the training (of Correctional Officers) to be reviewed and acknowledged by each participant annually.

2. Ensure that all educational materials are readily available on the learning portals for staff. New materials are to be reviewed and acknowledged in a timely manner, with notification of completion to be confirmed by the Correctional Manager.

To Warkworth Institution

3. Reinforce the policy requiring Correctional Officers to conduct security patrols at "staggered" or irregular intervals, ensuring the presence of a live, breathing body. Further, reinforce that if it is not possible for a Correctional Officer to ascertain if the offender is alive and not in distress, that they will interact with the offender in a manner consistent with CD 560 [the directive governing how staff should interact with prisoners].

The recommendation put forward by the Coroner's Counsel and the Correctional Officers' Union - that doors in the units be upgraded to allow greater visibility into the cells, particularly during nighttime security patrols – was not accepted.

The presiding coroner advised that the jury's recommendations would be relayed to the parties being addressed, and those parties were expected to submit a report within 6 months outlining the progress made in addressing the recommendations. It was not mandatory that jury recommendations be adopted, rather, inquests were mandatory when a person is in custody or being detained died (except when the death is due to natural causes).

A Social Problem

To many, death by overdose may seem insignificant. He did it to himself, didn't he? But people of that mindset fail to realize that drugs in prison are a major problem and staff members' lives are at risk unless strict measures are in place to ensure against their importation. Fentanyl is a particular problem. It is a powerful opioid (sometimes mixed with heroin, cocaine, or methamphetamine) to intensify the effects of the drug with which it is added. It is so powerful that if improperly mixed, even a minute quantity can be lethal. It is not self-induced suicide; it is an aftereffect of improper compounding used by unsuspected users to escape the day-to-day boredom of prison. It subjects staff in the prisons to unnecessary risk, yet it continues as a problem in Canada's prisons, with several additional deaths being recorded since Woodman overdosed. Throughout the three-day inquest, no one asked the question: How did the inmate receive the fentanyl he ingested?

The Conduct of the Inquest

It was all very matter-of-fact. The Correctional Service was on hand to advise the jury that it could not be blamed for Woodman's death. All three correctional officers who testified at the inquest maintained that it was their job to ensure that a living, breathing body was visible each time they made their rounds. The Correctional Officers' Union was on hand to ensure nothing could disparage the training or professionalism of the guards who made these hourly rounds.

No evidence was given as to why Jeffrey Woodman had ended up in prison in the first place. The inquest jury heard nothing of his background.

Woodman's Crime

Woodman's conviction stemmed back to September 2013, when Woodman was twenty-nine. Woodman and two buddies were observed shoplifting cheese strings, chocolate milk, and cigarette lighters from a Zehrs Supermarket on Weber Street in Kitchener, Ontario. The men were seen shoving the merchandise into their trousers. Woodman and his pals had been using heroin and crystal methamphetamine before entering the grocery store.

Waterloo Regional Police were called while the shoplifting was in progress. Two police cruisers arrived. It was night, and there were only a few people in the store and the parking lot. Nonetheless, the three thieves made a break for it. Security video footage shown at Woodman's trial depicted Woodman entering the driver's side of a black Hyundai, which took off with tires screaming. A high-speed chase ensued, which police later justified as necessary for public safety. Police testified that during the getaway Woodman was driving at speeds of 100 km/h on Weber Street in Kitchener running red lights. The car turned into a residential area on Montgomery Road, whereupon police lost sight of it.

Police scoured the area and caught sight of the car once again, this time in an apartment building parking lot on nearby Sheldon Avenue. Sergeant Eugene Fenton, a thirteen-year veteran of the Waterloo Regional Police Force, approached the vehicle with a gun drawn. He fired the pistol four times, smashing the car's windshield, and shouted for the occupants of the car to surrender.

Fenton approached the vehicle head-on while firing the shots. Instead of surrendering, the car's driver took off and struck Fenton. The officer told the Superior Court trial that he considered himself lucky to be alive. "I was tall enough and the car was small enough that I went over the hood and off to the side instead of under," said Fenton. "Otherwise the court may well have been hearing a murder trial." Fenton suffered a broken knee, other broken bones, and other injuries upon being hit. He was on crutches for eight weeks, underwent months of physiotherapy, and was told he could not expect his knee to completely recover.

The Defence

At his trial, Woodman was ably defended by prominent criminal defence counsel Hal Mattson. First Mattson had to deal with a less serious outstanding charge: Woodman had injured an OPP officer by hitting the policeman in the hand with the door of a minivan as he sped away from a Kitchener gas station. For that, he pleaded "guilty" while in jail on remand and was sentenced to seven months in custody on a charge of dangerous driving.

The main defence offered by Mattson was that although his client was involved in shoplifting and was the driver in a high-speed chase, he was *not* the driver who crashed into Officer Fenton. "The issue, in this case, is who was driving the car when the police officer was hit," Mattson told CTV News when interviewed outside the courthouse. Woodman said that after the high-speed chase ended, his cohort Kevin Sinson had taken the wheel. Therefore, he said, it was Sinson and not Woodman who had collided with the police officer.

Sinson took the stand to give alibi evidence, but his story was not as iron-clad as an accused person may have wanted. Sinson testified that he was high on heroin on the night in question and had no memory of who might have been driving. Sinson originally told police he was not the driver but speculated that he may have done so because he was on release from prison - and thus, to admit to being the driver would have resulted in his suspension and a return to prison.

The judge's charge to the jury included instructions that jurors need not believe any or all of a witness' statement. The jury obviously didn't believe Sinson and returned a verdict of "guilty" against Woodman. The crimes committed, aggravated assault and dangerous driving causing bodily harm, were the result of Woodman's driving, the jury concluded.

Sentencing

Although the trial was held in November 2014, sentencing was not completed until April 2015. When the day of sentencing arrived, the courtroom was packed with over 20 uniformed officers, including Police Chief Bryan Larkin. The officers maintained that they were there as a show of support for their injured colleague. No one knows if the sentencing judge, Justice Gerry Taylor, was influenced by this turnout. The police officers had a legal right to be in attendance and no one moved to have them excluded.

The Victim Impact Statement of Officer Fenton was entered into evidence. The lawyers for the prosecution and defence made their pitches. The court was told that Woodman had eighteen prior convictions.

Crown prosecutor Andrew Rajna asked for a penalty at the upper end of what could be considered reasonable. He said that

Woodman's behavior proved he was a "danger to society" and asked the judge to impose a sentence of eight years.

Mattson's Interactions with Police

No one would have blamed defence counsel Mattson for being intimidated as he entered a courtroom full of cops, as his own history with Waterloo Regional Police had not been positive. In early November 2010, Mattson had gone across the road from the courthouse to a Tim Hortons coffee shop. Mattson was arrested and detained for over three hours, accused of trying to convince a witness to withhold information during a preliminary hearing in a criminal case.

The charge was eventually thrown out as having no foundation, with a court later dismissing the charge as total speculation on the part of the police. But Mattson had not taken it lying down. He sued the Waterloo Regional Police Services Board, the Chief, and several officers for five and a half million dollars for wrongful arrest, detention, confinement, and assault by police. "I have a newfound understanding of how people feel when they're being arrested and put through the process I was," Mattson is quoted as saying in a *Law Times* article.

Mattson did what he could for Woodman, urging the court to see the accused as having suffered an unstable upbringing that in turn resulted in Woodman's inability to stay out of trouble. The prior convictions were for petty crimes. Mattson argued that the prosecution's recommendation of eight years would be more appropriate for a manslaughter conviction and that three years in prison would be appropriate.

The Sentence

In the end, Justice Gerald Taylor called Woodman a "career criminal" who was unlikely to be rehabilitated. It was all summarized in the lead paragraph penned by reporter Brian Caldwell in the next day's *Waterloo Region Record*: "A drug addict was sentenced Tuesday to the equivalent of six years in prison for deliberately hitting an armed police officer with his car as he ducked bullets and sped away."

Considering the time served in pretrial custody, the actual penitentiary sentence was just over four years and eight months. He could expect to serve two-thirds of that time until released under supervision to the street. Also considering that the main description of Brian Caldwell that Woodman was a drug addict, one would have expected that a prime factor to be listed in Woodman's correctional plan would be some form of intensive drug rehabilitation therapy. But when I informally interviewed Deputy Warden Henry Saulnier at the inquest, I was told that drug usage was not considered a criminogenic factor, or at least not enough of a factor.

Some would expect that drug treatment would rank high on what could be done to treat such an offender. But just as Woodman and his counsel met up with the "blue wall" at his sentencing hearing, he met up with a similar blue wall as his correctional plan was being prepared. In his book *Down Inside: Thirty Years in Canada's Prison Service*, retired Deputy Warden Robert Clark makes these damning comments:

> In my opinion, too few prison employees care about the prisoners under their care, other than to make sure they are alive and behaving. Any interest in a prisoner's well-being and their chance of becoming a law-abiding citizen is almost non-existent.

The inquest was held years after the inmate's death. If a jury's recommendation could have benefitted and contributed to saving the life of another inmate in the years since Woodman's death, the opportunity was lost by the delay. Indeed, a review of pending inquests in Ontario shows that a large percentage involve deaths in custody. It also can be seen that there is what might be seen as an excessive delay in holding the inquests.

The Blue Wall at Inquests

More significantly, the "blue wall" that is seen as protecting possible misconduct of police is mirrored in the situation that often arises where the only parties with any real knowledge of the prison system are the parties with standing seeking to prevent adverse findings by a jury. No one would accuse the Woodman inquest of making a false finding of fact or improper recommendations, but what if counsel, with their expert knowledge of the prison system in custodial inquests, were on hand to ask the tough questions? Would a more fulsome interrogation of correctional workers lead to better insights as to what might be done to prevent unfortunate deaths inside prison walls in the future? Should the issues of how drugs in general are introduced into a penitentiary and what steps are taken by the Correctional Service to prevent its introduction have been raised? They were not. A jury may have concluded by answering in a manner that would have embarrassed CSC. The jury heard only the blue wall of witnesses.

***

It is very possible that the Correctional Service did absolutely nothing wrong in the care and maintenance of this particular prisoner. Perhaps the wrong that happened was this country's over-reliance on jail as a corrective measure. As Hal Mattson said: "Imposing a lengthy sentence on such a young person, you crush their spirits and send them a message that they are not worth much. As a result, rehabilitating themselves is the last thing on their minds."

No one can deny that what Woodman did was wrong and deserving of incarceration. However, that prison sentence should not have become a death sentence, even if the cause of death rested with the inmate himself. Would Jeffrey Woodman be alive today if the trial judge had accepted the defence counsel's recommendation to consider the crime less seriously in the face of the blue wall in front of him? Would Woodman be alive today if more thought were to have been put into devising a truly rehabilitative correctional plan? We do not know, and the inquest gave us no answers since only the blue wall of corrections testified at the inquest.

It would be unfortunate if Woodman was a simple example of failure to prevent unnecessary death. CBC News reported in 2020 the death of twenty-six-year-old Jordan Sheard who died at the provincially-operated Central East Correctional Centre (CEDC) in Lindsay, Ontario, northeast of Toronto. The man had a history of prior drug usage and suffered from PTSD and depression. Sheard had entered the provincial detention facility on May 30, 2020, when his bail was pulled after he threatened suicide. On intake at the jail, he underwent a body scan meant to detect drugs concealed internally. Prisoners are known to try to import contraband by hiding foreign material in their rectums, a process they refer to as "suitcasing."

Sheard fell ill with a drug overdose as the suspected cause. He was transported to the hospital, where naloxone was administered. He remained hospitalized through May 31 and returned to the CEDC. Once again, he was scanned and readmitted to the prison. He died June 1st within hours of his readmittance.

It was learned after Sheard's death that a plastic bag containing twenty-six grams of fentanyl had ruptured and caused the overdose. Re-examination of the body scans showed the presence of the contraband had the scans been interpreted properly.

Drug Screening Policies

Ontario jails, like federal penitentiaries, are acutely aware of drugs entering the system. People entering correctional facilities undergo checks including metal detectors, ion detectors, drug-sniffing dogs, and metal detectors. In 2016, Ontario's provincial institution added body scanners costing the taxpayers nine and a half million dollars. Body scan images are accurate if read properly by trained staff. It appears that the two scans that Sheard underwent were improperly read, possibly by staff lacking adequate training.

Was the training inadequate? One can only hope that the question and its remedy will be posed and answered at an upcoming inquest, although I have my doubts.

It is not as though there has been a lack of public knowledge that foreign substances once imported into penitentiaries or jails can have serious consequences. A 1986 story by Toronto Star reporter Kathleen Kenna demonstrates this fact.

The Kenna report spoke of the January 2, 1985 death of twenty-five- year old inmate Danny Spilchuk in Millhaven Institution. On New Year's Day, a quantity of cyanide poisoning was fed to a mouse. The next day the poison was fed to Spilchuk. Spilchuk was said to have owed a substantial gambling debt. His killing was retribution for his inability to pay up (or con a friend or relative into paying up.) It was the first time cyanide had been discovered illicitly entering a Canadian prison. Kenna also discloses what an eye-opener the trial revealed as to the nature of drug importation and the procedures used. Eighteen witnesses testified at the trial.

One inmate's wife secured a quantity of the drug; another inmate's fiancee transported it in and made delivery during a visit. The evidence showed that refusal by an inmate or his supporters to cooperate with the trafficking of contraband could risk severe injury by beating or death.

When mechanisms are available to stop the introduction of contraband but those mechanisms are discarded or left unused, tragedy results.

CHAPTER 7

A CAUTIONARY TALE

Howard Massicotte and Exposure of
Inmate Slave Labour

> *The concept of using forced labour as punishment is against
> the international human rights principles embodied in many
> International instruments*
>
> **– Mary Robinson, Former Irish President**

"Drive by van Petegem's office!"

That was the instruction newly-paroled offender Howard
Massicotte gave to me, his driver, as the car in which Massicotte
was riding slowly moved toward the exit of the Beaver Creek
minimum-security institution's parking lot. As the car was parallel
with the administration building, Massicotte lowered the
passenger side window and extended his right arm with a tightly-
closed fist. At its closest point to the window of the
Superintendent's office, Massicotte extended the middle finger of
his clenched fist for the duration of the drive-by. It was a rude

gesture, likely unseen by Ted van Petegem, but Massicotte had even bigger plans in store that he had not shared with me.

Beaver Creek Institution

Beaver Creek Institution (or BCI as those who regularly deal with the Correctional Service of Canada refer to it) was a minimum-security Institution located in a forested area near the Ontario town of Gravenhurst, a hundred and ninety-three kilometers north of Toronto in the province's cottage country. It was the original site of a Norwegian Air Training Base used to train pilots to fight the Nazis in the Second World War. Close by was Camp 20, one of twenty-six prisoner-of-war camps established in Canada to house German officers and Nazi sympathizers during the war. Earlier uses of the land included a sanitorium for the treatment of tuberculosis. The clean air, trees, and nearby Lake Muskoka provided a tranquil setting for recovery from disease and later for the containment of POWs miles away from any major centre.

Although the region now hosts multi-million-dollar summer homes for, among others, American celebrities and sports stars, by 1961 the area was in economic decline. Canada's federal government held out the promise of economic renewal by experimenting with a new form of corrections, minimum security. Other minimum-security institutions were opened in Ontario (Frontenac and Pittsburgh Institutions, both on the outskirts of Kingston, Ontario) but BCI was different. It was to be a stand-alone prison whereas

Frontenac and Pittsburgh were built on the reserves of two other Kingston-area medium-security prisons. People in the City of Kingston were well-acquainted with prisons since so many were located in the city or its nearby towns. Beaver Creek was a new concept and it would be important to win the favour of the townspeople who were totally unaware that prisoners would be housed in a location without walls and fences and actually have access to the town. The fact that townspeople had good memories of the contributions made by the German soldiers in community work made the sales job of getting community support for a prison so much easier.

While the prison system has at its heart the task of rehabilitating offenders, the Beaver Creek experiment was also a public relations exercise. While the townspeople may have been uncomfortable welcoming murderers, thieves, and rapists into their community, the politicians presumed that the hearts and minds of the townspeople could be won if it could be shown that the money needed to construct facilities and watch over these convicts would not only provide an economic lift to a struggling community but also contribute to civic endeavours by engaging in charitable causes.

The Muskoka locals came to know and appreciate the hard-working young men (by and large they were young and muscular). They could be seen doing forest management in the bush that surrounded Beaver Creek Correctional Camp, as it had been named, and clearing snow in the winter and refuse in the summer from the streets in town.

The prisoners were accepted to work on projects for charitable and service clubs in the area. In no time, the NIMBY (Not In My Backyard) attitude of some locals had dissipated and BCI was considered an asset in the community.

Howard Massicotte

Howard Massicotte had been transferred to Beaver Creek from maximum-security Kingston Penitentiary. The former Montreal resident had been sentenced to seven years for committing a series of jewellery store robberies in and around his home city. Massicotte saw himself as a leader. He had established himself well in Kingston as the go-to person to right the wrongs his peers encountered. He became adept at writing up grievances, not only to vindicate wrongs he felt had been perpetrated against him, but also to advocate for fellow inmates. He soon learned the laws and spoke out against what he perceived to be an abrogation of the rights owed to prisoners at KP. The hundreds of grievances he filed had to be investigated and the situations that could not be justified were corrected once the complaints were upheld. It was a tremendous amount of work for the staff. His parole officer at Kingston Penitentiary urged his transfer to "camp" (the term inmates use to designate minimum security) probably not so much as to provide an easier transition to the streets when released but to end the legal challenges Massicotte continued to advance.

Massicotte initially revelled in his enhanced freedoms. He had his own room with a key he possessed, and the large concrete water reservoir to be used in the event of fire also operated as an inmate swimming pool. The water was cold but the opportunity to do a few laps or to lay "poolside" and get a tan was unavailable in the prisons Massicotte had occupied before. There was even a mini-put golf course the inmates had constructed. It was for many inmates the nicest place they ever lived. The papers called Beaver Creek Institution "Club Fed."

Exposure of Wrongdoing

But there was a darker side to Club Fed. Ted van Petegem was building a new home. He was also a part-time member of the National Parole Board (now called the Parole Board of Canada). It was rumoured that he would select inmates he deemed suitable for transfer to the Beaver Creek facility from those who had qualifications as drywallers, electricians, or some other trade that could be exploited as his house was under construction.

The offenders working on the house were paid at a rate greatly reduced from that of other tradespeople qualified to perform similar tasks. Furthermore, while a tradesperson in town could accept or reject a job, the inmates called upon to work at the van Petegem house would feel obligated to work lest there be retribution in their day-to-day lives as prisoners or encumbrances erected if they wanted parole. Massicotte quickly realized this was wrong and, once released, he took action.

Massicotte was now free to raise more than his middle finger. He contacted the *Toronto Star's* Kathleen Kenna. On a front-page story, the revelations of the use of "slave labour" surfaced on August 11, 1988.

At the time there were thirty-seven staff people at Beaver Creek. The *Toronto Star* investigated and found that correctional officials in Ottawa were able to confirm that thirty-five staff members had used inmate labour for personal services.

The *Toronto Star* article did not name Massicotte but the story contained numerous quotations that echoed Massicotte's sentiments on the issue:

"It's a work camp. They tell you that first thing when you arrive. No one minds doing work for the community but inmates do have a problem with what the staff are doing. It's unethical. I hate the fact that these guys are getting professional labour [from skilled tradesmen in prison] for next to nothing. They're laughing all the way to the bank off the sweat of prisoners. Why not? It's slave labour."

Kathleen Kenna also interviewed a former staff member, also unnamed in her reporting:

"I believe in forced work but I don't think inmates should be used and abused." That staff member charged that some staff, "especially the superintendent," did "save a bundle" through the use of inmate labour "because they can pay minimum wage instead of contracting a local tradesman."

It became obvious that the openness of the facility and the ability for inmates to get day passes to go off the grounds enhanced inmate freedoms and stifled the institutionalization that often crippled an inmate's return to the community. But it also opened the door to abuse. According to the *Star's* investigation, the abuse was rampant. Van Petegem's response as quoted in the *Star* failed to address the ethical issue. The Superintendent of the institution who walked with a cane tried to justify his actions, "I hire inmates more often than others. I'm incapable of doing things."

The response to the *Toronto Star* exposé was swift. Kathleen Kenna was able to do a follow-up report on August 12, 1988. She reported that Fred Mohlmann, a spokesperson for the Commissioner of Corrections, Ole Instrup, advised that the Commissioner had ordered an investigation to be undertaken by Inspector-General Jack Rankin of the Ottawa headquarters of the Service to determine if improprieties had taken place.

Mohlmann advised reporter Kenna that the use of inmate labour by staff was localized to the Beaver Creek facility only. The Correctional Service noted that inmates continued to be free to volunteer their work to service clubs, charities, and the public works departments of Gravenhurst and neighbouring towns. "We see that as a valuable part of their program. It develops employment skills and earns the trust of the community, both of which are necessary to help their re-integration into society."

Members of the Parole Board listen to inmates and are often critical when an inmate tries to lessen the extent of the inmate's involvement in a crime or the seriousness of the offence itself. For this, the Board has a term; it's called "minimization." I found it interesting to see how former staff members of Beaver Creek would deal with this one aspect of its operation.

Community Reaction

Charles Stickel worked for years at the prison including being named the last Warden of the prison before its merger with Fenbrook Institution to become a multi-level security penitentiary. He has written an excellent book on the history of the minimum-security prison, its development and operations over the years. The book, *The Inside Out Prison: The Story of Beaver Creek Minimum Security Institution*, also deals with this one aberration in what otherwise would be a remarkable success story to be studied for years to come by criminologists.

Stickel admits in the early years that some staff members hired inmates to work outside the institution making improvements on their private homes. He adds, "This was an accepted practice, of which the local community was well aware." He noted that in 1988, the practice came under broader public scrutiny. He then cites the story of a highly skilled tradesman that Stickel refers to as "Vic." Vic was paid minimum wage but in Stickel's recollection of events, other inmates became jealous. They reported the situation to the Citizen's Advisory Committee and the local newspaper but found their complaints falling on deaf ears. So, the inmates contacted a Toronto newspaper and "found a more sympathetic ear" in finding that staff were using inmates as slave labour. Stickel in one sentence notes that the Commissioner of Corrections' investigation curtailed the use of private use of inmate labour but concludes: "The local townspeople were somewhat upset as they felt the accusations of slave labour and unjust treatment of inmates was not justified." Nothing more is said. Perhaps it is human nature to minimize those things we find hardest to admit.

I raise this not as a criticism of Charles Stickel or any of the conscientious and hard-working people who were employed at BCI. What should be criticized is how easy it is to fall into the trap of accepting slave labour in a prison setting. Not all prison labour is forced. Much of the labour performed at Beaver Creek was a valuable community-centered activity done on a voluntary basis. It becomes exploitative when one was compelled to do something against one's will because failure to do so would result in the loss of something deemed more valuable.

The Nature of Abuse

We all loathe that from time to time we feel forced to do something we would prefer not to do. However, rarely are we forced to do something on the threat of violence or loss of liberty. Furthermore, a community's acceptance or rejection of the exploitive treatment of inmates should have no bearing in justifying the morality of the undertaking. The pressure put on inmates to perform work under duress is analogous to movie moguls pressuring would-be starlets for sexual favours to secure professional advancement. Modern slavery refers to forced labour and forced marriage when someone cannot refuse to comply or escape owing to threats, violence, and deception.

The relatively fast action by the Commissioner of Corrections in curtailing what went on is to be applauded. Yet this chapter in the Beaver Creek experiment can serve as a cautionary tale.

Slavery and Non-personhood

There is a tendency to think of prisoners as less than human. In May 2023, Matt Katz of WNYC News published a story recounting that for generations, New York State prisoners were buried in graveyards just outside prison walls, under headstones marked with prisoner identification numbers – but no names. The state directive outlining the corrections department's responsibilities when a person dies in custody was changed with little fanfare to now add names to all future burials. Some cemeteries are going further and adding the names of those deceased before the change of policy. It was noted that slave graves in the past did not include the names of those laid to rest. When we do not consider a prisoner as human, it grants us permission to treat the individual as subhuman.

Unfortunately, prison slave labour continues in the United States and elsewhere. It has been said that the thirteenth Amendment to the United States Constitution did not abolish slavery; it merely reformed it[1]. The International Labour Organization's own Federal Labour Convention, 1930 explicitly excludes prisoners by authorizing "any work done for service exacted from any person as a consequence of a conviction in a court of law." As a result, prison chain gangs continue to exist with solitary confinement being the alternative if one refuses to submit to the demand to work.

However, there is reason to hope in the United States. When Americans went to the polls for midterm elections in November 2022, voters in four states, Alabama, Oregon, Tennessee, and Vermont, approved ballot measures that will change their state constitutions to prohibit inmate slavery that forces prisoners to work against their will as punishment for their crimes. While the measures will be unlikely to change prison operations immediately, the Associated Press speculates that the initiatives may spur legal challenges when the pressure to work when there is a threat of punishment or loss of privileges when prisoners refuse the work. Potential losses would include family visits, phone calls, or time in solitary confinement.

Further, U.S. Senator Jeff Merkeley of Oregon and Representative Nikema Williams of Georgia have reintroduced a revision to the thirteenth amendment to end the slavery exception for inmates.

---

[1] The 13th Amendment reads: Neither slavery nor involuntary servitude, except as a punishment for crime whereof the party shall have been duly convicted, shall exist in the United States or any place subject to their jurisdiction." The exception for convicted criminals has been dubbed the "exceptions clause" by the New York Times and the "punishment clause" by USA Today.

Should Congress approve their proposal, three-fourths of the fifty states would have to vote in favour of ratification.

Even after the midterm vote, more than a dozen states have constitutions permitting inmate slave labour.

Slave labour continues as well in China, North Korea, and Eritrea. In China, there is widespread detention of Uyghurs. The detainees have been forced into producing goods that are exported worldwide.

The United Nations Office on Drugs and Crime has formulated what is often referred to as the Mandela Rules. The prohibitions in the Mandela Rules have influenced Canada's decision to drastically limit placing inmates in solitary confinement in excess of fifteen days. Yet the Mandela Rules go further. Rule 97 requires that incarcerated individuals "shall not be held in slavery or servitude" and further requires that any work performed be covered by the same wage, health, and safety standards applicable to all of a country's citizens.

When Howard Massicotte was in prison, he fought perceived injustices by the only tool he had – the filing of grievances. When Howard Massicotte was released from prison, he had another tool – popular opinion. The tactic of trying to mold public opinion by exposing an injustice does not always work. But this time it did. It is only when a substantial demand for justice is raised to spur political action or when injustice is proclaimed by the courts that we can expect any movement to curtail oppression.

CHAPTER 8

A JACKRABBIT PAROLE

Phillippe Clément and Terror in Cottage Country

> *The pain of running relieves the pain of living.*
>
> **- Jacqueline Simon Gunn**

No sooner is a custodial sentence pronounced than the offender's mind is turned to hope for release. That release need not be in the form of death from suicide, drugs, or assault within the prison. There is adequate health care so few inmates die of disease that cannot be remedied. In fact, rather than die in prison, there is the option of obtaining "parole by exception" so no matter when a person is eligible for parole, the dates can be adjusted to allow the inmate to pass peacefully at home. Otherwise, people, especially inmates that have worked their way down to minimum-security institutions can expect release through the process of parole.

Parole is usually available at the one-third mark of an inmate's sentence. The Parole Board must be convinced that an applicant for parole is a manageable risk in the community before granting day parole (release to a halfway house for 6 months or more) or full parole (allowing an inmate to reside at home).

Even when released, the prisoner is not totally free. He or she is still under state control, sometimes with Board-ordered conditions such as not using alcohol or drugs or not associating with persons known to be involved in crime. Violations of parole can result in a return to custody and possible full reincarceration after a post-suspension hearing before the Board.

A Simple Matter

It should have been a routine parole hearing.

Tuesday, September 15, 1992, started off with a leisurely drive to Beaver Creek Institution, located in Gravenhurst, Ontario, two hours north of Toronto in the heart of Ontario's cottage country. It was a pleasant sunny day as I parked my car and headed to the prison's V&C [Visits and Correspondence] building. I was early. My client, Phillippe Clément, was first on the list to be heard by the National Parole Board, whose hearing would start promptly at 8 a.m. I preferred to arrive at least a half-hour early, to meet with the client and kill off any butterflies that may be unsettling the client's stomach.

Beaver Creek Institution was a minimum-security prison, meaning that there were no walls or fences for the hundred and twenty or so inmates then residing there - just several residential units comparable to college residences where each person had the key to his own room. The meals were well prepared and delicious, and the prison even had its own mini-putt golf course. There were plenty of jobs for the inmates too, both on the prison reserve and in the nearby towns of Gravenhurst and Bracebridge. It was a site where only the most trusted inmates were housed – those who had demonstrated over the years that their good behaviour could be their reward and could earn them a chance at successful parole. Beaver Creek was considered a "releasing" institution, meaning that an inmate admitted to the prison would in all likelihood be paroled. For some, being free would be a hardship. For most, the lessening of state control over one's existence was well worth it.

It was set to be a routine hearing: to have the Parole Board consider a grant of Unescorted Temporary Absences. I had met with Phillippe Clément in previous weeks and had reviewed the paperwork that would go before the Board. The essential paperwork was a printout of the offender's criminal record and the A4D, the "Assessment for Decision," which was essentially a review of the institution's observations on the rehabilitative programming the inmate had undertaken. It also contained the recommendation of the prisoner's case management team that would go before the Board. That paperwork showed that despite Clément's conviction for second-degree murder, he had participated in psychiatric and psychology programs that addressed his criminogenic factors. The A4D, written in large part by the offender's institutional case manager (commonly referred to as the institutional parole officer), spoke glowingly of Clément's rehabilitation and concluded that he would be a manageable risk if released.

"This will be a quick and easy day," I thought, signing in as an official visitor at the V&C office. There were no metal detectors or ion scanners (routine fixtures in maximum and medium security institutions) one would typically have to negotiate before entering as existed in high-security institutions.

A Turn for the Worse

"Could you call Mr. Clément down so I can have a chat with him before the start of the hearing?" I asked the Correctional Officer behind the window of his office. It was a request I had made numerous times before. On the day of the parole hearing, clients generally wake up early (if indeed they slept at all) and would enter the V&C building with a nervous smile before joining me.

Fifteen minutes passed and Clément had still not arrived. I returned to the officer's window and asked to have Mr. Clément re-paged. Fifteen minutes later, Clément was still a no-show. A hearing assistant for the Board approached me in the V&C area and advised me that the Board was ready to proceed. I stated that my client had not attended a pre-hearing discussion and that I would appreciate a slight delay until I had a chance to do that preliminary interview. The hearing assistant was most understanding and said she would convey my request to the Board.

The hearing assistant returned almost immediately. She said that the Board members agreed that they would move on to the second case on the list, in order to give me the opportunity to consult with my client. I expressed my appreciation and made my third request to have Mr. Clément called down. Clément's institutional parole officer, Pierre Labonte, testified later that he had also requested Clément's presence at 9 a.m.

At approximately eleven a.m., I was still sitting alone in the V&C area. I was beginning to wonder if I had inadvertently offended someone at the Institution, and if the delay in my client's attendance was retribution for some imagined slight. Now the Board wanted to see my client, and at that point, the Board delivered its direction to have the offender attend.

The Reason for the Absence

Once the Board made the request, a team of correctional officers was dispatched to Clément's living unit. They knocked on his door but received no answer. A passkey opened the door to find a group of pillows arranged under the bed covers mimicking a sleeping body. My client was gone. There would be no parole hearing before the Board.

The grounds of the Institution were searched, and finally, the Ontario Provincial Police were contacted. It was obvious that sometime before seven-thirty a.m., Phillippe Clément had walked away from Beaver Creek Institution. He had ensured his own release - one that inmates call, "a jackrabbit parole."

* * *

Police Report

At about the same time as they were notified of Clément's escape, the Ontario Provincial Police received a call that a forty-six-year-old mother of five had been assaulted in her living room, several miles distant from the prison. A press release noted that a Bracebridge woman had discovered an unknown man in her home armed with a knife. The man was said to have grabbed the woman's breasts, then choked her and stabbed her. The woman's hands were tied together with shoelaces and blood streamed down her face. The keys to her car, along with about seventy-five dollars in cash were missing. This happened at about eleven a.m.

The woman's husband found her covered in blood, later recounting that his wife was "almost

unrecognizable" when he found her and that her whole head and neck were swollen to grotesque proportions. The husband showed incredible restraint, rushing his wife to the hospital and holding her, still with a blood-soaked nightie tied around her neck as a makeshift ligature, until he arrived at the hospital.

The same day, not far from the woman's home, police investigated another break-in. In this instance, two hundred dollars in cash and some food were stolen. Although police were suspicious that Clément may have been the culprit, they had insufficient evidence to lay a charge of a second break-in.

On September seventeenth, 1992, arrest warrants were issued on charges of attempted murder, robbery, aggravated sexual assault, choking, breaking and entering, and theft. The woman who had been assaulted was listed in satisfactory condition in the Bracebridge hospital and was continuing treatment for bruises and trauma.

Police issued a warning, asking residents to be on the lookout for the thirty-three-year-old escapee. He was described as six-foot tall, a one-hundred-and-seventy-pound man of athletic build wearing blue jeans, a black and red jacket, and grey shoes. He had dark brown hair, brown eyes, and spoke with a French accent. He had a leopard-head tattoo on his left bicep and should be considered armed and dangerous. Most disturbingly, it was reported that Clément was serving a life sentence for second-degree murder.

The description alarmed local residents. Les Judson, the prison's Warden, did not help the situation by advising the local press that Clément's was the third escape that month and that there had been seven walkaways the previous year. The Warden noted that the two previous escapes in September had resulted in the capture of the absconding prisoners within one day of their departure.

Discerning a Motive

The Clément case was more unnerving than the others though, as there had been violence committed on an innocent member of the community. Meanwhile, police were combing the area, especially in the forested areas surrounding the prison. Police had uncovered evidence that Clément had developed a crush on Correctional Officer Sue Langevin and feared that the escape could have been triggered by Clément's desire to make contact with Ms. Langevin at her home. Correctional Officers never tell inmates their home addresses, but in a rural community, it was fairly easy to locate where someone lived.

Over twenty police officers were tasked with combing the bush that surrounded the penitentiary. Cars on local highways were stopped and drivers and passengers were checked. A plane was deployed to have an aerial view of the area. The Ontario Provincial Police also engaged OPP Constable Doug Swift and his tracking dog, Duke. During the search, two butcher knives were found in a wooded area and the victim's car was located about three kilometers away. Police really had no clear information that Clément was even in the area. "We believe in the best flip of a coin he was going to be in the area," Detective-Sergeant Bill Patterson, head of the Barrie district crime unit, told local media. That hunch was reinforced when a citizen came forward to advise police that a man matching Clément's description had asked for directions.

Indeed, Clément had not taken long to discover Sue Langevin's address. He later told me he had been hiding in the bushes when police attended at her residence. But on September 18th, the jig was up as Duke caught the scent of the escaped prisoner. As Swift and Duke moved about three hundred meters into the bush, they discovered Clément lying on the ground.

"He put up his hands and decided he couldn't reason with this dog," a Corrections Canada spokesperson commented, seemingly wanting to share in the community's sense of relief upon Clément's capture.

The September 18, 1992 edition of the Orillia *Packet and Times* newspaper featured a front-page picture of a sullen and handcuffed Phillippe Clément being escorted by a frowning police officer in shirt and tie into police custody. Instead of returning to Beaver Creek Institution, Clément would be taken to the old Barrie Jail to await trial on the criminal charges.

***

Phillippe's Background

Although I had reviewed Clément's criminal history in preparation for his parole hearing, I was surprised at how much more gruesome his past sounded when it was laid out in print in the newspaper. The description set out by the Correctional Service was softer.

Clément and his sister had been raised on the outskirts of Montreal. Clément's father had been having nonconsensual sex with the children's babysitter. Clément's mother caught on to the affair, finally catching her husband raping the babysitter. Caught in the act, the father became so enraged that he stabbed and killed the mother, who had attempted to intervene to protect the babysitter. The children watched in horror as their mother was slaughtered. The blood and screaming were burned into the minds of these children.

The children were put up for adoption and were adopted together. They never received counselling, and Phillippe began to develop a bizarre response to the trauma he had endured. He would slip out of the house at night and stalk women on the streets of Montreal. At age thirteen, Clément assaulted women by grabbing their breasts. He was apprehended when his sister found several women's wallets in Phillippe's bedroom, and at the age of fifteen Phillippe was taken into youth custody.

Youth facilities such as the one he occupied were not secure facilities and he was able to slip out at night and sexually molest young women. From the age of fifteen on, Phillippe Clément would be subject to state supervision.

On turning eighteen, Phillippe met Suzanne Gregoire at a Montreal bar. Ms. Gregoire, a law student at the time, no doubt found Phillippe Clément personable as well as tall and good-looking. She agreed to leave the bar with him. When outside, Clément attacked Ms. Gregoire, sexually assaulting her by grabbing her breasts. When she objected, Clément repeated his father's brutality by beating the young woman and slitting her throat. He stabbed her eighty times.

Clément was arrested, tried, and convicted of second-degree murder. He was sentenced to life in prison with no parole eligibility for ten years. He spent five years in Archambault Penitentiary, a medium-security institution in Ste-Anne-des-Plaines that contains the Regional Mental Health Centre. At the time of Clément's placement, Archambault was considered one of the most violent prisons in Canada.

Eventually, Clément was placed in the Institut Phillippe -Pinel de Montreal, a two hundred and ninety-two-bed facility opened in 1970 to accommodate criminals who would otherwise be in penitentiary (but could be treated as psychiatric patients), as well as people who had committed criminal acts but had been found not guilty by reason of insanity. Clément was diagnosed as being an aggressive sexual sadist with homicidal overtones. That diagnosis was not transferred when Clément left that institution, nor was it disclosed that Clément had a sexual relationship with a prison nurse while undergoing treatment.

Clément told me he was abused and spent long periods in solitary confinement while at Pinel. I gave short shrift to his story, believing that the facility was well-managed and overseen by the Université de Montréal. But in 2006, a class-action suit was taken against Pinel, which the hospital settled in 2009 for a reported million-dollar figure. Only then did I become convinced of the isolation and abuse Clément experienced at the well-reputed hospital. I knew from my dealings defending Terry Fitzsimmons and the work done by experts like Dr. Stuart Grassian, that solitary confinement can result in disastrous situations, especially for people diagnosed with a mental illness.

Once discharged from Pinel, Clément continued his penitentiary sentence at a medium-security institution. Pinel did not forward crucial documents to the Correctional Service once discharged from the hospital. He spent two years at Cowansville prison in the Quebec region, where he attempted suicide and was placed in solitary confinement for the attempt. There was little focus at the time for the damage solitary confinement could do to individuals, especially those diagnosed with mental instability. Clément left Cowansville for an inter-regional transfer out of the Quebec Region to Warkworth Institution in Northumberland County, Ontario. Clément had a sister living in the region and had family and friends close by assisting in rehabilitation. Warkworth Institution was a medium-security institution, at the time housing the most inmates of any Canadian prison. It also hosted a new sexual offender treatment facility launched by Queen's University psychologist Dr. Howard Barbaree.

The sexual offender clinic was based on the principle of behaviour modification. An offender being assessed would be seated in a chair and a band would be placed around the offender's penis. The band was linked to a machine that could measure any expansion as the offender was forced to watch forms of pornography similar to the sexual episodes that brought the offender to prison. The instrument was called a plethysmograph, but inmates referred to it as the "peter meter." During treatment, inmates who responded with a measurable change in the volume of the penis would experience an unpleasant shock. The treatment would try to associate pain or discomfort with the visual cue that was found to be enjoyable. In theory, the antisocial behaviour would be alleviated once the brain associated deviant social acts with discomfort. When not undergoing treatment, some inmates were counselled to wear an elastic band around their wrists and snap the band whenever they had a deviant thought.

Whether the theory worked in practice became irrelevant as it applied to Phillippe Clément. He became enraptured with a young woman working in the clinic, who would later testify in court (and gave a TV statement) that she was not properly supervised while working there. Dr. Barbaree denied the allegation, stating he had ample documentation to show that his clinic had provided adequate supervision to staff. Clément, feeling he had developed a relationship with the female staff worker, signed on to repeat the course of treatment. Any notations that the inmate had romantic delusions for the clinic worker were not reported in clinical notes. When I later asked Clément how he was able to evade a telling sign when on the peter meter, Clément responded that he was unable to get an erection despite sexual thoughts. The Warkworth Sexual Behaviour Clinic ultimately signed off on Clément as a rehabilitated offender and considered him fit for placement at a minimum-security facility. Dr. Barbaree had developed a lucrative business processing sexual offenders and it would not service the business model if some patients were impervious to treatment. Thus, Clément was transferred to Beaver Creek.

Dr. Barbaree later told the *Toronto Star* that he advised against a transfer to minimum security because Clément was unable to reduce his deviant sexual impulses and if transferred from Warkworth, he should remain in a full-time sex offender treatment program.

Once Clément was transferred, he was confronted, perhaps for the first time in his adult life, by offenders who were for all intents and purposes "normal," i.e., not under extensive psychological or psychiatric treatment. Clément's first language was French and was therefore added to the caseload of a bilingual institutional parole officer. That parole officer would later be terminated and escorted off the grounds of the prison and charged with sexual offences as well.

Clément would later tell me that his institutional parole officer would have him recount his sexual misadventures and delve into the sexually deranged world of Clément's desires. The parole officer encouraged Clément by telling him that the female correctional officer, Sue Langevin, had a "thing" for Clément and was awaiting some sign of interest from Clément to move the relationship from professional to sexual. None of this was true, of course. But to Clément, the thought that this young woman was desirous of him put his imagination into overdrive.

Finding a Friend

On the whole, Clément was not well-liked by his fellow BCI inmates. One inmate that Clément met and liked was Julius

Melnitzer. Julius seemed kind to Clément and he felt he could confide in Melnitzer.

I had known Julius Melnitzer from my first days in legal practice in London, Ontario. Melnitzer was highly regarded in the London legal community as not only generous with his time with other counsel but a man with a brilliant legal mind.

However, Julius Melnitzer was later arrested and convicted of serious crimes. In 1992, he pleaded guilty to forty-two counts of fraud and forgery in relation to defrauding five Canadian banks out of sixty-seven million dollars, the largest personal loan fraud in Canadian history. He was sentenced to nine years imprisonment with eligibility for parole in three. As a first-time, non-violent offender, he was classified to start his sentence in minimum-security Beaver Creek.

Melnitzer later gave testimony in court about his relationship with Clément. He testified that he had developed close ties while in prison together. He said that Clément was obsessed with guard Sue Langevin. As an act of human kindness, Langevin's occasional provision of needlepoint supplies allowed Clément to continue with his sewing hobby. It was, unfortunately, seen by Clément not as an act of generosity and kindness, but as an unspoken tribute of her affection towards Clément.

Many Beaver Creek inmates indulged in crafts, which were seen as rehabilitative. Inmates without money sometimes had outside visitors provide craft supplies. However, for people like Clément, who had no visitors, getting the occasional gift of craft supplies was much appreciated.

The night before Clément's parole hearing, Langevin conversed with the inmate. Since she was working the night shift, she felt it inappropriate to enter his room, which Clément saw as an act of rejection. He told Langevin he might not be here the next day. Langevin asked what he meant by that, and Clément explained that he might be transferred to medium-security if things did not go in his favour before the Parole Board. Instead of consoling him and promising that all would end satisfactorily, Langevin went on with her work and simply reported the irregular comment to the institutional parole officer.

Clément spoke to Melnitzer, who realized that Clément was feeling rejected. According to Melnitzer, it looked as if Clément was ready to explode. With no bars on the windows, no walls or fences, and no guard outposts, walking away was simple. Melnitzer tried to console and ease the man's sense of rejection but acted appropriately and did not counsel escape.

***

Community Reaction

When the police notice was published that a man convicted of murder was on the run, citizens in the surrounding municipalities were naturally upset. Some reported locking their doors and windows and expressed fear of walking alone at night. Once

Clément was apprehended, it was expected that public concern would dissipate. Such was not the case.

The high-profile crime for which Clément was serving his sentence came as a shock to many residents. People simply assumed that murderers would never occupy a minimum-security institution. Few stopped to think about the fact that most inmates are eventually released. The Correctional Service exists not only to punish aberrant behaviour, but also to rehabilitate its charges. Rehabilitation requires participation in needs-specific programming and a demonstration of good behaviour. As long as the inmate's progress is acceptable, the reward is lower security consistent with public safety. For persons convicted of murder, the sentence starts off in maximum security. With suitable programming and good behaviour, the inmate could be sent to medium-security and enjoy greater freedom. Again, good behaviour and progress in programming could lead to placement in minimum security. And even then, a parole board looks to establish that the inmate is a manageable risk in the community – first by noting positive reports of prosocial behaviour on escorted temporary absences into the community, and then a follow-up that authorizes a series of unescorted temporary absences. Only then would it be likely that the prisoner could rejoin the community by again acting in a prosocial manner at a halfway house.

What few Canadians realize is that a life sentence is indeed a life sentence. A "lifer" is under the supervision of the state for the rest of the prisoner's natural life. Even a minor infraction of the law could result in a warrant of suspension and a return to incarceration, no matter how many years a person has been free in the community.

This is all fine in theory. The problem, in this case, was that people were scared. It came as no surprise that on Saturday, September 26, 1992, sixteen-year-olds Tracy Hemmings and Kyla Shulz, along with Tracy's fourteen-year-old sister, Jan, led forty area residents in a demonstration at the entrance to the Beaver Creek Institution, demanding better protection for their communities. Bracebridge resident Jan Hemmings told an area newspaper reporter, "This is our town and we don't feel safe here." The September 28 edition of the *Orillia Packet and Times* carried a photo of Donna Miller, who participated in the protest holding a sign with capitalized hand-scrawled letters reading "W.A.R." - or "Women Against Rape."

National Publicity

The case quickly drew national attention. CBC producer George James led a film crew for *The Fifth Estate* in covering a hastily called town hall meeting that featured Solicitor General Doug Lewis in a "Q and A" with local residents. As Solicitor General, Doug Lewis was responsible for the Correctional Service of Canada (CSC), and he hoped the public "bitch-session" would mitigate local hostility. A public hall in Gravenhurst was packed, and the crowd had no sympathy for the excuses proffered by the CSC.

Politically, Doug Lewis knew he was on thin ice. He was the Progressive Conservative Member of Parliament for the neighbouring riding, Simcoe North, the federal electoral district next to the riding in which Beaver Creek is located. It was the Conservative government of Prime Minister Brian Mulroney that was in the process of finalizing plans for the construction of a new medium-security penitentiary to be built in the wooded area behind the Beaver Creek facility. Public relations and political expediency demanded that the protests remain under control.

In January 1993, The *Fifth Estate* documentary aired, broadcasting the apparent incompetence of CSC officials for all to see. The Warden, Les Judson, told the media that mistakes were made and admitted that Clément was known to be missing at eight-thirty a.m. and that a thorough search of the prison grounds was made and the OPP were contacted at ten twenty-three that morning. A new procedure was unveiled, promising that in the future the OPP would be notified the moment CSC suspected that an inmate had taken off. Further, the OPP would be furnished with photographs of all inmates at the institution, which could save precious moments during the prospect of locating a suspected walk-away. A full CSC investigation into the walk-away was promised within the following week.

***

The Role of Defence Counsel

As a criminal lawyer and, more importantly in this case, a prison law lawyer, one must realize that an acquittal in these circumstances is impossible. Rather, the choices to be made in defence must be made to secure the best possible outcome for the client. Clément had very deep psychological issues that had not been treated (and one might even say are "exacerbated" by the prison system). When he assaulted the woman after departing the institution, he knew the nature and quality of his actions were wrong. Thus, he did not qualify for an insanity plea.

On the other hand, he was serving a life sentence and would be on that sentence for the rest of his natural life. An additional penitentiary term would not elongate the time he would be under state supervision. Obviously, consideration for parole would be lost in the near future. He had admitted to the police what he had done.

The main concern would be to secure a transfer to a region where he would not be known. Sex offenders can be brutally treated by fellow inmates in general population, and the last thing Clément needed was to spend years in solitary to avoid injury or death at the hands of other inmates. With all the local publicity, there was a strong possibility he would be beaten or killed anywhere in Ontario. That was the reason I commenced negotiation with Warden Les Judson for an interregional transfer either to the Atlantic Region, the Prairie Region, or the Pacific Region of CSC.

At the outset, I suggested a transfer to Dorchester Penitentiary in New Brunswick. There Clément could find more people who spoke

French than he might encounter outside the Quebec region. Return to Quebec was not considered; he had bad experiences in Quebec before, and there might have been long memories of his original murder conviction. It took a few meetings to bring the Warden who was on board with my suggestion for a transfer to initiate an interregional transfer. I met with Warden Judson a few weeks later who confirmed that the Pacific Region had agreed to accept Clément once he had been convicted of the new charges. Clément took it in stride that he would be calling British Columbia his new home.

Meetings with the Warden were matched with meetings with Crown Attorney Ken Anthony in his office at the Courthouse in Bracebridge. Anthony was feeling pressure to have Clément designated as a dangerous offender. However, that would require an extensive hearing and the calling of expert witnesses, a process that could tie up an already overburdened court system for weeks, not to mention the large sums of money required. It could also necessitate the calling of the victim, which would bring with it the fear that having to testify could add to her trauma. Instead, I advised Mr. Anthony that the client would agree to guilty pleas on attempted murder and aggravated sexual assault.

The Trial

On Monday morning, November 15, 1993, a year and two months after Clément committed his assault, he came before the Ontario Court General Division (now called the Superior Court) in

Bracebridge to enter guilty pleas and to be sentenced. Ken Anthony, assisted by an OPP officer, sat at the counsel table to my left. Phillippe Clément was brought into the courtroom, legs shackled, and took a seat in the prisoner's box behind me.

We stood as Mr. Justice John Goodearle entered the courtroom. After a few preliminary matters, counsel for the prosecution and defence were asked if we were ready to proceed, and we indicated in the affirmative.

"I'll ask Mr. Clément to stand while the clerk reads out the charges," the judge said. Clément rose in the prisoner's box and stood attentively as the charges of attempted murder and aggravated sexual assault were read. Clément answered that he understood the charges and entered his "guilty" plea when asked. The Crown Attorney commenced to give a synopsis of the facts supporting the charges. When asked if the summary was accurate, I had been instructed by Clément to indicate they were substantially correct.

We were ready to proceed to sentencing. As part of my sentencing submissions, I asked the Court to watch the *Fifth Estate* documentary. I had arranged for a television monitor and VCR to be brought into the courtroom to substantiate how the missed opportunities of Canada's prison system had not only led to this vicious crime but to the disillusionment of the entire community. I noted that while it could be said that Phillippe Clément was a victim too, his actions were sufficient to dispel any pity for him. I suggested that in passing the sentence, it might be worthwhile to indicate the Court's disappointment with how this offender had been treated over the years so that steps could be taken to ameliorate the system such that we could hopefully avoid the shock that the Muskoka community was forced to endure.

As usual, the judge asked the accused if he had anything to say before the sentence was passed. Clément rose from the prisoner's box and commenced by apologizing to the victim, her family, and the local community. He then added:" I feel the crime against the Gravenhurst victim was really a crime against the system. She was a victim of what I felt against the system, not against her or women."

"I regret very much what I have done and I am ready to take what goes with it," he continued with his French accent more noticeable than before.

Goodearle seemed impressed. He imposed a sentence of two concurrent life sentences with a future parole eligibility date of ten years. By allowing future parole eligibility, the judge said the system was partially to blame for the way it treated Clément. "Clément is not an evil person, and the system is to blame for the assault on a woman after his escape last year," the judge concluded.

Crown Attorney Ken Anthony came under attack from the lawyer representing the female victim. Anthony was chastised for failing to procure a "dangerous offender" designation that the lawyer argued would have ensured that Clément would remain locked up for the rest of his life. Anthony rightfully pointed out that it was highly unlikely any future parole hearing would release this accused person, and that the guilty pleas saved the victim the further trauma of testifying in court.

Clément was returned to the Parry Sound Jail to await transfer to a penitentiary in British Columbia. I confided in Ken Anthony that Warden Judson and I had worked hard to secure placement in a BC prison so that Clément would be out of the victim's immediate neighbourhood.

Some weeks later, we learned the victim had sold her Muskoka home and moved to British Columbia.

A New Federal Government

By the time the criminal matters were dealt with, the Progressive Conservative government (of which Solicitor General Doug Lewis was a part) was defeated in the October general election. The once-powerful governing party was reduced to a mere two seats in Parliament. Buoyed by the idea that the governance of Canada's prisons could be improved and having heard a powerful condemnation of CSC procedures from Justice Goodearle, I wrote to the newly-appointed Solicitor General, Herb Gray.

In a letter dated November 16, 1993, I wrote asking for an inquiry into the treatment of imprisoned sex offenders.

"We want to see if there can be a better response than there has been in the past by officials and the previous Conservative government," I wrote. "I call upon you, sir, to critically examine the method in which sex offenders are incarcerated and treated in the hope that new and more effective procedures can be established." I noted that the Ontario Judge had said in sentencing Clément, "The system failed you in the first place. There were people in the case that should be called into account."

I was joined in my request for an inquiry by Terri Follis, one of the founding members of the Coalition Against Violence in Muskoka. She said her group which had been formed on September 17, 1992, a day after Clément committed the assault, had been calling for more answers from prison and correctional officers. It was certainly an unusual situation to have a perpetrator's counsel standing alongside a victims' rights group demanding change.

***

Victim's Civil Action

Justice Goodearle's condemnation of Clément's past treatment also resonated with the victim, who brought a civil suit against Clément and those involved in his "treatment" in a lawsuit filed in the Ontario Court (General Division) in the spring of 1993. The lawsuit claimed multi-millions of dollars in damages and punitive damages against Clément, the Government of Canada, and certain individuals - most notably Howard Barbaree who established and was in charge of the Warkworth Sexual Behaviour Clinic.

The lawsuit, styled *S. (J.) v. Clément et al* was heard in Toronto. The plaintiffs were the woman who had been assaulted and her family members. Although Phillippe Clément was a named defendant, he had little to worry about. He was penniless; the deep pockets were with the federal government and Howard Barbaree. Since I was counsel for Clément and asked for his presence when I first arrived at Beaver Creek Institution, I knew that I would be called as a witness at trial. A lawyer cannot act both as counsel and witness for their client. To that end, Orillia civil trial lawyer Patrick Lassaline agreed to act for Clément.

I was called as a witness for the plaintiff, recounting my attendance at the institution and my frustration that the staff at Beaver Creek had not acted promptly to affect my early morning pre-parole interview. I considered everything I said rather uncontroversial and true.

I was therefore surprised when counsel for the federal government began his cross-examination of me by asking: "You hate the Correctional Service, don't you?"

Counsel for the plaintiff jumped up, objecting to the question. It was ruled improper; I never had an opportunity to answer.

Had I been allowed to be forthright in my answer, I would have acknowledged that the vast majority of Correctional Service Canada employees are hard-working and dedicated professionals. However, in some instances, mistakes and negligence happen, and the aftermath can be horrible as in the Clément case.

Madam Justice Susan E. Lang handed down her written reasons for judgment on February 9, 1995. The judge carefully recorded her findings of fact and determined there was Crown liability. She found that a risk of violence towards women in the vicinity of the prison from an escaped violent sexual offender was foreseeable, and further that the Correctional Service of Canada owed a duty of care to such women. Most tragically, CSC failed to conduct an immediate search for the inmate when he failed to respond to a page, and then CSC failed to immediately notify the police when it was realized an escape was probable. Failure to respond promptly constituted negligence.

The judgment also found that the plaintiff, only referred to as "J.S." to protect the victim's identity, was viciously beaten and sexually assaulted. She suffered from post-traumatic stress disorder, a loss of energy, and a loss of self-worth. She suffered a scar over her right eyebrow. Relationships within her previously happy family deteriorated as she withdrew from marital intimacy.

The judgment was for ninety-thousand dollars payable by Clément and Canada jointly and severally. This meant that J.S. could look equally to either Canada, Clément, or both to satisfy the judgment. Since Clément had no money, the entire amount would be a government expense.

J.S. was refused punitive damages on her claim that Clément had been dropped into her relocated home territory in British Columbia because the government was unaware of the plaintiff's move and the transfer was not motivated by malice.

Since the trial judge focused her concerns on issues of foreseeability, Howard Barbaree escaped liability. He may have participated in having Clément transferred to Beaver Creek, but it was too remote to suggest that an escape and an assault were inevitable.

The Tarasoff Principle

It was likely that Dr. Barbaree and those connected to the Warkworth Sexual Offender Clinic were able to dodge the bullet of liability because the trial judge never considered the Tarasoff principle, sometimes called "the duty to warn." Simply stated, the rule holds that when a therapist determines, or pursuant to the standards of his profession should determine, that the patient presents a serious danger of violence to another, the therapist incurs an obligation to use reasonable care to protect the intended victim against such danger. The new tort is widely used in the United States and has been considered at Europe's International Court of Justice. Some Canadian courts, while alluding to the concept, have not made it pivotal in awarding damages.

We are left to conclude that the evidence did not reveal that suspicion of the danger inmate Clement posed to the public was sufficient to trigger a duty to warn.

***

The government took note that there was genuine concern about how sex offenders are treated in Canada. A National Committee on Sex Offender Strategy was struck in 1993 and visited each of Canada's five prison regions over the course of 1994. Over a three-day meeting, March 28-30, 1995, four hundred and twenty-five attendees from Canada, the United States, and Europe met in Toronto to discuss issues related to assessment, treatment, and follow-up. Speakers included an impressive roster of experts delivering their expert advice on the state of sex offender treatment.

One of the experts speaking at the conference was Janice K. Marques of the California State Department of Mental Health. She reported that California was in the midst of a longitudinal study of sex offenders to test the newest, most promising, and most effective methods of sex offender treatment under a study referred to as the Sex Offender Treatment and Evaluation Project (SOTEP). The study was funded by the California Departments of Mental Health and Corrections and by the National Institute of Mental Health, and the treatment methods studied were those used in Canada and England. The program began in 1985 and was scheduled to conclude at the end of 2000. The data presented were not promising:

The 1993 panel of data showed that eleven percent of the treated group had committed new sex crimes or other violent crimes, compared with seventeen percent and fifteen percent of the matched offenders in the two untreated groups. 1994's data showed that twenty-five percent of the treated offenders had reoffended, compared with twenty-four percent and twenty-seven percent in the control groups. It was noted that conclusions as to the effectiveness of treatment with statistical precision were impossible to make until the program had been concluded.

A follow-up study published by Janice K. Marques and others in 2005 found that the treatment methods studied did not support their effectiveness in reducing violent or sexual recidivism.

Psychology papers published since offer hope that better interview techniques will allow an offender greater insight, but nothing provides a solution to identifying potential risks or ways to minimize the risk.

Perhaps our focus should not be centered on punishment/ rehabilitation modes of treating offenders convicted of such heinous crimes. As in medicine, maybe we should focus on prevention. The old saying that "hurt people hurt people" is demonstrably true. Perhaps attention should be given immediately after an individual, especially a young person, experiences or witnesses a traumatic incident. Anecdotally, I have observed too many cases where young adults have offended after witnessing or experiencing abuse. If a young man watches his mother being murdered, is it not logical to see that he gets counselling immediately?

Postscript

The following appeared in the August 1, 2007 edition of the Huntsville *Forrester:*

> During the evening of May 25, 2007, a little more than 15 years after he walked away from Beaver Creek Institution and brutally assaulted a Gravenhurst woman, Phillippe Clément died in prison.
>
> An inmate of Mountain Institution, Agassiz, British Columbia, Clément, 48, died of apparent natural causes after collapsing on the gymnasium floor.
>
> Mountain Institution is a federal medium security institution located 120 kilometers east of Vancouver.

In his entire adult life, Phillippe Clément spent three days away from state control

CHAPTER 9

TIMEBOMB:
PSYCHIATRIC PATIENTS
AND THEIR TREATMENT

Gary Leo Genereaux and The Experimentation
in a Psychiatric Hospital

> *The object of terrorism is terrorism. The object of oppression is*
> *oppression. The object of torture is torture, The object of*
> *murder is murder. The object Of power is power. Now do you*
> *begin to understand me?*
>
> **– George Orwell, 1984**

The news shocked residents of Kingston, Ontario when on March 10, 1973, the body of sixteen-year-old Shirley Bailey was found. Two days later, the remains of fifteen-year-old Robin Barrett were discovered.

Robin Barrett had been missing since October when she was last seen hitch-hiking from a friend's house. It wasn't until March twelfth, that a bottle-picker came upon what he first thought was a store mannequin to find the partly decomposed body of the Barrett girl.

Shirley Bailey, a high school student at Kingston's La Salle Secondary School, had finished her part-time work at a bakery in the Kingston Centre mall. Her body was discovered in a neighbouring County. She had been sexually assaulted and strangled with a pair of pantyhose.

Police had no leads on a possible suspect and no charges have ever been laid.

On May 22, eleven-year-old Michelle Keogh was getting off a school bus ready to walk to her home on a gravel road in Grafton, a hamlet a few miles east of Cobourg Ontario, and an hour's drive east of Toronto. Michelle never made it home. Her body was discovered by her father near the family home. She had been raped, strangled, and stabbed to death.

This time, the police had a suspect. Police arrested twenty-nine-year-old Gary Leo Genereaux and charged him with murder. Genereaux was from Trenton, Ontario, and had been released from penitentiary in 1972 after serving less than six years of an eight-year sentence for attempted murder. He had been working at a racetrack in Kingston.

Being released at the six-year mark of the sentence is unremarkable. He would have been eligible for parole after serving a third of his term. Obviously, he was not granted parole.

Instead, prisoners were automatically released after serving two-thirds of their sentence on what was then called mandatory supervision (now called Statutory Release). It was expected the final third of the sentence would be served in the community under the supervision of a community parole officer and subject to strict conditions of release. Breaching conditions (the prime condition being to keep the peace and be of good behaviour) could see release suspended and a return to federal incarceration.

What was remarkable with this release was that, while still in custody, Genereaux realized he had a serious problem and requested psychiatric intervention. The Correctional Service of Canada ignored his request, and he was released into the community without any obligation to seek psychiatric help.

In 1974, Genereaux appeared for trial in Cobourg before Supreme Court Judge Sam Hughes with Toronto lawyer Ronald Thomas defending him. Thomas was successful in obtaining a decision that Genereaux was not guilty of murder by reason of insanity. Thomas took the unusual step of reading Genereaux's criminal record into the record. The attempted murder charge was in relation to the assault on a Richmond Hill waitress at a pizza parlour who was stabbed 63 times but survived.

In support of the insanity defence, Thomas called two defence witnesses. The first was Toronto psychiatrist Gilbert Howie. Dr. Howie described Genereaux as "a seriously mentally ill individual" who hates women. He recounted a conversation he had with Genereaux in preparation for his testimony. Genereaux revealed that he sometimes dreamed of raping female corpses. He even fantasized about becoming an undertaker's assistant to act out his reveries.

Another psychiatrist, Dr. Ivan Sirechich of the Oak Ridges Division of the Ontario Mental Health Centre in Penetanguishene told Justice Hughes that Genereaux was schizophrenic and should be locked away in a psychiatric hospital, perhaps for the rest of his natural life.

Justice Hughes accepted the submissions and commented that Genereaux was a "time bomb" who could kill again should he go free. He would be sent to Penetanguishene's maximum-security unit on what was then referred to as a "lieutenant-governor's warrant." He could expect to remain in the hospital indefinitely until he could be declared sane. The judgment was good news for the grieving parents. Mike Keogh and his wife, Collette, were promised by local authorities that Genereaux would never be released into society.

Genereaux remained at Penetanguishene until 1980 when he was transferred to the St. Thomas Psychiatric Hospital. He found the hospital and staff at St. Thomas much more accommodating and he could start thinking of having the conditions of his lieutenant-governor's warrant loosened to escape the locked ward where he was housed.

My first contact with Gary Genereaux was in 1984. I met with Genereaux several times. He always appeared polite and low-key.

When I occasionally would visit my parents' home not far from where the Keogh murder happened, my father could be counted on to launch into a rant about the atrocity perpetrated by "the guy who killed the little girl in Grafton." To my father and to much of the community around him, "the guy who killed the little girl in Grafton" was the personification of evil.

On one visit I let it slip that my newest client was Gary Genereaux. The name did not ring a bell to my father. I explained, "He's the guy who killed the little girl in Grafton."

Shock and horror could be read on his face. "I hope you lose," he said, implying the matter was never to be discussed again.

I really didn't have a chance to lose. At the first hearing scheduled to consider a loosening of the warrant after I was retained, I learned the hearing would not start as early as I expected. No explanation was given. I looked over the paperwork while I was waiting. The recommendation to be put forward by the hospital was to loosen the warrant to allow Genereaux mobility throughout the hospital by removing him from the locked ward. He had exhibited model behaviour and the hospital administrators were convinced he could be trusted with further privileges.

Much to my surprise, when the hearing was about to begin, Genereaux was escorted to the hearing room bound in a straight jacket. Staff advised he had become unruly before the hearing was to begin and required restraint. The optics of proceeding with the client restrained were horrific. I requested and the Board readily agreed to an adjournment of the hearing until the whole situation could be investigated and re-evaluated.

Warrant Loosened

I did not have the opportunity to see the matter to its conclusion. I sold my London practice to take up a job teaching at the Queen's University Law School. However, Genereaux pressed ahead and had his warrant loosened gradually. In 1991, he was allowed unsupervised access to the community. He volunteered with St. John's ambulance and as an electrician's helper. For two years, he seemed to be integrating well into the community.

Genereaux was still under a warrant that could be re-activated if he engaged in suspicious activity. He failed to report that he had developed a relationship with a woman and engaged in cross-dressing. These aspects of his life became known when he was once again arrested. This time he was charged with sexually assaulting a developmentally handicapped woman.

When police arrested Genereaux in 1993, police found him wearing pantyhose. It was reminiscent of the article of clothing used to strangle one of his alleged victims. Genereaux claimed he was asleep when police knocked on his door. He sought to dress himself quickly by grabbing the pantyhose that a female friend had left at his apartment.

He had spent a year in jail awaiting trial. The pantyhose did not constitute similar fact evidence from a previous crime. The handicapped woman and her sister gave different descriptions of the attacker. Genereaux was acquitted of the 1993 charge in 1994. With the acquittal, he expected full release. But with the warrant still in place, Genereaux was returned to the St Thomas Psychiatric Hospital.

Several psychiatrists testified before a review board in January 1995. The expert evidence ranged from deeming Genereaux a "low risk" to other opinions that he had regressed. Genereaux argued on his own behalf that he should be sent to a medium-security hospital in North Bay where he could seek community release in five years.

The Next Hearing

In January 1995, The Ontario Criminal Code Review Board which took the place of the Lieutenant-Governors' Board of Review, met to determine if Genereaux should remain at St. Thomas or if he should be returned to Penetanguishene.

London Assistant Crown Attorney Geoff Beasley advised the Board that even though no charges were laid in regard to the two teenage girls murdered in Kingston, Genereaux had claimed responsibility for one of the deaths.

"He has admitted to killing a 15-year-old girl around the same time those girls were killed near Kingston," Beasley maintained. "As I recall, he was living at a halfway house and working at a racetrack and he picked up this girl hitchhiking. He killed her, dumped her, and then said where she was found," Beasley added.

But retired OPP officer, Neil Sigsworth, the investigating officer on the Barrett murder case pointed out it is not so simple as to make a bold allegation. Sigsworth continued to maintain that there was just not enough evidence to bring the matter to court. He stated, "You cannot go into a courtroom with just an admission and little or no evidence. The admission can always be recanted or ruled inadmissible. You have to back up what someone has admitted to. We believed he did it, but we had insufficient evidence."

Detective Constable Dave Galloway of the OPP Penitentiary Squad echoed Sigsworth's remarks in connection with the Bailey killing. Galloway was assigned to investigate the Bailey murder. "In my opinion, he was our guy," Galloway stated. "He admitted to people about the Barrett killing but not to the Bailey killing. He had a memory lapse."

Both Sigsworth and Galloway believed it would be futile trying to prosecute the charges since the likely result would be a finding of insanity as happened in the Keogh murder case.

The hearing also heard the opinions of three psychiatrists including Dr. Stephen Hucker and Dr. Samuel Swaminath.

Dr. Swaminath was disturbed that Genereaux was arrested wearing women's underwear, noting that both the Keogh girl and one of the Kingston victims were strangled with pantyhose.

Dr. Hucker, a specialist in forensic psychiatry, also warned against Genereaux's release. He stated, "We have a man here who has committed four violent, sexually-motivated crimes, two of which resulted in murder.... Mr. Genereaux has a serious pathology which is two-fold: He is sexually sadistic and psychopathic. The combination of these two is a particularly worrisome one."

Both Dr. Hucker and Dr. Swarminth urged the Board to hold Genereaux and not re-release him to the community. Hucker pointed out that a statistical risk assessment completed by Genereaux when he was originally confined at Penetanguishene indicated there was a one-hundred-percent chance that he would re-offend within seven years. Apparently, St. Thomas Psychiatric Hospital never took this into consideration when Genereaux was released into the community. Hucker agreed that Genereaux may or may not have killed one or both of the Kingston teenagers but, he warned, the killer, if not him, was someone like him.

Recommittal

On January 31, 1995, the Ontario Criminal Code Review Board handed down its decision. It found that Genereaux still suffered from a serious mental illness that made him "a significant threat to the safety of the public." He was ordered to return to maximum security at the Penetanguishene Hospital.

For a person to be committed to a psychiatric hospital after committing a criminal offense, one must accept the proposition that the aims of criminal law and psychiatry are different. Criminal law aims to enforce rehabilitation by removing an offender from society, usually for a given period. Deprivation of liberty is the only legitimate form of punishment accepted in Canadian society. When a person is proven to be insane, the principle is that the offensive act was committed by a person incapable of forming the requisite mental element that would constitute a crime. The act may be wrong and the offender ought to be treated for the mental health condition that caused the acting out. The aim is treatment, not punishment.

It is therefore somewhat surprising that Dr. Swarminth would agree that a maximum-security treatment facility would be necessary for cross-dressing. Obviously, the psychiatrist was of the belief either that Genereaux had assaulted the handicapped woman or that he was untreatable and deserved to return to the Oak Ridge facility, perhaps indefinitely.

Dr. Hucker, on the other hand, looked directly at Genereaux's mental condition and urged treatment at the Penetanguishene hospital.

Experimental Treatment

Although psychiatrists know or ought to know of the treatment regime they are recommending, members of the general public are largely unaware of what transpires within a prison or at a mental health institution. It is unlikely the psychiatrists who urged Genereaux's placement at the Oak Ridges facility had any real notion of the peculiar form of treatment with which the facility was experimenting. It is unknown if Genereaux was ever subjected to experimental psychiatric therapy. The nature of a program carried out at the Oak Ridge centre has come to light in a lawsuit originally filed as a class action in the year 2000 but disallowed in

2003. Lawyers reconstituted the action in 2006 as a multi-plaintiff proceeding.

The plaintiffs are men treated at the Penetanguishene facility who alleged that the "treatment" administered at the institution was torture. The program that drew concern was introduced by psychiatrists Gary Maier and Elliott Barker following Dr. Barker's visit to Mao Zedong's prison camps where coercion was used to reshape character.

More than two dozen inmates of the Penetanguishene facility were named as plaintiffs in the action, the defendants being the Province of Ontario and two of the doctors on staff. Damages claimed in the civil action were in excess of $100 million. In their claim, the inmates allege that between 1965 and 1983 they were confined in conditions amounting to torture in what counsel for the inmate claimed was "reckless human experimentation."

The two psychiatrists who were in charge of the special therapy unit (the STU), Drs. Elliott Barker and Gary Maier, named defendants in the suit developed programs of treatment called Defence Disruptive Therapy (DDT), the Motivation, Attitude, Participation Program (MAPP), and the Total Encounter Capsule Program.

DDT required patients to take hallucinogenic and delirium-producing drugs so patients could confront their abnormal behaviours by eliminating their defence mechanisms. Patients undergoing DDT were injected with LSD-25 or administered a variety of other mind-altering drugs. By late 1967, it was discovered that the risks of homicide and suicide were very real. Patients were not asked to sign consent forms before the drugs were taken.

MAPP required a regimen of perfect behaviour that included no unauthorized talking or movement. Participants of the MAP program were sent to solitary confinement for a period of time. Upon release, rotating groups of four to eight men were forced to sit on a bare terrazzo floor for about eight hours daily. They were made to sit motionlessly. Violation of the non-movement order resulted in heavy sedation, being placed in restraints, and being recommitted to solitary confinement. Other psychiatric patients were given the task of monitoring movement and reporting violations.

The Capsule Program involved chaining up to seven people together in a windowless 8 x 10 room with only one toilet. All of the men were naked. There were no blankets and the temperatures in the room fluctuated between extreme heat and cold. The men were fed liquids (sometimes soup and sometimes cold milk) by straw through a hole in the wall for days at a time. Of course, no "informed consent" was obtained. The participants in the experimentation were described by the doctors as "throwaways." Many had a history of childhood physical and sexual abuse.

Diagnosis of Torture

An American military psychiatrist, Brig-Gen Stephen Xenakis compared the treatment meted out by Barker and Maier at Oak Ridge to the torture and mistreatment of inmates at the U.S. prison at Guantanamo Bay in Cuba.

Justice Paul Perell held that such treatment was "an inexcusable breach of fiduciary duty for a physician to torture a patient, but his decision was appealed and the Ontario Court of Appeal overturned the ruling on the basis of unfairness in the legal process and ordered a new trial. After completion of the new trial, Ontario Superior Court Justice Edward Morgan found the two doctors and the Province of Ontario liable for assault and battery that violated both the doctors' and Ontario's fiduciary duty in knowingly assisting behaviour that constituted "a paradigm case of opportunity and power on one hand, and vulnerability on the other."

Could it be that psychiatrists such as Dr. Hucker were simply unaware of the techniques being practiced at Penetanguishene? Hucker had studied the Oak Ridge program and prepared a report for the Ontario Ministry of Health in 1985 entitled, *Oak Ridge: A Review and an Alternative*. The report led to the cancellation of some programs but Hucker continued to downplay the suggestion that the therapy at Penetanguishene was akin to torture. "The suggestion that the STU [Social Therapy Unit] program mirrored the experiments of the Nazi doctors tried at Nuremberg is in my view melodramatic and bears little relationship to the work of the Oak Ridge physicians," he stated.

Both Joel Rochon, the lead counsel in the successful lawsuit, and Stephen Hucker are highly competent and intelligent professionals. It would be wrong to label them based on the work they do. Hucker knowingly recommended Genereaux's return to the Oak Ridge facility aware of the nature of the therapy used but not believing it was torture. Rochon spent two decades championing the cause of abused patients. The distinction is at the heart of why our criminal justice and correctional system can be seen as dysfunctional.

Treatment or Punishment

Dr. Hucker sees the need to protect society from dangerous individuals, hopefully, to see their antisocial behaviour mitigated if not eliminated. Rochon looks to the individual and holds that no human being, whatever wrongs were done in the past, should be abused. No matter if we view society from the macro level (looking out to prevent harm to the population) or from the micro level (deciding that no human being should be harmed), policymakers must reconcile the divergent views if we are to be a safe but humane society. Regardless whether one takes the "macro" stance or the "micro" stance, the social norm in our society, whether it be a prison or confinement for treatment in a psychiatric hospitable should be the same" One goes to prison *as* punishment, not *for* punishment."

CHAPTER 10

GATING:
DOES THE PUNISHMENT
FIT THE CRIME

The True Case of Ross Evans

> *They also serve who only stand and wait*
>
> **– John Milton**

The 1994 movie *Natural Born Killers* suggested there was something in a person's DNA that led to a life of crime. Although eugenics has been disproven, it has always been easier (and more politically popular) to punish criminal behaviour than to seek out its societal cause. If the punishment is to deprive a convict of freedom, the question remains "How long?"

How does society deal with someone like Donald Oag? The Oag brothers' names came to popular attention during the 1971 riot at Kingston Penitentiary. Donald Oag, age 20, and his 25-year-old brother James Robert Oag, were part of the "Kingston 13," a group of offenders ranging in age from seventeen to thirty-nine who had taken the opportunity during the uprising to assemble a group of suspected sex offenders and informers into a circle in the prison dome and brutalize them. One inmate died and the group of prison vigilantes were charged with murder. A plea deal was worked out after a month-long trial and James Robert had his charge reduced to manslaughter and was given an eight-year sentence concurrent to his life sentence of non-capital murder that had been imposed in 1968.

Donald, however, also pleaded guilty to the lesser and included offence of manslaughter and had three years added to the six-year sentence he was serving for attempted arson, originally imposed in 1966.

On four occasions since his imprisonment, Donald Oag escaped. During his 1975 escape, he committed serious offences including armed robbery and unlawful confinement, During the 1975 escape he took a prison officer hostage and placed a sharpened knife to the officer's throat, threatening to cut his neck. He had also threatened another individual at knife-point. In 1977 he committed attempted murder by repeatedly stabbing another inmate. In 1982 while at Edmonton Institution, he threatened to kill guards and their families. He had also resorted to self-harm, slashing his arms with razors and sharp objects. He had numerous disciplinary charges while in prison. Donald Oag ran up his list of convictions to include attempted arson, escaping custody, and assault causing bodily harm. In total his sentence was increased from six to eighteen years.

In accordance with the way sentences were calculated before the *Corrections and Conditional Release Act* was proclaimed, inmates were given days of remission each month as a reward for good behaviour. If a prisoner earned full credit, a release date on "mandatory supervision" could entail the offender serving the last third of the court-imposed sentence on the street under supervision of a community parole officer. Days of remission could be lost if an inmate failed to abide by prison rules. Every time a loss of remission occurred a new sentence calculation was required. A body of law developed as to how these computations were made and errors sometimes happened.

In early December 1982, the maximum-security institution where Oag was being held realized an error had been made and he had already reached his mandatory supervision release date. An emergency letter was forwarded to the Chairman of the Parole Board outlining Oag's past and requesting instruction to issue a notice of breach of his release. While waiting to board a plane to return to Ontario from Edmonton, police arrested Oag and delivered him back to the prison. The procedure of arresting someone immediately upon reaching a mandatory supervision date, i.e., immediately upon exiting the prison gate became known as "gating."

In Ontario, a similar situation arose. Marlene Moore was due to be released on mandatory supervision on December 14, 1982. Immediately upon her release, the Chairman of the National Parole board signed a warrant of suspension and Ms. Moore was returned to Kingston's Prison for Women.

Both Donald Oag and Marlene Moore separately brought motions for *habeas corpus* to challenge their further detention. The remedy allows someone illegally held in custody to be freed. In the case of Marlene Moore, the inmate was successful both at trial and on appeal. Oag was successful at the first instance but the decision that he should be released was overturned by the Alberta Court of Appeal. This set up a challenge heard in the Supreme Court of Canada,

On May 17, 1983, Chief Justice Bora Laskin, on behalf of the nine-member court, ordered that Marlene Moore's release was proper and the appeal judgment against Donald Oag was to be set aside and his immediate release ordered.

Now that gating was determined to be illegal, shock waves resonated throughout the correctional system. Could the public be kept safe if dangerous criminals were to be let loose?

Justice Minister Bob Kaplan in the John Turner Liberal government tried to ease tensions by announcing the government was ready to amend the *Penitentiaries Act* to give the Parole Board an opportunity to legally do what the gating procedure failed to do. However, one day before the scheduled summer recess of Parliament, NDP Member of Parliament Svend Robinson failed to get the support of his party's caucus. The matter was not considered. Parliament was adjourned and the legislation died on the order paper.

In early September, 1984 there was a federal election in which the Liberals were swept from office and Brian Mulroney's Progressive Conservatives took power. One of the new government's first acts was to introduce Bills C-67 and 68 in the House of Commons. The intent was to allow the National Parole Board (later renamed the Parole Board of Canada) to detain dangerous inmates beyond their mandatory release date until the full sentence was served. It was initially indicated that the new procedure would be applied to only the worst inmates in Canada.

It is against this backdrop that I met with Ross Evans

***

Being the unwanted child of a young woman, pregnant with another man's baby, was not the way most toddlers face the future. Years later, a court would hear that Ross Evans was handled by every social agency in Toronto. He was evaluated at the Cleveland Children's Clinic for behavioral health. Evans went through about thirty-five different foster-home placements. He was rejected by his father who had a family of his own. He also was abused by several babysitters.

It is not surprising that Ross Evans grew up on the streets and ignored the norms of society. He was charged criminally at age eighteen in the summer of 1981. Evans had broken into a homeowner's garage and was in the process of ransacking a car. The owner caught Evans in the act. She was attacked and sexually assaulted. The woman realized Evans was a threat but he fled down the street and escaped.

Breaking into a home is considered one of the most serious crimes in Canada. At Evan's first adult court appearance, most observers expected a period of incarceration. On November twenty-third, 1981, he was sentenced to a term of seven years imprisonment for rape, possession of a dangerous weapon, and robbery.

Evans received little, if any, counselling while an inmate at Kingston Penitentiary. He spent most of his sentence in solitary confinement. He was due to be released on August fifth, 1986 on mandatory supervision (as statutory release was then called). As the term "mandatory" implies, the release would be automatic. It did not need Parole Board approval. The last third of the sentence would be served under the supervision of a community parole officer. Any violations of the law or breach of the behavioural norms expected by the parole officer could result in a suspension of the release and a return to prison. The inmate would be allowed to participate in a post-suspension hearing where the Parole Board could re-release the offender to complete mandatory supervision or reincarcerate the prisoner setting a new parole eligibility date for future consideration.

Unlike Donald Oag and Marlene Moore, there was now legislation that set out the basis for continued detention. The procedures to be followed were vague. The new legislation would allow more time for dangerous inmates to receive treatment programs and thus be "street-ready" when finally released. Some prison-reform minded critics argued the proposed law would simply dump dangerous individuals on the street if no more work on their rehabilitation was done in the last third of their sentences than was done in the first two-thirds. Despite objections from some of my colleagues, I testified in support of the legislation before a Parliamentary Committee. At the time I testified, I assumed the government would develop regulations so the process could be fairly applied and that serious attempts would be given to step up treatment and counselling for those to whom the legislation applied so they could be ready for release and not face the prospect of a return to prison.

The legislation was ultimately passed in a special one-day recall of Parliament and took effect on July twenty-fifth, 1986. Five days later, the legislation took aim at Evans. Although it was never revealed how the referral to the Board was made, it was presumed that the Commissioner of Corrections had referred Evans to the Board on July thirtieth.

At half past eight in the morning, Evans was pulled from his cell to attend a special hearing of the Board on July thirty-first. He had already signed the paperwork required to release him to the street and was told by penitentiary staff he could expect to leave the prison on August fifth, the date of his mandatory release.

On July 31st, he was asked to sign another set of documents that would waive his right to an assistant at the hearing (as legal representation is called although an assistant need not be a lawyer), his right to review documentation, his right to bring forward additional documentation of his choice, and his right to adequate notice of the hearing. He was told that if he refused to sign, his August 5 release date could be extended a month so that the paperwork normally shared with an offender could be generated and supplied to him. With only a fourth-grade education, Evans quickly agreed to waive his rights.

Evans went directly into the meeting with the Parole Board. In a perfunctory hearing, Evans was ordered detained until his warrant expiry date in prison. He had become the first man "gated" under the newly-enacted amendments to the *Parole Act*.

Evans called my office at Queen's University and explained what had happened. I agreed to bring a *habeas corpus* application on his behalf. Although I had testified in support of the legislation, I was being called upon to challenge it. I saw no conflict. What I supported was an attempt to get serious about providing the tools for rehabilitation. I never argued on behalf of a "throw away the key" mentality.

Evans was the first of three inmates who had been detained wanting to challenge the decision to hold them in prison. The Evans case was heard in Ottawa on September fifteenth, 1986. The following day, Kingston Prison Law lawyer Fergus "Chip" O'Connor brought a similar application in Federal Court. On September twenty-fourth, Toronto Prison Law lawyer David Cole (later appointed as a Provincial Court Judge) launched a broad attack on the entire mandatory supervision scheme for his client who was out of prison serving his time under supervision in the community.

The Evans application was heard by Justice Smith of the Ontario High Court in Ottawa. The decision was in favour of Evans. Justice Smith enunciated the procedural rights allowed an inmate and - rather than making an Order of habeas corpus – invoked section 24(1) of the *Canadian Charter of Rights and Freedoms*, elevating the duty of the Correctional Service of Canada to act fairly in such circumstances to a constitutional imperative. He ordered a new hearing.

I then acted for Evans as his assistant at the new hearing. With proper procedures followed, the Board ordered Evans' release and he was set free the following day. He was to reside at a Toronto-area halfway house.

I was out of town for the weekend and didn't get the news until I tuned in to a Kingston radio station upon my return. The host was asking callers to phone in the name of a person deserving praise (in which case a whistle would sound) or a person deserving to be hit with a bat (in which case they'd play the sound of shattering glass). The rest of my drive was spent listening to people calling in to say that John Hill deserved to be hit with a bat. The continuous sound of breaking glass became unnerving.

Later, I picked up a copy of the day's *Kingston Whig-Standard* at a local variety store. Just below the headline, "Evans Rapes Again," was my photo. I was devastated.

I learned that Mr. Evans had been returned to custody after only a day's freedom and charged with a new sexual assault. This time the victim was a thirty-year-old Scarborough mother, who had been assaulted at knifepoint. Fortunately for the woman, her husband and a friend returned home in time to interrupt the attack.

What I thought had been a good piece of lawyering had resulted in the public blaming *me* for sexual assault by proxy. I had already been blamed for unnecessary government spending when acting on behalf of inmates to gain access to hot water and cable TV at Kingston Penitentiary, so this latest uproar reinforced my realization that sometimes the public cannot separate the actions of a lawyer from the criminal actions of the client.

When I returned to the Law School, the reaction of my colleagues was frosty, to say the least. Few spoke to me for several days, and no one, with the notable exception of a Professor of Psychology, Dr. Bill Marshall, had written to the *Whig-Standard* in support on my behalf.

At the trial for sexual assault, Evans hired David Cole to defend him. The Crown Attorney moved to have Evans declared as a "dangerous offender." A two-day hearing ensued with testimony given by two psychiatrists who stated that Evans had little hope for responding to treatment. In the end, lawyer Cole joined in a joint submission put to Toronto District Court Judge Sidney Dymond that Evans be imprisoned for an indeterminate period. Cole told Toronto media that he interpreted the decision to mean that Evans would spend at least the next ten years in a penitentiary. It was an optimistic prediction since the average number of years spent in prison following a dangerous offender designation was seventeen.

Judge Dymond said she was satisfied "beyond any doubt, not just beyond a reasonable doubt" that the requirements of the section of the *Criminal Code* establishing dangerous offender status had been met. She stated in her verbal remarks that Evans "constitutes a threat to the life, safety, or physical and mental well-being of other persons." However, perhaps as an acknowledgement that prison had not rehabilitated Evans in the past, the judge recommended that Evans be given "psychiatric, psychological or other unconventional treatment" that might be appropriate.

After an eight-month delay, the Federal Court agreed with the decision handed down by Justice Smith in the Evans case that the gating legislation was constitutional. The law was upheld but procedural safeguards were put in place that exist to this day. This man with a grade 4 education, despite his reincarceration, had been instrumental in changing the way the correctional/parole system operates.

***

Donald Oag once released continued his crime spree. In 2002 he picked up another four-and-a-half-year sentence for kidnapping his ex-wife in British Columbia and driving her, bound and gagged and covered by sleeping bags, to Ontario. He was once again released in 2007 and took up residence in Oshawa, Ontario. Over a two-day span in 2009, he continued to assault and cause bodily harm to a woman with whom he was living. He remained in custody from the time of his 2009 arrest until he was declared a dangerous offender in 2014.

Marlene Moore had a much more tragic ending. Once released, she was soon rearrested for possession of a weapon. She was declared Canada's first female dangerous offender. Psychiatrist Peter Garfield told a court in commenting on the "most scarred arms I have ever seen" that "They are walking evidence of her means of relieving her frustration." Marlene Moore killed herself at Kingston's Prison for Women by hanging herself with strips of fabric ripped from bedsheets.

The legacy of both Donald Oag and Marlene Moore was their fight that ultimately changed the law in Canada. Ross Evans' contribution was lending his name to a case that spelled out the proper procedures for dealing with inmates subject to detention. None of it was genetic. None of them were natural-born criminals. Ultimately their legacies were to secure procedures far fairer than the methods used to keep them in prison.

Flash forward to April 2020. A *Globe and Mail* report tells of Ross Evans having his wheelchair pushed to a lineup outside the health services building at Bath Institution, a medium-security penitentiary twenty-five kilometers west of Kingston. Evans has become very familiar with Canada's Corrections and Conditional Release Act. He knows that it sets out as a guiding principle that "offenders retain the rights of all members of society except those that are, as a consequence of the sentence, lawfully and necessarily removed or restricted." Evans is angry that he usually waits forty minutes to receive medications needed to control his diabetes and heart problems. The wait subjects him to conditions including wind, rain, and snow while he waits clad only in a thin polyester jacket and sneakers.

"I don't think you would ever see a hospital or pharmacy treating patients this way," said the fifty-six-year-old inmate. "But us, they treat us how they please. It's like we are not even human beings...." Evans with the assistance of the Queen's Prison Law Clinic (QPLC) took the conditions of his captivity to the Canadian Human Rights Commission; as one of the individuals the clinic represented, he was looking for a legal remedy to force the Correctional Service to stop outdoor medication lineups that discriminate against older and disabled inmates. Bath Institution has a disproportionately higher number of older prisoners. In December 2022, after mediation the Clinic reached agreement with the Correctional Service of Canada that included the following terms:

The basic terms are that:

1. CSC promised not to return to an outdoor medication distribution line-up, and confirmed that its medication distribution will take place indoors going forward.

2. CSC publicly apologized in writing to the Bath population for the old outdoor line up.

3. It recognized that causing prisoners to wait outside for medication during inclement weather was indeed an unnecessary hardship.

4. CSC commit to a process by which people can apply for and receive individual accommodation if picking up their medication would cause them particular hardship.

5. No damages were awarded in aggregate under the representative complaint, but the resolution of the representative complaint did not bar individuals from seeking individual financial compensation through the human rights process based on their experience of the medication line, and does not bar QPLC from assisting such individuals in doing so.

Now that the representative complaint has resolved, QPLC is now offering assistance to individuals who wish to bring individual complaints seeking damages in relation to their experience in the line, and it hopes to bring a significant number of such complaints and pursue a mediated global resolution in a consolidated proceeding.

The way medical services are delivered to inmates is becoming the new frontier in the fight for prisoner rights. A class action lawsuit has been filed by prison law lawyer Jeffrey Hartman challenging the way inmates at British Columbia's Mission Institution were treated when COVID-19 became a threat to everyone's health, but especially the health of Canada's vulnerable inmate population. Prison visits are considered essential for rehabilitation and inmates coming from larger virus-prone areas are visited by friends and family from areas of high contagion even though the prisons themselves may be in remote areas or communities with low COVID rates. Yet if an outbreak occurs it jeopardizes the entire community since staff go home and into the community at the end of each shift.

The latest Evans case came while Canada was under lock-down during the COVID-19 pandemic. It focused on the way that Canada's prisons are ill-prepared for a public health emergency. Prisons are overcrowded and social distancing is all but impossible. Inmates are required to buy their soap and shampoo from their own funds at the prison canteen. This leads to far less handwashing than might be expected during a public health crisis. Moreover, hand sanitizer contains alcohol and is considered contraband inside prison walls or fences. Prisons become petri dishes for the growth of infections jeopardizing not only inmates, prison visitors but staff and the families of staff that enter and leave the facility daily.

Evans has spent all but a few days of his adult life and much of his youth locked away. He has never had a real taste of freedom. Yet this man, with no more than grade 4 in formal education may have benefitted the prison population, by being one of a number of prisoners lending their names to cutting-edge cases challenging prison practices.

CHAPTER 11

GETTING NOTICED

Vlado Maljkovic and Alan Kinsella's
Tactics to Get Justice

> *There is no such thing as bad publicity except*
> *your own obituary.*
>
> **– Brendan Behan**

M any people regard prisons as the trash heaps of society. Whenever the garbage truck carts away our refuse, we forget about what has been discarded even though the items thrown away once had purpose and meaning in our daily lives. I argue that the analogy holds for people who have been convicted of crimes, even serious crimes such as murder. In fact, it is a challenge for each of us to name more than a handful of prison inmates. The "fifteen minutes of fame" that these newly branded criminals achieved remains forgotten after the names of alleged criminals are sentenced and the news cycle passes on to something more alluring.

However, for the thousands of people condemned to our jails and penitentiaries, life goes on. How can a perceived injustice, either in the conviction itself or in the treatment they are accorded inside lockup, be challenged when inmates must get recognition of the merit of their claim? One way is through traditional legal challenges such as bringing suit against the jailor or seeking judicial review of decisions affecting them. A less traditional way is to set out to seek publicity in the hope that an injustice will be recognized and corrected.

What follows are two true stories offered as examples of these means of getting noticed.

A. Legal Challenge: The case of Vlado Maljkovich

The neighbours of the Maljkovich family described them as "the most normal family." That was until the twenty-ninth of October, 1993. On that Friday evening, the flashing lights of numerous Toronto police squad cars illuminated the exterior of the family's Rusholme Road home in Toronto's west end. Inside, police found the lifeless bodies of Nada Maljkovich, forty-one years old, and her daughter, Rosemary, twenty-two. Both women died of stab wounds to their neck. Police also found two injured men, Rosemary's boyfriend and Nada's husband Vlado. Vlado also suffered a neck injury but that was treated at Toronto General Hospital under police guard.

The Maljkovich family had owned the residence and lived in one of the units for fifteen years. In the summer of 1993, Vlado and Nada separated. Vlado moved out and into an apartment at another unit he owned on nearby Rusholme Park Crescent.

No one could have expected such tragedy. The Rusholme house where the Maljkovich family had lived and where the children grew up contained five apartments. All the occupants described Vlado as a mild-mannered and gentle landlord. He was thoroughly liked. It came as a shock when Vlado was charged with the murders. It came as a severe shock to Vlado's son, John, who was away continuing his studies at the University of Waterloo when he learned of the tragedy.

Vlado went to Court and pleaded guilty to second-degree murder, thus avoiding a lengthy trial. Prosecutor Ian Scott described the accused's actions as "a tragedy of epic proportions" and "the ultimate act of spousal violence." Justice Edward Then obviously agreed and sentenced Maljkovich to life imprisonment without eligibility for parole for 14 years. The conviction was imposed on August 29, 1995.

Penitentiary must have seemed surreal to this mild-mannered property owner who was now under state control for the rest of his natural life. He was first taken to maximum-security Millhaven Institution and eventually cascaded to medium-security Fenbrook Institution. It was at Fenbrook that I encountered Vlado Maljkovich for the first time in 2004.

At the time I spoke with him, smoking was allowed in Canada's prisons. Inmates were not allowed to hold onto cash, thus as a result, cigarettes became the currency within the system. Seventy per cent of inmates smoked, and some would be described as chain smokers. Short of drugs, nicotine was the way to deal with boredom and alleviate stress. With demand for the product, tobacco was a marketable commodity.

Fenbrook was Canada's newest prison. It was built on property that had previously been bushland behind minimum-security Beaver Creek Institution. In a rush to complete construction, engineers overlooked one crucial design element. Although the prison was constructed with non smoking areas so people who did not smoke, like Vlado Maljkovich could reside, the air circulation was not separated. Therefore, smoke from ranges where smoking was allowed was simply recirculated to non-smoking ranges. Everyone was susceptible to second-hand smoke.

It was not just breathing in the fouled air that Vlado disliked. The air was also giving him breathing problems. He reported experiencing significant and immediate discomfort, including headache, nausea and irritation of the throat. Maljkovich told me that he was allergic to cigarette smoke and had suffered from this allergy for more than twenty-five years. Moreover, he had a note from his medical doctor confirming it. Yet Vlado saw himself in a no-win situation. He could simply put up with his situation and not have to fear antagonizing smokers on his range and continue to suffer the ill-effects, or he could continue to file complaints, which at best result would lead to making enemies with other inmates and being transferred to a range where air quality would be just as bad.

Maljkovich agreed that he would be best served by allowing me to bring an action in Federal Court seeking damages and hopefully getting a judgment that would alleviate his situation. Maljkovich made clear it was not the money he was after; it was preservation of his health that mattered most. Accordingly, a Statement of Claim was filed in the Federal Court using Simplified Procedure Rules (the Federal Court equivalent of Small Claims Court) where the maximum amount of damages claimed would be $50,000. Using this procedure, the litigation process could be put on a fast track which was equally important to the client.

A judgment was handed down by Madam Prothonotary Martha Milczynski on October fifteenth, 2005.

The Court held that the Correctional Service of Canada was completely at fault for denying the plaintiff his rights to be treated in accordance with the standards of health care required by statute and common law. Damages assessed would have been greater except that the Department of Justice filed a memorandum with the Court stating that effective the end of January, 2006, smoking inside all federal institutions and correctional centres will be prohibited. The Department of Justice attempted to make clear that the tobacco ban was not brought about because of the Maljkovich suit, but it was a policy that had been under consideration for quite some time. As a result, a sort of reward to the Correctional Services, damages were set at a nominal five thousand dollars.

Vlado Maljkovich was ecstatic; he had his situation noticed and remedied by legal means. He could spend his remaining years in prison without suffering from second-hand smoke allergy. That is not to say there was no residual fallout. The smoking ban destroyed the unit of currency within the prisons. Those who might have racked up cartons of cigarettes in gambling debts were left bankrupt by the change of rules and guards who smoked were upset.

However, there was an upside. I received congratulations from secretarial staff at the prison that the judgment would assist their endeavours to have a scent-free workplace. The case received national publicity and once again reminded the country of the destructive force of one unprecedented man's loss of temper. One newspaper referred to the case as an example of "frivolous lawsuits brought by extortionate lawyers." Yet not one newspaper mentioned that the Maljkovich family successfully brought a motion to divert payment of the judgment sum to the survivors of his outrage. The Correctional Service saved millions in not having to re-engineer its air supply and ventilation system at Fenbrook (now called Beaver Creek Medium Institution).

Vlado Maljkovich was never paroled. Eventually he was transferred to Pittsburgh Institution, a minimum-security penitentiary near Kingston. Because of his suit, Maljkovich was noticed by the courts and because of the suit his name was once again given notice in the news. The *Kingston Whig Standard* reported that on Tuesday, March 29, 2022, the then eighty-two-year-old, Vlado Maljkovich died of apparent natural causes at Millhaven Institution's Regional Treatment Centre in Bath.

B. The Publicity Stunt: The Case of Allan Kinsella

The Village of Bath is a quiet little community on the shores of Lake Ontario, just west of the City of Kingston. Nothing much out of the ordinary happens there and residents like it that way. Bath is not like Kingston, a city to the east with its multitude of penitentiaries. For the townspeople it became worrisome that after the 1971 riot at Kingston Penitentiary many of the inmates were transferred to the newly-constructed Millhaven Institution. Millhaven was a maximum-security prison constructed on the outskirts of Bath. Millhaven had high security fences and appeared well fortified. It was not so with the new minimum-security prison built right next door named Bath Institution. But it was a recent event that caused municipal councillors of Bath, Ontario to become upset at their meeting held on October 26, 1994.

Prison populations had grown since 1971 and by May of 1994, the minimum-security Bath Institution was being converted into a medium-security prison. That involved increasing security, including the addition of fences. The actual reconstruction was still in progress but not yet complete when the prisoners who were transferred into it began arriving. Things did not proceed as planned and this became apparent at the council meeting.

"The biggest fear is not knowing," commented Bath Councillor Kelly Hineman. He was responding to a presentation made at the meeting by Bath Institution's Warden Sam Brazeau. The Warden tried to assure councillors that security was well in hand.

The Brazeau explanation was necessitated because a few days previously, on October nineteenth, two convicted murderers, Allan Kinsella and Serge Damien escaped from Bath Institution. The Warden's message was that an investigation was underway and would answer the community's fears of how potentially dangerous people escaped and what would be done to ensure it did not happen again.

Allan Kinsella was fifty-three years old and Serge Damien was forty-nine on October 19, 1994. At sometime during the evening hours that day, the two made it over the newly-installed three and a half metre (twelve foot) fence at Bath Institution. As the former minimum-security institution had no walls or fences, the installation of the fence was part of the changes necessary to complete the prison's transition to higher security. The pair's absence was not discovered until a head count some three hours later. A construction worker's ladder was found and suspected as being the means of escape. Two large knives were also reported as missing.

Serge Damien was a former Montreal police officer who was convicted of killing a credit union cashier with a sledgehammer in 1983. At the time of the killing, Damien had been working as a security officer at the credit union. The motivation was cash, and he made off with a sizeable amount.

Allan Kinsella was also serving time having been convicted of first-degree murder for the 1978 killing of twenty-four-year-old Kenneth Kaplinski. Kaplinski had been on duty as a hotel clerk at the Continental Inn north of Barrie, Ontario, a city north of Toronto, when Kinsella's pal, Ted Sale shot the young victim with a .22 calibre gun in the head and made off with the cash in the till. Kinsella had been drunk and asleep in Sale's car when the robbery occurred.

Kinsella refused to believe he committed murder. Ted Sale confided to Kinsella that he had discharged the firearm while Kinsella was asleep in the car at the time. Nonetheless, the two were apprehended, charged with, and convicted of first-degree murder.

Kinsella exhausted all his legal appeals, but it was no use. At the time, being with a murderer when a murder was committed could set one up as an accomplice, and when it could be shown the two men set out with a gun intending to score some quick cash, both could be found guilty of murder. Then, in 1989, the Supreme Court of Canada changed all that. It held that "constructive murder" could not be the basis of a first-degree murder charge. Kinsella wanted that charge expunged from his criminal record. Even with another life sentence for robbery, a parole board would take a kinder view to a nonviolent offender than to one who killed another human being.

Kinsella wrote to Canada's Attorney-General asking that the murder conviction be reviewed. But it was no use. Nobody would listen to him. People would rather believe the myth that the justice system never errs than to admit that mistakes can were possible.

Serge Damien escaped from Bath Institution to recapture the freedom as best as he could find it on the run. Kinsella's motivation was not to gain freedom. He just wanted publicity so that the public, once it became aware that Kinsella was being treated unjustly, would force the politicians to act by reviewing his conviction and overturning the murder charge.

He could have tried to make it to the Canada-U.S. border or armed himself and lived up to his reputation of being "one of the most dangerous people in Canada." That was the label attached to his name after October 19, 1994.

The press had been aware of Allan Kinsella since he was unsuccessful in bringing a "fifteen-year review" in December of 1993. I had acted for Kinsella during this application. It was a seldom-used procedure that required a jury to be impanelled in the county town where the offence that led to the prisoner's conviction was committed. The provision was set out as section 745 of the *Criminal Code of Canada* and commonly referred to as "the faint hope clause." If successful, a jury could recommend that the mandatory twenty-five years of parole ineligibility be reduced to fifteen years. Since Kinsella had already served eighteen years of his life sentence, he would be entitled to immediate consideration from the parole board.

At first, things went well for Kinsella at the faint hope hearing. The prosecutor, Ken Anthony, during pretrial motions, indicated that he would be calling two witnesses to which the defence objected. One of those witnesses was the sister of Kenneth Kaplinski, the deceased victim. Another was Liberal Member of Parliament John Nunziata. Nunziata was one of only forty Liberals elected after the then-governing party was decimated by the Progressive Conservative Party in the 1984 general election. He, along with a few colleagues such as Hamilton's Sheila Copps, became outspoken and highly publicized, nicknamed by the press as the opposition's "rat pack." But when the Liberals returned to power and the Progressive Conservative elected only two members, Nunziata was not admitted to the Jean Chrétien Liberal cabinet. He then towed a much more conservative line. One of his policies was the repeal of the faint hope clause. The objection raised to the inclusion of these witnesses was that the prosecutor, by calling the victim's sister to testify, was trying to retry the original trial. It was simply an attempt to draw up emotional sympathy for the victim. It ignored the specific purpose of the hearing which was to see if a jury could be convinced that the prisoner was rehabilitated sufficiently, and that a jury could reasonably conclude he was a manageable risk to continue his life sentence in open society. The objection to Nunziata was relevancy. It was not the jury's duty to engage in political debate. Kinsella was pleased that the judge ruled in favour of rejecting both proposed witnesses. Neither witness was allowed to be brought before the jury.

However, Crown Attorney Ken Anthony was also prepared to fight Kinsella and to derail his attempt to be entitled to be seen by the parole board early. Once the jury had been selected it was the applicant's responsibility to tender evidence showing his rehabilitation. In Kinsella's case we were able to show that he had engaged in correctional programming and that he had been escorted to lecture high school students on the importance of staying out of crime. However, Ken Anthony disparaged that those attempts were of recent origin. Kinsella hadn't taken any programs before 1990. His participation, Anthony argued, could as easily have been seen as a means to con jurors into believing he was rehabilitated. The jury rejected Kinsella's move for early release consideration.

Once the hearing was over, even if he was not allowed to go before the parole board anytime soon, he was still subject to Correctional Service control. His participation in rehabilitation programming was sufficient to earn him a transfer from Warkworth Institution to Bath Institution where rehabilitative programming could continue. Not all institutions offered programming of the same nature and quality. It was up to the Service to make an adequate fit for the type of programming required and where it could best be administered.

The proposed transfer in light of the media attention of his faint hope hearing caused a political firestorm. Ken Anthony wrote to the Solicitor General who was the Minister overseeing corrections warning that he believed Kinsella to be dangerous. He claimed not to have received a reply from the Commissioner of Corrections or anyone on the Commissioner's behalf.

Michael Code, the provincial Deputy Attorney General also wrote to the federal Minister complaining that Kinsella was unfit for transfer to minimum-security. The Minister replied that the provincial concern was unwarranted. Bath Institution was no longer a minimum-security institution but rather had been remodelled into a medium-security prison. It was not a case of security reduction; it was a lateral transfer.

On the same evening of the escape but before anyone was aware of it, John Nunziata filed a private members bill in the Canadian House of Commons that proposed repeal of the faint hope clause.

Once the escape happened, police notified the public warning that two armed and dangerous inmates were on the lam. Police provided protection to Kaplinski's sister and to John Nunziata.

Damien and Kinsella went through the bushes and followed the railway tracks all the way to Belleville, a city to the west. It would take thirty minutes to drive the distance between the two towns but it took Kinsella and Damien three days on foot and on the run. They had to stay hidden and be on the lookout not to be recaptured. On the third day, Kinsella awoke to find that Damien had departed. The two had not discussed splitting up but Kinsella believed that it might be to his benefit, since Kinsella's aim was not freedom but public attention.

Kinsella was able to avoid being recognized and successfully hitch-hiked rides into Toronto. There he camped out under a freeway and tried to contact me.

I had recently moved from Cobourg to Toronto. My office phone continued to be answered by my assistant, Maureen Temple. Maureen advised Allan of my home phone number in Toronto. It was by this means we were able to keep up communications. Of course, during each call I was sure to tell Allan he should surrender himself to the police.

I contacted a Toronto newspaper reporter, Alan Cairns, who I knew to be highly ethical. I could count on him to give the public the information Kinsella wanted me to convey in such a manner that a gun-toting posse would not be out to harm Kinsella. There was daily news coverage of Kinsella on the run and how he had been wrongly convicted of murder. During my calls with Kinsella, proposals for his surrender were discussed and through the newspaper coverage Kinsella's position was conveyed to the Solicitor General of Canada. I never heard personally from the cabinet minister but could gauge his response by watching the nightly TV news. It was as though we were negotiating through the media.

Finally, a breakthrough. Although the Solicitor General, Herb Gray, would not meet or talk with me, a trusted and highly-regarded Liberal Member of Parliament, Warren Allmand, told television news coverage that he, acting not as a government agent but in a personal capacity, would take a look at the Kinsella situation and consider further action.

On my next telephone call with Allan Kinsella, the news was most welcome. He was cold, hungry and had run out of his Type 2 diabetes medication. His only concern was that should he turn himself into police, he would be savagely beaten. He had heard stories while in prison of such police brutality. If I could get assurances from the police that he would be treated fairly, he would surrender. But he still wanted full coverage. I made a few calls and it was agreed that he would surrender himself in the atrium of the CBC broadcast centre. The television network would be notified to allow it to have full national TV coverage for its newscasts.

I was also being hounded by various police forces (R.C.M.P., the Ontario Provincial Police Penitentiary Squad, and Metro Toronto Police) regarding a surrender. It was Larry Dee of the Metro Police who immediately gave his assurance that if Kinsella surrendered, he would be treated respectfully. He impressed me with his professionalism. It was only after speaking with Kinsella and assuring him that I placed my full trust in Dee that Kinsella consented. Kinsella advised he would contact his son Kevin to walk with him and provide directions to the CBC building where the surrender would occur.

I was able to see on that night's news that Larry Dee and his partner had encountered a young man followed by a dirty and dishevelled older man who identified himself as Allan Kinsella.

They had not arrived at the CBC building as I had advised Dee but somewhat before. I was told by Kinsella that Metro Police were honourable and professional and actually treated him very well.

Allan Kinsella was charged with escape and returned to maximum-security Millhaven Penitentiary. For the next year, I continued with the Kinsella case. He eventually pleaded guilty in Superior Court not to the charge of escape but to the charge of being unlawfully at large. It seemed like a minor distinction but that was key to Kinsella resolving his situation. He felt that this time someone listened to him and that he was not made to believe a lie dressed up like a truth foisted upon him.

While at Millhaven, he continued to publicize his situation. He granted an interview to the *Toronto Star* reporter Harold Levy who, in an exclusive report, published Kinsella's exact account of his adventure. This is what he told Harold Levy:

"I didn't leave to get away. I left in order to try to get the attention that was needed to bring about change in my life. And I wanted to get across to the victim's family that it wasn't me that killed their son."

He continued, "That day, the fellow that I ran away with told me there was a ladder, and maybe I should check it out. I took the ladder at about 2:30 p.m. and moved it from one side of a garage to the other, where it wouldn't be detected. During supper I thought about what I was going to do. I decided I'd leave and come to the Toronto area, and that I'd try to stay out long enough to get somebody to support my cause."

Kinsella was clear about his cause: "I wanted to try to get out the fact that I am innocent of the murder charge, that I had been constantly screwed for eighteen years, and that I wasn't going to take it any more. There was another course available. The borders weren't that far away. Many people in Toronto will sell you guns if you're looking for guns. Or if you want out of the country . . . I mean, I was supposed to be one of the most dangerous people in Canada at the time. If I was violently inclined, I could have expropriated a car or left the country or I could have done whatever I wanted. But that was never my intention. In fact, I had never planned to run away, but since they had kindly availed me of the ladder, and I was getting nowhere at the institution, I took off."

There was a plan involved: "But I knew I would give myself up. I wanted to get across to the victim's family that it wasn't me that killed their son. I had wanted to write to the Kaplinski family on many occasions and tell them that I hadn't done anything wrong, that I had proof of that, and that I was willing to under go anything, polygraph or whatever, to prove it."

"I didn't have much money out there. I left with about twenty dollars, five rolls of cough drops and two rolls of lifesavers. I had enough medicine for my diabetes to last me for the week. That's all I had. I was out for about two weeks. I was eating out of some dumpsters behind stores."

"One night, I had a sleeping bag and I was on the side of a hill. The sleeping bag slid off the garbage bags it was on and started going down toward the expressway. If I didn't have one foot on each side of the sleeping bag, and it was stopped by a small tree, I would have been out on the expressway. So that was the big event."

"I didn't have any close calls in terms of being discovered. That went surprisingly well. But I was alone out there. Nobody assisted me. I decided to turn myself in after I phoned Peter Mansbridge at the CBC and I told him that I would give myself up if they could talk Warren Allmand [chairperson of the Commons justice committee and former solicitor-general] into reviewing my case. He's probably the most honorable person in Ottawa right now. Everybody in prison likes him because of his decency and his concern. I read in the paper that he did say that he would look at my case. The man's word was good enough for me."

"So I phoned and made arrangements that I would deliver myself to Catherine Oughtred, a producer on CBC's National. But I never made it in. I was on my way with my son, Kevin. He was to show me how we were to get down there. We were walking on the street, on the way to the CBC, when a policeman that knew my son arrested me. It was pure chance."

Kinsella described the events of his arrest: "And when the policeman arrested me, he said, 'Mr. Kinsella, I know all about you. I'm not here to hurt you.' He says, 'Just follow my directions and everything will be all right. No one will hurt you.' He arrested me at gunpoint - there were two of them - and took me down to the station, 51 Division. They treated me very well, and a lot of officers shook my hand, and commended me for being out there and not committing a crime."

"One officer said, 'Gee, you really stink. How long have you been in those clothes?' And I said, 'two weeks.'

'Well, I'm going to open the window,' he said, 'and air the place out.' So, he opened the window, and he gave me a wink, [while] he was walking away. And as soon as he opened the window, everybody was there with cameras, outside on top of police cars, taking pictures."

"The reason I used the opportunity provided by the ladder to escape and get the message out was that I was never allowed to raise my innocence at my fifteen-year review in December. I put a lot of hope in the review. I thought it would open the door to parole and that it would allow me to tell the world that I was innocent of the murder. My co-accused was even willing to take the stand and exonerate me. But the judge would have none of this. I knew I didn't have much of a chance. This was made clear when I first entered the Newmarket courtroom and found four special forces policemen and two York Regional officers. Since I had been allowed to go on day passes with a single escort, this seemed to be designed to send the jurors a certain message."

"It was also made clear to me when Crown Attorney Ken Anthony launched a vicious attack on me and my witnesses. At one point,

Anthony [said]: 'That man right there, that murderer sitting right there,' - now he's got me branded as being the murderer – 'killed that boy's father, that girl's brother, and that women's son, and he's asking for mercy!' What was the jury going to do after that? So, it was back to the pen for at least another ten years. I'm back behind bars again, and I've lost all of the support that I built up in eighteen years in prison. I want something to come out of this, but even if it doesn't, I can live with it because a burden has been removed from my shoulders. I've told the Kaplinski family that I'm innocent, whether they believe me or not."

***

Serge Damien was apprehended at the Niagara Falls border crossing in April of 1995 by U.S. Immigration officials as he tried to cross into the United States.

The press coverage given to Allan Kinsella did not sit well with Scott Newark, who at the time was an executive officer of the Canadian Police Association, then representing thirty-five thousand rank-in-file members. He was publicly critical of any internal report the Correctional Service might provide and demanded a full public inquiry into the prison system.

Shortly after *The Toronto Star* published Kinsella's description of events to Harold Levy, another Toronto news story emerged, this time suggesting Kinsella had been the source of a tip. The tip to police was that three other inmates associated with organized crime planned to assassinate Ontario Premier William Davis, then-justice minister Roy McMurtry and former police chief Jack Ackroyd.

The newspaper never named its source for the information, but to me it seemed a plot to ensure the placement would be made in the vilest institution in which Kinsella could be placed. He was immediately transferred to Kingston Penitentiary for his own safety.

Why do I believe the transfer was misinformation? If it were true that years ago, Kinsella ratted out his fellow cons, it would have been considered noble to the outside world, but should it become known inside that Kinsella was indeed a snitch, it would amount to a death sentence. It would have been an inexcusable breach of security for the Correctional Service. Moreover, I do not believe it is true because Allan Kinsella never revealed any such information to me while I was preparing to impress a jury on what a rehabilitated inmate he had become. To me, the story lacked credibility in its entirety. Yet the damage had been done and Kinsella's safety would have to be secured until his release. We all have to live with the lies prevalent in our communities.

Six months after Kinsella had been captured, I received a notice indicating that my home phone had been tapped by police. A warrant authorizing the monitoring was because an affidavit had been filed saying my business phone number, that would be exempt because of lawyer-client privilege, was still located in Cobourg. My Toronto number was for residential service. I had wondered why Kinsella had been picked up *en route* to CBC and not upon arrival as had been the plan with Kinsella.

The contractor doing the work for the Correctional Service at Bath Institution was fired. Blaming others is always a convenient way to escape criticism.

A final report that Bath municipal council required to assure townspeople could rest safely reported that security had been inadequate with seven inmates escaping within four months of the upgrade to medium security. The prison was now secure.

But Allan Kinsella had made his point. He had garnered the publicity that people now understood he was not the violent killer that the mere reading of his criminal record sheet would imply. After many years of imprisonment, Allan Kinsella has been released and is living a crime-free lifestyle.

CHAPTER 12

DRUGS IN PRISON:
FIGHTING FALSE ALLEGATIONS

Michael Johnson and Kim Eldridge

> *Nobody stays recovered unless the life they have created is*
> *more rewarding and satisfying than the one they left behind.*
>
> **– Anne Fletcher**

Abuse of alcohol can certainly land someone in prison. Drug convictions have swelled our prison populations. Substance abuse is not curtailed by imprisonment. Drug use by inmates can lead to explosions of violence. Staff, as well as inmates, are put in harm's way when violence erupts. It is completely understandable that prison staff come down hard on inmates who abuse drugs.

One Inmate's Experience

Almost twenty years ago, Tracy Curry, an inmate of the federal female prison, Grand Valley Institution in Kitchener, Ontario had just returned from an unescorted temporary absence when she was confronted by the drug-sniffing dog, Skipper. The dog indicated that the scent of narcotics was present on Ms. Curry. A frisk search found no contraband. The inmate protested that she was not carrying any narcotics and consented to an X-Ray and pelvic search conducted at the St. Mary's hospital. Neither the X-Ray nor the internal probing detected any contraband. On her return to the prison, she was again searched. This time too the drug dog indicated narcotics. Tracy Curry was stripped and placed in a dry cell, a solitary cell without plumbing where the inmate is constantly monitored and any excrement is closely examined. She remained there for almost twenty-four hours but even though she had a bowel movement, no drugs were found. Nonetheless, the inmate suffered severe emotional distress because of the ordeal that was later diagnosed as post traumatic stress disorder. A subsequent law suit found that the Correctional Service acted negligently *but not illegally* and awarded Ms. Curry monetary damages for her ordeal.

The use of dry cells is authorized by law, but unlike an X-Ray or body cavity search, the inmate need not consent although the Warden must be satisfied that holding an inmate in a dry cell is likely to result in contraband being expelled.

The use of dry cells to collect proof that contraband illegally imported into a prison stem from a belief that foreign material will be excreted with bowel movements in a relatively short order. But what about a situation in a women's prison where it is believed the illicit substance is hidden in the vagina?

A Recent Challenge

That situation and the constitutionality of the law authorizing use of dry cells was decided in the Nova Scotia Supreme Court in a case called the *Adams v. Nova Scotia Institution* case handed down on November twelfth, 2021.

Lisa Adams was confined in a dry cell for over fifteen days on the Warden's authority. Although several bowel movements were examined, no contraband was detected. The institutional authorities believed that vaginal concealment could require additional time until a menstrual discharge took place. While a dry cell is another form of solitary confinement and Ms. Adam's stay clearly breached the rule that no prisoner spent more than fifteen consecutive days in solitary, the Department of Justice argued that the section 52 authorization of dry cells continued to be enforceable. According to Department of Justice counsel, holding Lisa Adams in solitary was illegal but it was simply "maladministration" on the part of the Warden of the Nova Scotia Institution for Women that should not result in finding section 52 of the *Corrections and Conditional Release Act* as unconstitutional.

But in his sixty-three-page judgment, Justice John Keith found that the section is discriminatory in that it could impose more extreme treatment on women than on men. Thus, the section is in violation of the equality rights of women under section 15 of Canada's *Charter of Rights and Freedoms*.

In finding the Charter breach, Justice Keith did not legitimate importation of contraband into an institution. He reasoned that the wording of the prohibition needed to be changed and it would be the responsibility of Parliament to do so. The Court therefore suspended the declaration of invalidity for 6 months. The use of the dry cell is informed by the definition of "body cavity" and it will be up to federal legislators to devise a regime that does not infringe Charter values.

For too long there has been a failure, indeed a refusal, of our criminal legal system, from police, prosecutors, defence counsel/lawyers, judges, correctional services to ignore abuse and other forms of misogynistic violence. The Nova Scotia judgment will cause our parliamentarians to take a fresh look at a troubling situation that has been brewing for at least twenty years.

Drugs and Prison Violence

Prisons are violent places. In 1984, a six-member correctional service group was set up to study a rash of homicides in Ontario prisons during the previous two years. The conclusions reached were not surprising. It concluded that "a high proportion of these incidents can be attributed to prison commerce and, in particular, drug trafficking, a 'bad' supply, inability or unwillingness to deliver drugs, inability to pay and power struggles over the drug market." It is obvious the investigation centred its concerns on the black market that exists inside penitentiaries where cash is forbidden and an ability to deal in drugs becomes the new currency.

The study estimated that in some penitentiaries, anywhere from 65 to 90 per cent of the prison population was using drugs. A Toronto Star report in 1986 quoted Constable Rod Carscallen of the Ontario Provincial Police as saying: "If you get rid of the drugs and the money that goes with it, you'd eliminate seventy-five to ninety per cent of the problem." Those statistics may be accurate; no one knows since, try as they might, prisons have been unable to eliminate smuggling in contraband and inmate usage of banned substances.

My Fight Against Overuse of Powers

It is not that prison authorities have never tried. The problem has been that correctional authorities have used a sledge hammer for a problem requiring a scalpel. As a case in point, I recall the case of inmate Michael Johnson. Johnson was returning from a pass that allowed him the opportunity to enter the community to assist in his reintegration upon parole release.

It was the contention of correctional authorities that the inflow of drugs could be stanched if everyone venturing back into prison after an escorted or unescorted pass could be X-Rayed. That, authorities believed, would ensure that no contraband could be secured inside a body cavity. It meant that male and female inmates would be subjected to radiation and would be deterred from attempting drug importation. No hospital visit or equipment was needed as the X-Ray used by the institutional dentist could be used by a correctional officer to deter offenders from attempting to bring drugs back to the prison. Consent to the procedure could be obtained easily; by telling the inmate that it was either consent to the X-Ray or spend time in a dry cell.

A dry cell is a segregation cell that lacks a toilet. An inmate is forced to defecate into a pail and his excrement will be searched by correctional staff to ensure no foreign matter was being transported. For female inmates, the time in a dry cell could be much longer since it could extend until a menstrual period had passed before a decision was taken that she was "clean." [A prohibition for subjecting women to such procedures was not announced until the spring of 2022.]

Michael Johnson at the time was twenty-seven-years-old and returning to Ontario's Joyceville Institution from an open visit where physical contact with another person was likely. The year was 1986 and I was just nicely ensconced in my job as Director of the Correctional Law Project at Queen's University. When I was contacted by Johnson, I knew immediate action must be taken.

I issued a Statement of Claim in the Federal Court and sought an interim and permanent injunction to halt the procedure. Fortunately, there was a meeting of Anglican bishops in Kingston. I was able to convince this group to intervene with the federal government in opposition to the newly-announced X-Ray program. I knew that the Correctional Service was extremely sensitive to publicity about unusual procedures. The bishops did a fine job of making it known that the non-medical use of X-Rays would be condemned from the pulpit. The end result was that the Johnson case was settled with the proviso that X-Rays could be taken only with the consent of the inmate and with the authorization and under the direction of an accredited radiologist. The prison X-Ray programme was effectively curtailed.

The Challenge of Urinalysis

It was within the same time period that the correctional service instated the use of urinalysis. Convicts under supervision, whether incarcerated or on parole, could be subject to random urinalysis to screen for the presence of prohibited substances in their urine. The Correctional Service contracted with a private company to provide kits allowing designated officers to complete tests to determine if an inmate had ingested narcotic substances.

A positive test for an inmate inside one of Canada's prisons could have drastic consequences: cancellation of family visits, increased scrutiny during the daily routine, a disciplinary charge and possibly time in segregation. For offenders on parole, it could mean a return to federal custody on a warrant of parole suspension, and even revocation of parole.

Urinalysis: A Case Study

No one knows the effects of a negative urinalysis test better than Kim Eldridge. She was only eighteen when she was convicted of first-degree murder during a drug deal gone bad in New Westminster, British Columbia. She had no part in the actual killing but she had set up the drug deal for her boyfriend. An appeal court reduced the charge to second-degree murder but conviction for murder, whatever the degree, carries with it a life sentence. She would be under state supervision for the rest of her natural life. She was paroled in 1989 and moved from prison to St. Catharines, Ontario. She obtained a variety of jobs while on parole, working in a bar and working at a department store. She was proud of the fact that she was living a crime-free lifestyle.

That is until 1995. With Christmas fast approaching, she invited several new friends to celebrate the holiday. She planned to prepare a special dinner and invite her new friends to enjoy a home-cooked meal. She spent time purchasing groceries and preparing a turkey for roasting. She was happy and looking forward to what she believed to be a very special get-together. As the hours ticked away, she received one call after another from the invited friends cancelling out on the dinner invitation. What she had hoped to be a joyous occasion turned to despair. She dumped the turkey and the side dishes in the garbage and left her house wallowing in self-pity. She stopped by a bakery and instead of feasting on turkey and all the trimmings, she gorged herself on poppy-seed bagels.

The very next day she was subjected to a random urinalysis test by her parole officer. The results came back positive for heroin. Kim, of course, denied any drug usage but the test results were there in black and white for correctional service officials to see. A warrant of suspension was issued and Kim Eldridge was returned to Kingston's Prison for Women or P4W as it was known.

She lost her job in the community and her life appeared to be in tatters. While awaiting a post suspension hearing before the Parole Board, she spoke to *Toronto Sun* reporter Alan Cairns. Cairns in turn phoned me to ask if I had any way to help this woman who he truly believed to be innocent.

Urinalysis was fairly new to Canada's prison system and I had no doubt that everything would be done to ensure the Parole Board upheld the result the Service had paid for. I agreed to interview Kim Eldridge and see if there may be a possible defence. I arranged an appointment at P4W and listened to the inmate as she recounted the sorry events of her ruined Christmas gala.

As the facts of the situation were ruminating in my mind, I seemed to recall a story of an American inmate who had been charged with using drugs after eating poppy-seeded bread. There was a constitutional challenge in the United States about a inmate who was sent back to prison after testing positive for morphine after consuming a "salt-stick bagel" that contained poppy seeds as an ingredient.

The year was 1987 and the American inmate in question was Anthony Clarizio of Stanford, Connecticut. Federal half way houses in the United States have what is called a "poppy-seed rule." Inmates are forbidden to eat poppy seeds because they tend to result in false positives on drug tests. If false positives can be the result of eating products containing poppy seeds, surely there must be a way of establishing that the urinalysis Ms. Eldridge endured was similarly flawed. If false positives were a known fact in the United States, why was it seen as conclusive for Canadian correctional officials to take the drastic step of parole suspension when an investigation could verify a parolee's excuse.

What has been called "the poppy seed defence" has been verified by several studies worldwide. Hair analysis is considered an accurate means of testing for heroin use as it is impossible for poppy seed ingestion to result in a false positive. Even though poppies are the source of heroin, the opioid in poppy seeds does not stay in the bloodstream long enough or in high enough concentrations to be found in hair follicles in quantities sufficient to measure. Hair follicle analysis is a means of identifying when drugs are used. As the body processes drugs, metabolites are carried in the blood stream and form part of the hair strand being formed and growing at the time the drug was used. Obviously, it cannot give a time and date of drug usage, but becomes a true indicator of the substance ingested.

I contacted a private lab that was capable of providing hair analysis and carefully reviewed the instructions on how a hair sample must be taken. The hair sample should be clipped as closely as possible from the scalp. Since hair grows at a predictable rate and since Kim Eldridge had been in prison for almost six months, I need not worry about being overly concerned with how close to the scalp I should be in taking the clipping.

The lab provided me with a self-addressed postage paid envelope to return the sample, a piece of aluminum foil with which to wrap the hair and instructions regarding how the sample should be taken. To ensure that I could not be accused of corrupting the sample, I notified the prison and obtained its authorization that when I visited the institution, I would be permitted to bring in a pair of scissors, the test kit that included the foil and to be doubly sure, I asked that a Correctional Service of Canada employee attend with me and the inmate. Ordinarily a visitor or even a professional visitor (the term the prison system uses for lawyer) would not be allowed to bring such objects into the visiting area.

Once in the visiting room, I had the CSC employee read through the lab instructions and be able to acknowledge, if called upon later to do so, that I had complied with the instructions to the letter. Kim Eldridge winced a bit as I selected a small tuft of hair from the back of her head and cut it leaving a bald spot smaller than a dime. "It'll grow back," she said as she turned towards me and smiled.

I carefully wrapped the sample in the foil as instructed and placed the bundle inside the envelope. I made sure all parties were watching as I sealed the envelope. I then asked everyone to initial the back of the envelope and affix the date and time the sample was taken. I requested the corrections officer to post the envelope in the day's outgoing mail and she agreed. I had full confidence the correctional officer would not sabotage the test by refusing to mail the envelope.

The Test Results

After what seemed an eternity, the lab produced its report. There was no evidence of any narcotic substance in the sample submitted. I immediately made copies of the lab report and conveyed the results to the Parole Board and to the Warden of the Prison for Women. It was just a matter of waiting for the post suspension hearing to be scheduled.

It was July 5, 1996 when the hearing took place in a windowless room inside the old prison. The hearing proceeded as expected with the Correctional Service recounting how a urinalysis had been requested and the test came back positive. The urinalysis certificate was produced as the iron-clad evidence necessary to return Kim Eldridge to prison indefinitely. But Kim Eldridge spoke clearly and forcefully that she had been a law-abiding citizen during her six years of release and that she not only never used drugs in the Christmas season of 1995, she had never used drugs all the while she was out of prison. Of course, the hair analysis report was tendered as proof supporting her claim.

This was the first time hair analysis had been used in a parole hearing. Would the Board uphold my contention that the hair analysis was more accurate than a urine sample? If urinalysis was found to be inaccurate returning false positives, what would that do in continuing to use the procedure? How would it impact on the contract the Correctional Service signed with the private company that provided the test kits? These were the questions going through my mind as the hearing finished and it was time for the Board to deliberate.

As usual, everyone was asked to vacate the hearing room to allow the parole board members to vote and produce written reasons for the Board's decision.

The Decision

When called back into the hearing room, the Board decision was read aloud. The board did not mention either the urine sample that tested dirty or the hair analysis report that showed Kim Eldridge to be clean. Instead, the Board said that it was not satisfied that the prisoner had violated conditions of her parole. Kim Eldridge would be free to leave prison and resume her life outside its walls.

Alan Cairns published a major spread on the subject in the *Toronto Sun*. Although urinalysis testing was not found faulty in the Parole Board's decision, the Cairns report was sufficient to have the public draw that conclusion.

The Correctional Service was forced to return Kim Eldridge to society but it did not do so gracefully. An order was issued that henceforth no lawyer should be able to bring scissors or a test kit for hair analysis inside a prison. Further, no staff member should henceforth be put in a position of becoming a witness for the inmate.

The company contracted to provide urinalysis was greatly upset that the case received national publicity. Several meetings were held to clarify what had happened.

Corrections Canada rejected the use of hair follicle analysis for drug-use screening. Karl Niemann, the prison official in charge of urinalysis in Ontario is quoted in *the Kingston Whig-Standard* of October 12, 1996 as saying: "There was considerable discussion after that happened, simply because of the publicity."

Niemann then noted that in the year in which Eldridge was re-incarcerated, roughly ninety-five hundred prisoners had been tested but he did not mention that Kim Eldridge was the only one to challenge the findings. Without any scientific basis for his conclusion, Niemann told the *Whig-Standard* that the Correctional Service had investigated hair testing and was told that it was less reliable when used on long hair samples and only shows chronic drug use.

The Correctional Service dug in its heels and would not consider that its procedures could be wrong. Kim Eldridge's life was uprooted and accusations were made against her resulting in six months of needless incarceration. There are no media reports that she ever reoffended.

CHAPTER 13

THE MAN WHO
NEVER RETURNED

Michael Gwynne's Fight against a
120 -year Alabama Sentence

> *But did he ever return?*
> *No he never returned and his fate is still unlearned*
> *He may ride forever 'neath the streets of Boston*
> *He's the man who never returned.*
> *Lyrics of M.T.A.*
>
> **– The Kingston Trio**

Who could foresee that a ten-minute telephone call in early 1984 could have life-changing consequences? Certainly not Alabama housewife Gypsy Capell. Capell would later testify that an unknown male caller stunned her by announcing that he was holding her 15-year-old daughter, Elizabeth, hostage. The anxious mother refused to believe it. She argued that Elizabeth was at school. "That's not so," the unknown caller replied. "We have her, and we want $500."

Not knowing how to respond, Capell blurted out that her husband was just driving into the driveway. The caller hung up. Indeed, Elizabeth was at school and totally unaware of the commotion at home. Gypsy Capell and her husband were frantic until they were told the truth about their daughter's whereabouts. Nonetheless, a police report of the incident had to be made.

That was not the only call that was reported to Alabama police. Another call of a similar nature was also reported. In neither case was any hostage taken nor did any money change hands. It was just the cruelty of the calls that demanded the laying of charges.

Police investigated and arrested forty-two-year-old Michael Lucian Gwynne for making the prank calls.

Gwynne was no stranger to criminal proceedings. He was born in Trois-Rivières, Quebec on the twelfth of January, 1942. He had been sent to a residential school in Ontario and at that school suffered traumatic physical and sexual abuse. In his mid-teens he was released from the school without treatment or therapy and soon afterward committed his first crime, the theft of an automobile. He was returned to the residential school for another year and a half. Thereafter, he moved to Montreal.

Between 1963 and 1966, Gwynne was on a crime spree. During his twenties, Gwynne spent most of his years in prison. He was convicted of armed robbery for taking cash from stores and a bank in Quebec with a .32 calibre handgun. He also performed a series of break and enters of private dwellings.

One of his more serious crimes occurred when Gwynne and three of his cohorts came across another man who owed money to one in the group. The man was travelling with his sister. When the four confronted the debtor, the bullying tactics to secure payment devolved into taking the sister into a car and abducting her.

Gwynne was eventually paroled for his misdeeds but with time yet to serve on his Canadian sentence, he absconded to the United States in 1972. He re-offended soon thereafter. He served two and a half years in prison in Colorado with two years being spent at a state hospital in Colorado where he participated in rehabilitative programming. He escaped from prison in Colorado in 1980 but shortly after breaking loose, he surrendered himself. He was paroled the same year.

Upon release, Gwynne relocated to Alabama where he gained employment with a Birmingham hotel chain. That occupation allowed him access to names and telephone numbers he used in making threatening calls, not for extortion but to satisfy his own desires of hearing women in distress.

The telephone calls to Alabama women resulted in two counts of attempted extortion. He was found guilty of the crimes in the Montgomery County Circuit Court on May 22, 1984. Those offences would ordinarily carry a sentence ranging from one to ten years. However, his Canadian sentences and his conduct in

Colorado were also considered in the State's desire to label Gwynne as an Habitual Offender and seeking enhanced punishment. On July 13, 1984, the presiding judge-imposed sentences of sixty years each consecutive for the felonies. Gwynne faced one hundred and twenty years in prison but realized that the term would mean he would die inside a penitentiary.

Michael Julian Gwynne was now facing having to do time in the notorious Alabama correctional system. He would later describe his introduction to the system as follows:

"Following my sentence, I was placed in Kilby Correctional Facility. Kilby has the reputation amongst Alabama prisoners of being one of the more brutal prisons. Because it is a receiving centre the staff want you to know immediately upon entering that they do not tolerate any back talk, any foolishness, any violation of their rules. The first day there we were standing in line, stripped naked, ready to be sprayed with bug spray and take a shower and get our hair cut. The guards all carried long billy clubs, about two and a half feet long. One fellow was told to get a haircut. He didn't want a haircut. The guards immediately set on him with the billy clubs, knocked him unconscious, dragged him into the barber shop and shaved his head bald. That was my introduction to Alabama's prison system."

Once introduced to the system, Gwynne was then transferred to Holman Prison in southern Alabama. Holman was a maximum-security institution known for its death chamber containing an electric chair. It would not be until 2002 that Alabama inmates were permitted death by lethal injection. Gwynne's next two years (1984 to 1986) would be spent at Holman.

> "Holman is an old prison. My first perception was of a cement tomb with paint peeling off the walls, off the ceiling. It was infested with cockroaches, spiders, snakes, rats, and mice. I was placed in a dormitory of approximately one hundred people, double-bunked with the bunks set three feet apart with no partitions between them. The toilet facilities were against one wall, wide open, no partitions surrounding them. If you had to use the bathroom, you used it in full view of one hundred people. The shower arrangement was similarly wide open with no curtains and no semblance of privacy. The showers opened around 6:30 p.m. - 7:00 p.m. in the evening and you had thirty minutes to shower. There would be three people under one shower nozzle taking turns soaping, getting out, rinsing, and letting someone else soap. There was nowhere to put your soap, nowhere to put your washcloth, nowhere to put your towel except on the floor. The whole arrangement at Holman was very primitive and embarrassing."

Gwynne was suffering emotionally. It was not only the violence that Gwynne abhorred; the infestation of the institution with insects and rodents caused him distress.

"On my first night in Holman I was lying in bed and I felt something crawling over me. They were cockroaches. This became a daily thing for the next nine years. You wake up in the middle of the night, cockroaches crawling down your neck, on your arms, under your bedclothes. The place was infested. You can't get rid of them. "In Alabama there are a number of poisonous snakes and spiders everywhere. It wasn't unusual for rattlesnakes to slither through the fence into the yard, into the buildings. Black widow spiders, brown recluse spiders are everywhere. A black friend of mine was lying in bed and he got bit above the knee by a black widow or brown recluse. The flesh rotted and a plug of flesh about the size of his thumb, maybe a quarter of an inch deep, a little deeper, came out of his leg. He received very little treatment for it. You always had to be careful. On one occasion, this was in a different prison but it was still in Alabama, I sat down on the toilet and I had my trousers down around my knees, of course. I caught a movement out of the corner of my eye and there was a water moccasin curled up beside the toilet on the cement floor. It was damp, it was cold and that's the kind of climate they like. Water moccasins, cottonmouths, they are similar snakes, and you can die from their bite. Needless to say, I jumped up off the toilet with my trousers still around my knees and got out of the area. Finally, someone grabbed a piece of a hoe and came over and killed the snake. You always had to watch out."

If it was not the dangers of the vermin that caused concern, one also had to be mindful of the dangers posed by fellow inmates.

If it was not the dangers of the vermin that caused concern, one also had to be mindful of the dangers posed by fellow inmates.

> "I believe it was my second day in Holman and there was a commotion on the far side of the dorm. One inmate was chasing another one around with a knife. This went on for several minutes before the guards even bothered to come in. At that point the fellow with the knife stopped, the guards clubbed him pretty badly and dragged him off by the heels and threw him in the hole, threw him in segregation. I quickly learned that violence is a part and parcel of the Alabama prison system."

Then there was the ever-present prospect of death. As Canada had abolished the death penalty, there are no death rows in Canada. Watching prisoners facing death was a new experience for Gwynne.

> "One of the worst experiences for me as a Canadian in Holman prison was the realization that I was in close proximity to the death chamber and knowing that it was not simply a relic of the past, of another age, but was an active part of a contemporary prison system. "It's really difficult to explain. It's a very fearful thing. When you know an execution is scheduled and you see the person walking by going to the hospital to be checked over to make sure he's in good health to be

executed, and you see the shock on his face two or three days before the execution, it's a terrible feeling. It isn't a feeling that I've ever experienced before. At the point of execution the prison falls quiet. Even the most hardened criminals just fall silent. They just can't cope with the idea that the state is going to kill someone. It's a feeling of anguish, it's a feeling of wishing you could do something, it's a feeling of dread. You don't want midnight plus one minute to arrive because you know what's going to happen. It's probably one of the worst feelings I've ever experienced in my life. It's scary. It just really, really causes a person to think deeply, I guess, and wonder how society can do this to another person in the name of justice. Granted, the person may have murdered someone, but Alabama has life without parole which means you never get out, there is no possibility of parole. The southern states were notorious for the practise of stuffing the potential victim's anus full of cotton right before the execution so he wouldn't soil himself in the chair and the guards wouldn't have to clean it up. This was in the newspapers. It's just total inhumanity towards another human being. It's a dreadful situation.

Gwynne spent two years at Holman before being transferred to West Jefferson, another maximum-security penitentiary in Birmingham, Alabama. He was held there for three years.

The brutality continued.

"I had a short-sleeved shirt at Holman but you're not allowed to wear any of your own clothes. It has to be prison whites with

Alabama Department of Corrections stamped on the back of your shirt and on your pants. Holman allowed short-sleeved shirts which was all I had. When I went to go to the meal line at West Jefferson with a short-sleeved shirt shortly after my arrival, an officer said, "You can't go to the chow hall dressed like that, you need a long-sleeved shirt". I explained that I had just arrived and I didn't have a long-sleeved shirt. He said, 'Well, you can't eat.' So, I asked for permission to go and see the lieutenant or the keeper to explain my situation and he said, "No, you're not seeing anybody; you get your goddamn ass back in there." So, I was returned to the cell block and told I couldn't eat. I had no way of getting a long-sleeved shirt. It's against the rules to borrow a shirt from someone else. You have your number printed on them and if you're caught, you're charged and you go to the hole or segregation. I called my wife who in turn called the Canadian Consulate in Atlanta, Georgia, a Mr. Jack Silverstone. He called West Jefferson Prison and asked why I wasn't allowed to eat. I mean, the most basic of rights is to be able to eat your food. At that point because outside people had become involved, especially an embassy from a foreign country, the sergeant called me up to his office, had three or four dirty long-sleeved shirts that he had found somewhere, I don't know where, and gave me the shirts and told me I could eat. Of course, it was too late to eat that day so I'd have to wait till the next day. It wasn't so much that I missed the meal as the way I was treated. I had no control over my shirt. I had no control over my clothes. When I asked to see a higher authority a rank guard told me to "get my goddamn ass back in the cell block". If I hadn't, I would have been hit over the head with a billy club. It's very disturbing to enter into an atmosphere like that. Several times my wife had to call the Canadian Embassy to try and keep me safe."

In Alabama prisons, as in prisons everywhere, loss of personal care of one's belongings causes a great deal of stress. A maxim that is universal in prisons everywhere is "little things become big things."

"When I arrived at West Jefferson, I had a few boxes and a few bags of my own personal belongings. I was brought into a cell block unit. West Jefferson, unlike Holman, consists of two-man cells, not than the dorms I had previously. There are no dorms. I was assigned a cell to share with another inmate. I set my boxes down while I was looking for my cell. I turned my back and when I turned around one of my boxes had disappeared. Someone stole it within minutes of my arriving in the cell block. I finally found my cell, put my things away, met my cell partner and noticed that the prison was cleaner than Holman in many respects. It was a newer prison, but I wasn't prepared for the violence at West Jefferson, not only from the inmates but in particular on the part of the staff, the guards. They were as brutal as brutal can be."

Seemingly common situations can lead to horrendous brutality. Gwynne recalled an episode as one inmate attempted to take a shower at the West Jefferson prison.

> "The showers are out in the common area and all you have to do is push a button and they come on for 30 seconds and then you've got to push the button again. I witnessed one situation where a prisoner had been working and he was filthy, and he went to take a shower, but it wasn't shower time. Shower time was at four p.m. at West Jefferson. He got in the shower and he was full of soap. Two guards came up and told him to get out of the shower. He said, 'just let me rinse the soap off me,' and he went to get back under the water. The guards dragged him out, beat him for several minutes with their billy clubs and tore patches of hair off his head. His scalp was bleeding, his face was bleeding. They used his towels to mop up the blood and handcuffed him and took him off to segregation.
>
> "I have also witnessed other prisoners being hit by the guards on the back of the neck, on the vertebrae, with these billy clubs, then handcuffed behind their back and dragged unconscious by their heels face down on a cement floor off to segregation. This is not uncommon. I've seen people beaten so badly they used bed sheets to wipe up the blood."

Facing a sentence of one hundred and twenty years, Gwynne soon realized that penitentiary is no place to age.

"There was an old fellow at West Jefferson who I befriended and several months after, I was there he had a stroke and was partially paralyzed on one side. The man was close to sixty years old. On one occasion he was locked in his cell, his cell partner was gone. The guards popped his cell open from the bubble, several inmates ran in with knives and they had socks filled with rocks, terrorized the old man, robbed him, took his personal pictures, photographs of his wife, his children, took the wristwatch off his arm, took whatever smoking products he had, food, cleaned him out. This inmate went and complained to the lieutenant. The lieutenant knew who the inmates were because they run in gangs and they do this all the time. The lieutenant made them give him back his personal photographs but allowed them to keep his watch, tobacco, whatever else they took. It was a joke."

A predominant feature of the Alabama prison system is the extent to which it is infused with racial discrimination. The effects of racial discrimination weighs on the minds of those who experience it.

"Gregory Fawcett was a friend of mine, a young white fellow. He had an argument with a Black inmate who had a history of stabbing white inmates, hitting them over the head with a rock as big as a grapefruit, hitting them with chairs. This is documented in complaints at West Jefferson Prison. Gregory Fawcett was in his cell asleep, a Black guard popped his door open, this Black inmate ran in, stabbed Gregory Fawcett several times in the neck, in the chest area. Gregory Fawcett didn't die, he lived. I saw him come out of his cell, blood pouring from his neck. I filed a lawsuit on his behalf because this inmate had

done this repeatedly. He wasn't segregated. He was a danger to every other inmate in the institution. During the course of discovery procedures I found all the other reports on this inmate that stated he had attacked several white inmates over a course of a few years."

There is certainly violence in prisons in Canada as well as in the United States. However, to Gwynne who had served time on both sides of the border, the extent of the violence in the Alabama prison was the worst.

"Although at West Jefferson you had more privacy than at Holman because you had a two-man cell instead of a dormitory, the climate of violence was worse than Holman. We were standing in line at the mess hall one day. We were stuck in a long hallway, no exits, no way out. A person pulled out a butcher knife and started chasing another fellow in and out of the line, up and down the hallway. It's a pretty terrifying experience. You have nowhere to go and the guards are not there very quickly to stop it. "You live with that fear constantly. You never know when something's going to happen and it rarely happens in your face. Most stabbings are done when you're asleep; most stabbings are done when your back is turned. I went out to walk the yard one day to give my cell partner, Otis Brown, a little bit of privacy. He slept on the top bunk. While I was gone three men ran into the cell with knives to rob us. Otis wasn't about to let them just get away with it. He jumped off the top bunk. One of the inmates stabbed him in the forehead for his effort right above the eye. At that point they panicked, and they left. They left the cell, they ran out. When I came back in stuff was scattered all over the place. Otis had a bad cut across his forehead less than a half an inch away from his eye. It was a common occurrence. It's always there. You never escape from it. "One of the most oppressive features of West Jefferson was the intimidation which took place with prisoners strong arming and threatening other prisoners for what little personal property and personal items they had in their cell. The level of intimidation is probably based on the fact that in the Alabama prison system, you are not paid a salary for the work you do. Consequently, there is very little money. You are paid one dollar a month no matter what job you do. If you work breaking rocks for eight hours a day or if you work in the tailor shop, laundry, or the kitchen, you are still paid one dollar a month. You are not given shampoo, deodorant, or things that you are given in the Canadian prison system. You have to buy those things. Most of the prisoners in the Alabama prison system come from dysfunctional families who do not have a lot of money. They have no family to send them money. The only way many of these people have to get anything is through intimidation, violence or just taking it. It is rampant through the system."

In 1989, Gwynne was once again transferred; this time he was sent to St. Clair Institution, another maximum-security prison located near Birmingham. Gwynne appreciated that the cleanliness of the institution was "a notch up" on Holman and West Jefferson but was constantly frustrated that there was no decrease in the high degree of brutality on the part of custodial staff and inmates. Gwynne was given a job in the kitchen since he maintained that his work in a hotel chain "on the street" gave him credentials for a job requiring more than physical labour.

Gwynne worked in the stock room where he received incoming food supplies. The work was indoors, and he was not subjected to the heat of Alabama summers. It also gave him time to think. The more he thought the more he became determined to find a way out. He had either escaped or walked away from earlier prisons or paroles. What if he could devise a plan to get back to Canada that would not put him in personal peril? What if Canada could extradite him so he could do his time in what he considered the relative luxury of a Canadian prison?

It took a phone call to land him in Alabama's correctional system. Perhaps another phone call could result in his release.

* * *

It was in late May 1989, as I recall, that I received a call at my Cobourg, Ontario office. The caller was Michael Gwynne, and he was calling from the St. Clair Penitentiary in Alabama. He inquired if I was indeed the John Hill who worked on behalf of prisoners and I assured him he had the right person.

He told me upfront that his aim was to secure a return to Canada, and he had already explored the possibility of making an application under Canada's *International Transfer of Offenders Act*. This was legislation that enabled Canadian offenders serving time in certain foreign lands to serve their foreign sentence in a Canadian prison and under Canadian prison rules. The treaty between Canada and the United States required that the agreement to transfer be signed by three parties: the offender proposing to be transferred, the receiving state, and the sending state. Gwynne was certain that Alabama would never agree even if it were a party to the treaty.

Gwynne devised another solution that would force Canada to seek his extradition. In order to do this, he told me, it would be necessary to raise the profile of his case to the point that everyday Canadian citizens would demand that their government seek his return to Canada. He then proceeded to outline in broad strokes the information that he could provide for dissemination.

Since Gwynne's story was centred on the lakeside city of Kingston, Ontario, I set out to negotiate with the city's newspaper, the *Kingston Whig-Standard,* and found early on that the paper would be entirely cooperative. Its cooperation would involve having one of its key reporters, Paulette Peirol, being temporarily appointed as my law clerk and our travelling by plane to Alabama to interview and take a statement from Michael Gwynne.

The day after our arrival in Alabama, Paulette Peirol and I headed by rented car to St. Clair Institution where arrangements had been made for a lawyer-client interview. As we approached St. Clair prison, we were shocked to see chain gangs and shackled inmates picking up trash from the ditches on either side of the highway. "This is *Cool Hand Luke* all over again!" I blurted out as Paulette stared out the window at the sight. Kingston is home to a number of penitentiaries but neither of us had ever witnessed the forced labour of an actual chain gang.

As we approached the prison, we spotted a structure composed of a cement slab floor and bound by wire. We were later told this was a "dog run" where inmates who refused to do work on the chain gang would be caged with minimal clothing to bake in the summer sun or get chilled to the bone in winter months.

Entering the prison was the standard format for entering any maximum-security facility wherever one might seek entrance. We were identified as the individuals authorized to conduct an interview and searched to ensure we were not introducing any contraband. The guards appeared to be polite and efficient, and in short order, we were seated in an interview area and Michael Gwynne was brought to us.

Gwynne was smiling as he approached us. I estimated he stood six feet tall, with graying hair, and appeared to be in decent physical shape, but not as buff as younger prisoners tend to be in their early years of incarceration. He was dressed in prison garb. He took a seat beside us ready to launch into the story he had been rehearsing in his mind for days. He seemed unprepared for the usual pleasantries that mark the first meetings of strangers.

I interrupted to introduce myself and Paulette. A round of handshakes followed. I started out by saying that I had to give a warning before we went further. I noted that Paulette was appearing at the meeting as my law clerk. As such she bore the same responsibility as the lawyer to keep everything said in complete confidence. However, I added, the privilege was one that belonged to the client, not the lawyer, and could be waived if the client so chose. I also reminded him that Paulette was a reporter with the Kingston newspaper. If he wanted her to write an article on what he was about to tell us, he would have to waive his solicitor-client privilege. That would release both me and Paulette from our obligation of secrecy.

"That's what I want you to do," Gwynne stated firmly and authorized the both of us to go public with his story.

Gwynne said he had never told his story before, not even to his wife Rosalie. The reason he was divulging his memories was that he wanted out of the Alabama prison system. He had tried every legal means he could conceive including lobbying and court proceedings, all to no avail. He was upfront with his criminal past, both in Canada and the United States.

"I want to be extradited to Canada," he said forcefully. "The only bargaining chip I have is the story I will tell you. All the police will have to do is start digging." I never expected that Michael

Gwynne was speaking literally and not figuratively. "My only hope now is for extradition."

Gwynne then began relating the story of a missing person. It was the story of Judith Zicari, a former North Bay resident who went missing on April 7, 1972, just before her thirty-first birthday.

Throughout the years, police had no knowledge of the whereabouts of Judith Zicari, or Judith Bailey as she was known as an inmate at Kingston's Prison for Women.

Gwynne said he and a former wife were renting an apartment for a hundred dollars a month at 384 Alfred Street in Kingston. Gwynne stayed in town after serving time in Kingston Penitentiary and Collins Bay Institution before being granted parole on his ten-year sentence. The Alfred Street property was a five-bedroom, three-story house rented out to Queen's University students who wanted to live off-campus and ex-convicts on release from the area's many penitentiaries.

"Since I had a house with a lot of room, it became a meeting place," Gwynne explained. It was there that he had first contact with Zicari who, he believed, was on parole. He described Zicari as a woman of medium build, five feet, three inches tall with short black hair and brown eyes. Zicari, Gwynne claimed, had a drug problem. Indeed, he said, drugs were her "reason for living."

Gwynne met Judy Zicari through a male friend whom Gwynne believed to be on day parole. Gwynne described Zicari as "a rounder" who "hung around with criminals at least half her life and may have been married to two or three of them." Zicari seemed to have bonded with Gwynne's friend. The two appeared to be intimate. Zicari was his "serious girlfriend or common-law wife, as much as they could be common-law while they were still on day parole. They spent a great deal of time together. I made a room in my house available to them." Gwynne described how the two would go to the second floor, next to the master bedroom that faced the street. "They'd go up and I never bothered to enquire what they did up there. They just went up and it was their business."

I asked Gwynne to name his friend. He refused. He realized what he was saying would be made public. He referred to his friend simply as "a well-known criminal in Canada who dealt in drugs for many, many, many years." It was obvious Gwynne would not allow the release of the story if it meant ratting out his friend.

The drug-dealing friend one day confided to Gwynne that he suspected Zicari was ripping him off. He would send her out, but she had not returned with sufficient cash for the sales she made. The friend concluded that Zicari was giving free drugs to bikers in the Kingston area. Gwynne said that at that time the bikers (Satan's Choice or Devil's Disciples motorcycle gangs) controlled the drug trade in Kingston at that time. There was an eerie truce between the bikers and the ex-cons in town. There was the feeling that Zicari might be responsible for altering the accord between the two groups.

Gwynne asked his friend what he intended to do about it. The reply was, "I don't know, but I need to confront her about it."

It was sometime later when the friend came in with Ms. Zicari and took her up to their second-floor bedroom. The two began arguing. "The door was open, and they were arguing pretty violently. She was high on something, I don't know what, but she was totally messed up. I mean she'd start screaming and yelling and swearing and doing all kinds of things.

"At one point, he hollered out to me. I was coming up the stairs and he said 'Get a piece of rope' . . . I don't remember his exact words, but she had jumped on him, tried to scratch him up, and was, you know, just really, kind of wild.

"So, I went and routed around and found a piece of rope maybe two feet long, or two-and-a-half feet long, and I brought it to him. And he tied her elbows . . . the rope passed from elbow to elbow behind her back. She still had full use of her hands and her feet but couldn't jump up and try to claw his eyes out or anything."

I asked Gwynne to describe the rope. He thought it may have been a white clothesline.

Arguing continued in the bedroom for the rest of the afternoon. Gwynne said that from observations he made, Zacari was consuming blue-colored pills, possibly Valium, from a brown bottle she was holding, and she would occasionally "pop some into her mouth" with her free hand.

He said he couldn't hear or tried to ignore the voices but witnessed parts of the turmoil when he came upstairs to use the toilet or to go into his own bedroom.

"I'd stop sometimes for five, six, seven minutes and stand in the doorway to see what was going on," he said. "I might have stood there for 10 or 15 minutes on two or three occasions. Then I'd go about my business."

Early in the evening, about 7:30 p.m., Gwynne's friend left the bedroom and told Gwynne not to bother Zicari. Gwynne understood that Zicari was allowed out of prison with permission as a person on day parole and would be required to return to the prison at a specified time or risk being found unlawfully at large and losing her pass program or worse.

Gwynne's friend explained the situation. "He said 'She's asleep. Just let her sleep.' He said 'Don't worry about her going back in tonight; She's messed up on drugs.' He said, 'She's going to have to spend the night out and we'll worry about that some other time.'" Gwynne realized that returning to the prison high on drugs would also jeopardize her future leave privileges.

It was about 3 a.m. or 4 a.m. when Gwynne awoke to use the bathroom. He decided to look in on Zicari again.

"She still had this rope holding her elbows and she was lying with her face in the pillow, kind of off to one side a little bit, and her knees were drawn up just a little bit, not a lot.

"So, I flicked the light on and walked in to take a closer look and there was some mucus coming out of her nose, and it looked like a string of mucus this big around, as big as that pen." Gwynne also noticed purple marks on her skin. "I called her name and shook her, and she was just as stiff as this table. I mean she was dead and had been dead for a good while because rigor mortis had set in and the discoloration of her skin was pretty livid.

"I made sure she was dead, and at that point, I didn't know what to do, so I sat down and smoked a cigarette and thought about it, and probably smoked several cigarettes. And I thought: well, I can call the authorities, but if I call the authorities, I'm on parole, she's on day parole, I'm already in trouble for letting her stay in my house beyond the time she's supposed to be back in because I know she's supposed to be back in.

He claims not to know how Ms. Zicari died. "I won't even speculate on what happened to that girl," he said. "It was just another day until the wee hours of the morning when I found her."

I asked, "Did you kill Judy Zicari?" Gwynne said, "No. I didn't."

"If I called them, I don't know for sure what she died of, but whatever it is, it's going to come back to haunt me, because this is my house and I'm here."

There had to be something he could do to extricate himself from the dilemma he found himself in.

"So, then I thought, well, I'm going to take her down to those bikers she likes so well and break into their house and put her in there. They can't afford to get caught with a body any more than I can, so they'll have to do something with it. Let them take care of it.

"Then I thought: bad idea, that's not going to work."

He then developed Plan B.

"Eventually I said, 'Well, I'm just going to have to conceal this body, pretend I never saw her that day and didn't know what happened to her.' So, I took her down to the basement, and got a shovel and started digging a hole . . . Once I decided what to do, I worked until daylight."

Mr. Gwynne described the basement as a "damp, dark basement" with a dirt floor and hard clay beneath the surface. There was a low ceiling of exposed beams, plumbing and wiring, and a furnace that looked like an octopus, he said. There was an uncovered window at ground level, facing Alfred Street that had to be blocked when daylight entered. He couldn't have a passerby seeing what he was doing.

"I got a narrow trench dug about as long as she was, and I figured it was about as wide." The plan was to remove all her clothing to get rid of any evidence. He had trouble with her pants. They fit "like a second skin." He just gave up. Gwynne had no recollection of finding a wallet or identification papers on her. "I buried her as is," he said.

"I don't remember if I took the rope off the back of her elbows. I just don't remember any of that. But the thing I do remember doing is putting her in the hole, covering it up with the ground, and just concealing the body," he said. "I just buried her the way she was."

In the morning, Gwynne's friend showed up at the house once again. He asked about it. Zicari. He was told she was dead. The friend never asked how Zicari died. He just wanted to know "What did you do with her?"

Gwynne realized that his friend had set him up.

"The thing that bothers me, looking back, is he knew I wouldn't say anything about it, but that's leaving me in a hell of a fix."

Gwynne asked his friend to relocate the body two times, and twice, nothing was done. Fearing that the police might come looking for the missing female inmate, Mr. Gwynne decided to skip town. He took a sailboat to the United States and, except for a brief stint in Mexico, has remained in the States ever since.

I questioned further about the body, "Is there any chance it has since been removed?"

"I think the possibility of that is extremely doubtful, next to non-existent," he said.

At the conclusion of our meeting, I had Gwynne sign a summary of what he told us at the meeting using exact quotes where possible.

"Do you think Canada will want to extradite me?"

"It's not a murder confession," I cautioned, "but any decision in that account will be up to how the police and the Crown Attorney react to the news you just shared." We left the prison for the flight back to Canada.

***

Immediately upon arrival in Canada, I scheduled a meeting with the City of Kingston police. The following day, I handed over Gwynne's signed statement. Perhaps I was expecting a sign of gratitude that an outstanding missing person case or possible homicide could be closed. All I received was a bureaucratic acknowledgment that the document had been delivered and would be considered.

Shortly afterward, on June 5, 1991, Paulette Peirol published the first of several articles dealing with the missing woman and Gwynne's account of her disappearance. It was not until two weeks after the initial publication of the story in the newspaper that Kingston Police gave a comment. The media spokesperson for the police was simple: "No information can be released that may prejudice its outcome." The spokesperson did disclose that no excavation had yet been undertaken at the site. That statement was published on June nineteenth.

On June twenty-first, Kingston police made this statement, "This phase of the investigation has been exhausted and all evidence indicates that human remains do not exist in the basement of 384

Alfred St." RCMP Sgt. Bob Stair confirmed that the federal police force had assisted in the investigation and added, "We've basically ripped the basement apart pretty well, to make sure there isn't anything there." He added, "We were pretty convinced, once we got down to two and a half to three feet that we were in a non-grave situation." Case closed on the Zicari lead.

Gwynne called my office, and I delivered the news he did not want to hear. "They didn't dig deep enough," he pleaded. "I can draw a map pointing out the exact location." It was obvious from my conversation that police had never contacted Gwynne directly and they had no intention of doing so. I heard the disappointment in Gwynne's voice.

His hopes of extradition to Canada were dashed. If he couldn't get back to Canada by legal means, he was certainly skilled in obtaining his ends in a non-legal fashion. Gwynne had to figure out another plan to leave Alabama behind after my final call with him. Sometime in 1993, he cut the fencing at the St. Clair prison and escaped. He made his way and somehow secured passage on an Amtrak train and eventually headed for Vancouver.

Now in Canada, he was later arrested and sent to maximum-security Kent Institution in British Columbia. He still had an unexpired penitentiary sentence to complete in his homeland.

The American authorities were advised. While he had hoped to use extradition as a means of returning to Canada, he now faced another obstacle. American authorities now served Canada through diplomatic channels with a notice that the United States was seeking Gwynne's extradition to complete his one hundred and twenty-year sentence there. Thus, began a three-year legal battle with Gwynne opposing extradition.

Canada's Minister of Justice ordered Gwynne's extradition to the United States. The legal battle that followed was in essence an appeal brought by way of judicial review of the Minister's decision. Gwynne retained prominent British Columbia counsel: Stan Guenther, a veteran Vancouver practitioner, and Professor Michael Jackson, who taught law and more particularly prison law at the University of British Columbia.

Refusal to transfer from Canada on an extradition request was rare to non-existent. The only reported case of a Canadian court's refusal to extradite someone wanted in the United States was the case of *United States v. Cobb* in 1997. It was a case where American authorities urged Canada to hand over the person accused of telemarketing fraud. The Court accepted evidence that an American prosecutor appeared on Canadian television demanding an end to the challenges to extradition, threatening, "You're going to be the boyfriend of a very bad man if you wait out your extradition." Abominable prison conditions had never been the basis to deny an extradition request. The *Cobb* decision was later overturned on appeal.

In a strange twist of fate, the man who had pinned his hopes that extradition might secure his transfer from Alabama was now opposing an extradition request that could result in his return. The appeal was held in Vancouver on October 16, 1997. Judgment was reserved and written reasons of the three-panel court were handed down on February 4, 1998.

The evidence reviewed by the Court involved a statement by Justice Minister Alan Rock claiming that the United States had a fair system for the administration of justice and as long as an accused was treated fairly upon arrest and in the judicial proceedings, it was not up to Canada to criticize how a sentence short of the death penalty ought to be served. Minister Rock explicitly stated: "Canadian citizens who commit offences in the United States, can expect to be housed in correctional facilities akin to those in Canada." This was another way of saying the old maxim "If you can't do the time, don't commit the crime."

His affidavit also contained this statement:

> "Mr. Gwynne voluntarily went to the State of Alabama and thereby chose to submit to its laws. While such a law may not be appropriate in Canada in like circumstances, that alone would not make it unconstitutional to return him to the state where he chose to commit his offences."

Material put forward by Gwynne drew comparisons between his treatment in Alabama and his treatment in the Canadian prison system. It is highly unusual for a Canadian prisoner to laud his prison experience in Canada. However, it was his hope that the judges reviewing his case would be horrified that any prisoner of whatever nationality would have to endure the inhumane conditions he had experienced in Alabama.

On top of this, Gwynne pleaded for mercy for himself and his family. In his affidavit filed with the court, he stated:

> "I will die in the Alabama prison system. I realize I have a long criminal record but I'm also fifty-four years old and my time of crime has long gone by. My last conviction in 1984 was not for a violent crime. I would gladly stay here in a Canadian prison if I could have a transfer from the Alabama system to here. That would bother me a lot less

than going back to Alabama. If you send me back, you're sending me to a death sentence. It's an inhumane system. It's something that you cannot believe unless you're actually there, and it's a death sentence for my wife and me. That's as blunt as I can be about it. That is exactly what it is, a death sentence. There's no forgiveness for what I did. You do not escape from Alabama and not pay the consequences of it. I will die in an Alabama prison. And if you have any compassion, not perhaps for me as a person, but for my wife who has waited for twelve years hoping for a small ray of sunshine to come into our lives, if you have any compassion at all, I would ask that you take seriously the inhumanity of my past treatment in the Alabama prison system and the terrible consequences I will face if I am sent back to serve my one hundred and twenty-year sentence and rule in my favour."

The decision delivered by the court was not unanimous. Madam Justice Southin provided a strong dissent to the opinion concurred in by the two male Justices, Cumming and Goldie. The majority opinion stressed Canada's role in the community of nations and its honour would be at stake to renege on its international obligations. The majority on the bench agreed that the Alabama prison regime allowed conditions that were "subjectively abhorrent" and may have been in violation of constitutional rights enjoyed in the United States by those subjected to its laws.

The dissent agreed with Gwynne that the conditions in Alabama were so shocking that they could not be countenanced under section 7 of Canada's *Charter of Rights and Freedoms* that guarantees the right to life, liberty, and security of the person, and the right not to be deprived of thereof except in accordance with the principles of fundamental justice.

Despite a split decision, the Supreme Court of Canada refused to grant leave to appeal the decision of the British Columbia Court of Appeal. By the time the legal proceedings had ended, Anne McLellan had taken over the Justice portfolio from Allen Rock.

Gwynne's British Columbia lawyers wrote to McLellan asking her to seek the Justice Minister's assistance in dealings with Alabama to allow Michael Gwynne to remain in Canada. Newspaper reports note that McLellan refused and on October 9, 1998, turned down the request for compassion.

It was reported that Michael Lucian Gwynne returned to Alabama three days before Christmas in 1998. The news reports stated that Gwynne's three-year battle to remain in Canada was for naught.

"He's gone with the wind," a Correctional Service of Canada spokesperson at Kent Institution claimed.

Gwynne's broken-hearted and wheelchair-bound wife, Rosalie, told reporters from her home in western Canada, "In my heart of hearts, I don't ever expect to see him again." She reiterated that she knew her husband always maintained a dread that he would die in Alabama.

Newspaper accounts stated that Gwynne was collected by US officials at daybreak on December 22, 1998, and was expected to arrive back in Alabama later that day.

The case of *Gwynne v. Canada (Justice)*, 103 BCAC 1, as it is recorded in the law books, stands as an unfortunate precedent to others who might seek to avoid extradition. No follow-up stories have been reported in Canadian newspapers.

The outstanding question is what has become of Michael Gwynne almost a quarter century later. Has he coped with the dreadful conditions inside Alabama's prisons? An investigation of Alabama's state prisons for men conducted by the United States Department of Justice, Civil Rights Division, published July 23, 2020, demonstrates the horrible conditions of Alabama's penal facilities continue. Did Michael Gwynne successfully learn to cope or did he, as his wife feared, die inside the prison barriers?

The stories that ran in Canadian newspapers describing Gwynne's extradition to the United States were reminiscent of the Irish traditional ballad *The Fields of Athenry*. In that song, a poor Irish farmhand is transported to a penal colony in Australia by the English for pilfering some corn so he could feed his famine-stricken family. In Gwynne's case, the newspaper accounts were dripping with pathos. A disabled wife weeps as her husband is transported to a brutal prison system where he will most assuredly die.

The story, as reported without follow-up by the press, would be heart-wrenching except for one important detail. It is a lie.

I looked for indications online that might show Gwynne's present whereabouts or news of his demise. All without success. I wrote to the Canadian consulate in Atlanta, Georgia on March 8, 2021 seeking any news that the office might have on the Canadian prisoner. The following day, I received a one-line reply: "We are not aware of the whereabouts of Mr. Gwynne and as a result, we are not in a position to respond to your inquiry."

That prompted a request to the Alabama Department of Corrections on March 9, 2021. The response was almost instantaneous: "He is serving time in Canada. It does not appear he ever came back to us after his escape."

I then contacted the Acting Senior Communications Advisor for the Correctional Service of Canada. That official confirmed the information I had been given by the Alabama Department of Corrections. The CSC spokesperson wrote: "CSC has a Michael

Lucian Gwynne under its jurisdiction. Due to the privacy act, I am not able to share where Mr. Gwynne is located other than he is in Canada."

Through the assistance of the Correctional Service of Canada, I was able to speak with Michael Gwynne at his home in an undisclosed location. He was able to fill in some of the blanks that had been unreported until now.

Gwynne said that he escaped from the Alabama prison with a fellow prisoner he calls Johnny. The two inmates holed up for a while in Birmingham and eventually made their way to Savannah, Georgia. They later took the train to New York State where they made their border crossing into Canada. Border security did not challenge their excuse that they were crossing the border to take in a baseball playoff game. Gwynne made his way to Toronto staying first at a B&B and later renting a small apartment on Church Street. Johnny had a drug addiction and returned to Alabama where he found it easier to feed his habit. Michael Gwynne stayed in connection with Johnny's girlfriend. Gwynne relocated to another province.

Unfortunately for Gwynne, Johnny was caught with another woman. His girlfriend reported Johnny's whereabouts to police who apprehended the escapee. The girlfriend also gave information about Gwynne. Police knocked on Gwynne's door and took him into custody. It was while in prison at Kent Institution that the Americans sought his extradition.

He was returned to Alabama as newspapers had reported notwithstanding what I had been told later by the Alabama Department of Corrections. It was while he was in the US prison that he got word that Rosalie was diagnosed with leukemia. She passed away a few days after he was sent back to Alabama.

Professor Michael Jackson continued to work to have Gwynne return to Canada and was successful. The Alabama prisoner was brought back to Canada in an RCMP plane and jailed in Kingston Penitentiary until he could secure an interregional transfer back to Kent. Eventually, his security level was reduced, and he was then sent to medium-security Mission Institution and later to minimum security. From there, he was paroled.

Now, almost eighty years of age, Gwynne resides alone but misses Rosalie immensely. He takes care of two cats he adopted 14 years ago.

In 2018, Kingston police sent two officers to interview Gwynne and try to see if they could obtain further information on where Judith Zicari's body could be located. Gwynne could tell the officers no more than what had been reported in the *Kingston Whig-Standard* many years before.

Why had stories of Gwynne's return not been published in newspapers across Canada? Gwynne is unable to offer an explanation for the secrecy. It should be big news that he had been allowed to transfer his sentence to Canada. Even though most people would agree that compassion should be shown in such circumstances, it would have been politically risky to tell the public that hardworking Justice officials and diplomats were diligent in protecting this Canadian's life and devised a transfer allowing Gwynne to serve his sentence in Canada. A significant section of the Canadian public wanted the government to be "tough on crime." To avoid political fallout, the safest route is to avoid publicity.

Michael Gwynne did not spend his final years in an Alabama prison. In accordance with a court order, he was sent back to an American prison, but eventually came back to Canada, this time for good. He has been spending the duration of his hundred and twenty-year sentence abiding peacefully and lawfully. He never returned to criminal behaviour. He died at home in Canada in July 2023. In that respect, he is truly the man who never returned.

CHAPTER 14

EXILED

Daniel Cody Morgan and the
Sentence that Never Ends

| *Who knows why were we taught to fear the witches,*
| *and not those who burned them alive.*

When Daniel Cody Morgan went to bed on April 12, 1993, his mind was racing. When his feet touched the floor the following morning, he knew it was the last time he would be in a cell at Kingston Penitentiary. It should have been a happy day. He was due to go home to Peterborough, Ontario as a free man. But Daniel Cody Morgan was not happy.

Morgan had been released in 1992 on what was then called "mandatory supervision." He had tried to establish himself in the Peterborough area. But a new allegation while he was on release led to his parole suspension. He was returned to prison and a new mandatory supervision date was calculated, two-thirds of the time between his return to custody and the warrant expiry date. Even though a new mandatory supervision date was set and he could have resumed his release and continued to be supervised while living in the community, he decided to reject freedom and spend every last day of his sentence in the penitentiary. But just before his warrant of committal expired and release was inevitable, Morgan found that the Peterborough police had issued a warning describing him as a "dangerous offender," even though no court had made that designation. The police notice included his photo and his criminal record. Morgan had authorized me to take legal action against the police.

Suing the Police

On Morgan's behalf, I issued a Statement of Claim against the Police Services Board of the City of Peterborough. The *Toronto Star* described the action as "the first legal action of its kind to be taken against a Canadian police force for a practice that is becoming widespread across North America to the outrage of defence lawyers and civil libertarians."

The Statement of Claim sought damages from Peterborough police for one hundred and twenty-five thousand dollars for psychological distress, lost job opportunities, damage to his reputation, and invasion of his privacy. The Statement of Claim had been served on the police on February twenty-sixth and generated publicity of his upcoming release. Morgan was unconcerned with that. He was adamant that making him a pariah in his hometown was intentional and, although nothing could be done to have the police retract the action they had set in motion, the chill of a lawsuit might help those inmates in similar circumstances fare better in the future.

The police claimed they were justified in advertising Morgan's eventual release. The force had received a notice from the Correctional Service of Canada on January twenty-ninth containing the photograph and a memorandum characterizing Morgan as a "high risk/dangerous release."

The police notice stated that it was expected that Morgan would be living in Peterborough. The Statement of Defence was filed in response to the lawsuit describing Morgan as a "pedophile whose offending pattern is quite alarming." It is true that the then forty-three-year-old had an extensive record dating from 1963 that listed six convictions for sexual assault or exploitation. The police warning to the community failed to report that Morgan had undertaken extensive rehabilitative programs in prison and that the Parole Board considered him to be a manageable risk. The police discounted their role in Morgan's suspicion that he would be unemployable as a consequence of his criminal behaviour in the past.

The lawsuit was eventually settled but nothing could undo the hostility and disdain some members of the public felt realizing a former child molester was about to walk the streets of their fair city. In a press interview prior to his leaving prison, Morgan is quoted as saying, "It's going to be difficult, very difficult to adjust." He continued, "I doubt I can get a job in Ontario. I'm expecting a mob of protesters to be waiting for me outside the gates."

Release from Prison

April thirteenth arrived. Morgan readied himself to exit Kingston Penitentiary. He had accurately predicted what awaited as the large grey wooden door slowly opened and the entrance bars were unlocked at the prison's north entrance. He simply had to walk across the sidewalk to a car driven by a John Howard Society volunteer parked on the street directly in front of him.

A large group of citizens had assembled. The first arrivals had gathered in the dark at half past four in the morning in case the Correctional Service of Canada tried to sneak Morgan away. The protesters included men and a group of women that called themselves "Voices for Children's Rights." There were also reporters wanting to take note of any interaction between the offender and the mob.

Despite Morgan's intention to walk swiftly to the waiting vehicle, he could not help himself from making a public statement: "What I think is really the worst part of this whole thing is that for me it doesn't make a lot of difference. But it does for the people who are going to be coming out who should be integrated into the community slowly." Furthermore, he declared, "They need to be under supervision and these people aren't going to get that. They're going to walk out the door. They're going to be mad and they aren't going to have anywhere to go."

Morgan feared that even those who had become rehabilitated inside prison will in the future, because of police notifications, be "red-flagged." They will be considered dangerous regardless of their real situation.

One of the reporters covering Morgan's release was Canadian Press reporter Gloria Galloway. Her story was published on April seventeenth with these two opening sentences: "When convicted pedophile Daniel Cody Morgan was released from federal prison this week, Virginia Foster was there to meet him. And she didn't bring the Welcome Wagon."

Reporter Galloway goes on to explain that twenty-eight-year-old Victoria Foster and her group called Voices of Children's Rights consisted of some twenty members that had banded together since the previous November to draw attention to the release of what they considered to be potentially dangerous sexual offenders. Foster explained the origins of the protest group to Galloway: "It all started with a news report in the *Toronto Star* about [convicted pedophile] Wray Budreo getting out of prison." This came as a shock to group members. "We just sat down," she added, "and said 'This is it'. We can't tolerate this anymore. You can't let out a man who is this dangerous."

That incident led to a sit-in outside the prison walls and drew national media attention. The group considered it a success when the Parole Board denied Budreo a release. That success inspired the group to lobby on to protest the release of several other child sexual abusers. One of the people that Foster's group lobbied against was Guy Paul Morin. Morin had been convicted of the rape and murder of nine-year-old Christine Jessop. Morin was later exonerated as having had no part in the killing. But this group never looked past the headlines. The group was satisfied that vigilante justice be administered to continue the punishment that the law did not allow.

Morgan tried to resettle, this time ruling out the Peterborough area. He didn't feel welcome. He moved to Atikokan, a small community some two thousand kilometres from Peterborough and two hundred and ten kilometres northwest of Thunder Bay.

Less than a week after his release, Ontario Provincial Police in Peterborough charged Morgan with an incident that supposedly occurred between March and May of 1992 when Morgan had been on release in the area. The nature of the sexual assault involved a thirteen-year-old boy. Morgan called me upon learning of the charge. After our telephone conversation, Morgan chose to surrender himself to the police.

Morgan's Preliminary Hearing

Morgan was taken into custody. He waived the reading of the charge and remained in lockup until his transfer to Peterborough to face the charge. Since Morgan remained in solitary confinement for fifty days awaiting trial, it was urgent that we press to expedite proceedings. The matter came on for a preliminary hearing, the first step before going to trial. The purpose of a preliminary hearing is to determine if there is sufficient evidence to bring the matter to trial. For Morgan, it was just another delay and continued time in solitary. Morgan was anxious that there should be minimal delay in proceedings. His stint in isolation cells, presumably to protect him from other prisoners, was becoming mentally unbearable. Morgan saw it as a form of torture.

The day scheduled for the beginning of the preliminary hearing arrived. The Crown prosecutor, Brian Gilkinson, seemed troubled. He asked the court to delay the proceedings for a short period so he could consult with his witness, presumably the teenage boy. It seemed like a long time-out but eventually Gilkinson returned. I was sitting at a counsel table, Morgan was in the prisoner box out of earshot. Gilkinson stood beside me and leaned over advising that his witness was refusing to give evidence. I obviously could not indulge the prosecution by agreeing to an adjournment should the witness change his mind. I said simply, "Let's get on with it."

Once the court was back in session and the case was called, Gilkinson rose to address the court. He let it be known that his witness was being uncooperative. He admitted that without the witness the Crown had no case, thus he opted to withdraw the charge. Morgan, once again, was a free man.

Morgan was far from home. It was late in the day and any hopes of getting a bus or a train were out of the question. I drove Morgan from the courthouse in Peterborough to my office location in Cobourg. I found Morgan a room at a Cobourg motel where he spent the night. The room rate for the motel was low, indicative of the lack of amenities. But it was clean and a place to rest his head.

Morgan hoped that the pressures of the lobby group, the publicity, and what he felt was police harassment were over. Maybe now he could sleep peacefully and get on with his life. He was about to move again. That was the last time I saw Morgan.

Trouble in Jasper

In July of 1994, I received a call from the RCMP in Jasper, Alberta. I had no idea why I was contacted. I was informed that Morgan had relocated to a Western Canadian city. He had volunteered to work for a community television station. Of particular concern was that Morgan's volunteer work involved his working with children. It was also noted that Morgan was giving a lift to "young boys" in his pickup truck.

Once again, police decided it was their duty to warn the community. American jurisprudence had evolved to allow the release of private information if there were reasonable grounds to believe that an individual posed imminent harm to the community or a particular member of the community. This had become known as the "Tarasoff principle." It came about when a psychiatrist at a California University was told a student that he was treating was threatening to kill or to inflict harm on a female student with the surname Tarasoff. The psychiatrist believed he had an ethical duty to remain silent. The psychiatrist's patient acted out violently and killed the female student. Tarasoff's family sued the University and won. The Tarasoff principle was born and became enacted as law in several American jurisdictions, though never in Canada. When a counsellor becomes aware of a person's intent or potential to place others in clear or imminent danger, care should be taken to give threatened persons warning sufficient to avert foreseeable harm.

There is a very fine line between the very civic-minded allowance for the disclosure of private information as allowed by the Tarasoff principle and the spreading of vicious rumours. The key in the Tarasoff principle is that the danger must be clear or imminent.

The RCMP disclosure of Morgan's volunteer work in Alberta seemed to fall short of the mark. When the story was reported, once again the name of Daniel Cody Morgan made the national news. This time, however, no charges were laid. A story printed in the *Kingston Whig-Standard* dated July 23, 1994, included a comment from the executive secretary of community television station JCTV saying Morgan posed no harm to the children. Other adults are always present when children are involved in broadcasts.

The Jasper story as reported in the Kingston newspaper added fuel to the fire of the lobbying group, End Violence Against Children. The group was now seeking an Ontario law allowing police to release photos of child sex offenders and the communities to which they are being released, Spokesperson Hazel Huneault was quoted as saying, "Do we not have a right to protect our children, to know that these people are out there?" She was frustrated that the laws do not allow such disclosure. As she saw it, "His sentence has expired; he's free to do whatever he wants. That's a flaw in the justice system."

Once again, Morgan had to get out of town.

Budreo's Release

The offender whose case initiated the formation of the lobby group, Wray Budreo was coming up for release. On November 18, 1994, Peterborough police issued a "public safety warning" that Budreo would be staying with someone in the city. A small group of protesters took up their station at half past four in the morning, ready to greet Budreo when released.

This time, the Correctional Service tried to avoid a side-show atmosphere. CSC spokesperson Ron Fairley said, "Budreo left the penitentiary at five after eight in an unmarked Ontario Provincial Police car driven by the OPP Pen Squad. We do not know where he was headed. Once he pulled onto King Street, our jurisdiction ended. The car exited the prison grounds through the staff parking lot along the east wall of the prison, out of sight of the protesters."

The lobby group felt jilted. "They had no right to help him," lobby group member Lyne Bergeron exclaimed to the Kingston newspaper. "The fact that someone snuck him out is an absolute outrage. They had no right to do that. When [Daniel Cody] Morgan was released last year, he walked out the front door and the John Howard Society was there to pick him up. But at least he walked out to face us. Corrections Canada didn't have the balls to do that this time."

"We have never given them any indication that we'd be violent or reason to believe we'd hurt anyone," Bergeron continued. "Society has the right to know what this man looks like now. I think Corrections Canada went above and beyond the call of duty."

Fellow protester Sharon Wallis added, "We want a picture of him. Why they are helping him out now that he's a free man is beyond me. He was supposedly under supervision the last time he offended and he still did it. It's going to happen again and I think someone should be held accountable. It's the children who get a life sentence."

Morgan Resettles

While all this was going on, Morgan relocated from Jasper, Alberta to Valemount, British Columbia. He was met with what was becoming familiar to him, community distrust. Once again police laid charges of Morgan's sexually assaulting two young men. Residents had put up posters citing his background. Time to pack his bags again!

Next stop was Fort St. John, British Columbia. Once again, the RCMP decided it needed to be proactive. RCMP Sgt. Randy Munro told the Canadian Press in late November 1995 that "The community should be aware of him. He seeks out young boys with low self-esteem. The majority are young offenders." The police notice did not mention that the British Columbia Supreme Court had dismissed the charges of assaults on the two teenagers.

The fact that Morgan had never been convicted of any sexual offences since his release from Kingston Penitentiary gave no pause for concern to Fort St. John Mayor, Steve Thorlakson. "As a parent I am personally disturbed by this. I have an eight-year-old son. I had a very, very, very, very serious conversation about the importance of not talking to strangers," the mayor said.

The mayor and one of his councillors did a lot more than talk to strangers. They talked to CBC National News. At the anchor desk, host Peter Mansbridge introduced the story on November 25, 1995:

"He is a sex offender who preys on boys, and since his release, Daniel Cody Morgan has been chased out of town and cities in three provinces. Now the people of Fort St. John, B.C. have learned he's living among them, and the city council has launched a campaign to drum him out of their town, too."

The story continued with a news clip of Fort St. John Councillor Pat Pimm saying, "Whatever it takes to make this gentleman move on, that's what we have to do in this town."

Reporter Ian Hanomansing asked Morgan for his reaction to council's move to expel him. Morgan said, "Worried. A little scared....And, at the same time, pretty frustrated." Morgan continued his explanation to the national television audience, "At some point, everybody has to be able to make a living, has to live somewhere. The…the constant harassment makes it harder, makes it more likely that any person is going to return to some type of crime because they can't make it legitimately, even if…no matter how hard they try."

Nonetheless, Fort St. John council voted to design and photocopy hundreds of posters for local groups to distribute, first in areas in the vicinity of schools. The mayor told the *Vancouver Province* that the motive was to force Morgan to leave town.

What the Town of Fort St. John and the RCMP were not counting on was the involvement of the federal and provincial privacy commissioners. Once the commissioners got involved the mayor was forced to stop distributing the posters.

Thorlakson had already faxed information to Alberta and the Yukon when B.C. Privacy Commissioner David Flaherty called persuading the mayor to discontinue the publicity campaign. The mayor commented: "We are left in the rather ironic position that, pending clarification from Mr. Flaherty, we are not currently able to spread this information around to our fellow local governments in British Columbia."

Nonetheless, the council-backed tactic of intimidation worked. Morgan was last seen hitchhiking out of town.

The Rule of Law

Most everyone would agree that Canada operates under the Rule of Law. It is the law and not caprice that determines what is a fit penalty. We have institutions that administer the law and ensure that laws are maintained. The police play a pivotal role in the administration of criminal law. They are an essential component of ensuring that our institutions remain legitimate so that the Rule of Law can be respected.

The courts are also institutions that ensure law and order are maintained. But sometimes there are pressures that if unchecked could supplant the Rule of Law as a hallmark of our legal system. We have all heard of appeals to the Court of public opinion. Public hostility to law enforcement can undermine the basic principles and institutions that form the basis of our democratic society.

Canada can also be seen as a "child-centered" society. Parents and other right-thinking people would deplore child abuse in any form. The court of public opinion is easily outraged at any notion that child abuse is tolerated.

In the Morgan case, we see a prime example of how the police have stepped over the line in enraging the public. It is a call for vigilantism. It would be politically unpopular for politicians to deter this sort of police misconduct. Morgan's harassment continued when Doug Lewis, a Progressive Conservative was Solicitor General and in charge of Canada's policing and it continued when he was replaced by Liberal Herb Gray.

We cannot look for a political answer to curtail the abusive treatment of an offender who had served out every last day of a sentence considered sufficient by the courts but deemed too lenient by many who would rather have seen him dead.

A Better Way

There must be a better way! In the first few days of January 2008, James Alfred Cooper was released from prison. He had been sentenced in Hamilton fourteen years previously.

He had been arrested and convicted of sixteen counts of sexually and physically abusing five former stepchildren and a neighbour's daughter. The victims' ages ranged from seven to fourteen.

He received no sympathy from the trial judge who said of Cooper, "You are a low-down, mean, despicable, evil manifestation of a human being that preys upon little children." He received no sympathy in the imposition of a thirty-year term of imprisonment. It was the harshest sentence ever meted out to a child-abuser in Canada. The Court of Appeal altered the sentence to twenty-one years. After serving fourteen years, Cooper was to be released on statutory release to serve the final third of his court-imposed sentence in the community.

When the then seventy-two-year-old Cooper emerged from a Kingston-area penitentiary, there as no mob demonstrating against his release. Even though his intended destination was Peterborough, no police warning was issued. Instead, he was met by Dan Haley, a chaplain and manager of Circle of Support and Accountability.

Dan Haley also met with Wray Budreo when he was released and intended to live in Peterborough. The police warning stirred so much hostility that Budreo lasted only two days in the city. Haley relocated Budreo to Toronto and assisted Budreo in successfully reintegrating into the community. Budreo died in September of 2007. He had never reoffended.

Cooper also chose to relocate to Peterborough because of the Circle of Support chapter in the city. The *Peterborough Examiner* gave Cooper's release front page coverage. This time there was no outpouring of community rage.

Haley told the *Hamilton Spectator*, "I think people are better educated now. It understands that in our judicial system, sex offenders can't be locked up forever. And when they do get out, those who do find support from a Circle have a lower rate of recidivism."

In October, 2022, The Supreme Court of Canada struck down a 2011 amendment to the Criminal Code requiring sex offenders to be added automatically to the sex offender registry as unconstitutional. Prior to 2011, the Crown prosecutor would have to ask a judge to impose an order under the Sex Offender Information Registration Act (SOIRA). A judge could make the ruling if it was the case that disclosure of the offender's privacy and liberty was in the public interest. Cancelling that discretion made certain that the badge of dishonour and public humiliation would no longer remain a constant in the offender's life. Striking this legislation down is one way the Supreme Court has signalled discontent with the offender's having to endure life-long banishment from the community.

The better way is to refrain from appealing to our basic instinct of wanting vengeance for past misdeeds. It is ensuring that released offenders are able to conduct their lives as normally as possible. Of course, their past crimes deserve our condemnation but exiling an offender and not offering the opportunity to live a reformed life is begging for further misconduct. If police agencies could concentrate on law enforcement and refrain from inciting a mob, justice will also be served.

CHAPTER 15

WHAT IMPRISONMENT
IS REALLY LIKE

A First-Hand Account by Convicted

Businessman David Dorson

By David Dorson[1]

About one in eight Canadian adults have a criminal record, yet most Canadians have little or no sense of what it is really like to be arrested, convicted of a crime and serve a prison sentence. The impressions we get from TV or movies can be highly misleading.

For anyone who does want to know more, many people have written about the experience of imprisonment, in a wide variety of ways. There are chronological accounts, focusing on events as they

---

1 *David Dorson is the pen name of someone who went through arrest, case disposition, imprisonment and parole in Ontario a few years ago. He has been granted anonymity because he offers a unique perspective on a subject that matters deeply to many readers, and revealing the author's identity would make re-establishment in the community after serving his sentence much more difficult than it already is.*

took place; psychological accounts, focusing on emotions; social accounts, focusing on the effects of incarceration on family and friends; cultural accounts, focusing on the nature of the world inside prison. Each of these has its own value and integrity. Each tells part of a complex story. And each person will have a somewhat different experience so also a different story. (One of the best places to find such accounts is in the Journal of Prisoners on Prisons, published by the University of Ottawa, to which I have also contributed, anonymously.)

As a former prisoner who also has a strong background in research and policy, I struggled with what I might best contribute. My experience is that our criminal justice system, despite its rhetoric about rehabilitation and deterrence, is actually largely about punishment and even vengeance, with the result that we do much damage to people in the name of justice, and probably creates more overall harm, even as we do not provide nearly enough support to victims of crime.

To make needed improvements in the justice system requires a systemic stance informed by research evidence. But criminal justice policy is driven by emotion to an extent rarely matched in other fields of public policy. So, to change policy means moving people's hearts and minds to want those changes. That in turn requires attention to personal experience. So in this essay, I write from an individual and experiential perspective, but also in an effort to show what could and should be done to make improvements.

I suspect that some people, those who consider themselves 'tough on crime,' will read this account as one-sided and self-centered. I do understand that the interests of the accused are certainly not the only ones at play, and return to that issue in the last part of this chapter.

From arrest to imprisonment

Imprisonment is only one part of the process that any person found guilty of a crime experiences. As soon as I was arrested, I entered a new world in which who I was, the life I had, and even what I did and why were essentially of no interest to anyone outside my personal circle. All the other groups involved were, it seemed, consumed with their own interests.

The presumption of innocence, which is talked about as a cornerstone of our legal system, exists in reality only in a very narrow and limited way. In the eyes of the police, prosecutors, and the public, and often in the eyes of employers, landlords, colleagues, and even friends, an accused person is considered guilty from the start.

Being arrested for the first time is a huge shock. My arrest was not nearly as bad as many I heard about. I was not faced with drawn guns or physical violence, which happens in many arrests, including, from what I was told, many cases where the crime was not violent. Police justify these approaches by saying that they are necessary for safety, even when this is manifestly not the case. This is one of many instances in which the actions of people in the system are guided by 'what is the worst that could happen and how do we prevent that' rather than by 'what actions seem reasonable under the circumstances.' Criminal justice is a risk-averse system and high levels of risk aversion generally lead to bad outcomes.

I was fortunate to know enough to know that I did not need to answer any questions from the police. I knew from criminal lawyers that I should say as little as possible and get legal assistance as soon as possible. Many if not most accused do not know these things and so are subject to manipulation by police that can seriously harm their ability to defend themselves.

After my arrest, the police focused on making themselves look good by making me look bad. They issued more than one press release about me, which were dutifully reported in the media without any qualification as if everything the police said was undoubtedly true. Police also used their stock phrase of believing 'there may be other victims' even though in my case no individuals ever came forward or were identified as victims of any actions of mine.

I was rather shocked to discover that in Canada being arrested and convicted of a crime does not require that there be any victims. I had naively thought that a crime had to involve creating harm when it actually has much more to do with what society fears or dislikes. Many crimes involve little or no harm to any other person, while many actions that cause great harm to other people are not crimes.

Despite its obligation to seek justice, not a conviction, the crown in my case focused on how they could convict me of the most damaging charges with the harshest penalties. Without any evidence, they made outlandish suggestions about the extent of my criminal activity (also dutifully reported in the media without qualification) and opposed my release on bail.

The judge set bail conditions not based on my possible innocence, but rather on the assumption that I was guilty. This is a common practice even though the Supreme Court has spoken out against it more than once (for example the *Antic* and *Zora* cases). As the regular furors about bail show, anger stoked by the media leads to cries for harsher treatment of those accused. It is no doubt one reason that so many people in Canada are in jail without having been found guilty.

That rush to judgment happens all the time even though nearly fifty percent of criminal charges in Ontario do NOT result in a conviction and some portion of those that do are wrongful convictions. (We will never know how many wrongful convictions there are, but there are clearly many more than are ever investigated.) Even in murder charges, only about half result in a conviction, something one would never know from media accounts.

All this means that you may, while still officially innocent and waiting for the disposition of your case, be required to abide by highly-restrictive conditions on where you can live, where you can go, whom you can associate with, what you are allowed to do and what you are required to do. Your family may be required to act as your supervisors and, for all practical purposes, jailers. You can lose your job, lose access to your children, be forced to attend counseling, be subject to a curfew, or be prohibited from consuming alcohol, whether or not any of these had anything to do with the charges against you and all before you have had any chance to defend yourself. Again, these problems have been identified many times, including by the Supreme Court, but the situation has not changed. In Canada, many people are regularly arrested and charged for violating bail conditions that would not be crimes for anyone else.

There is much more I could say about problems in the legal process, from the endless delays while your life is on hold or worse, to the giant costs of a good legal defence, to the way the system is rigged to have you plead guilty. Anyone who thinks that our system favours the accused clearly has not experienced it! In reality, the Crown has huge advantages, which is the reason that more than 90% of criminal convictions come after guilty pleas. If every accused person actually insisted on having a trial, our court system would collapse completely; we can barely cope with ten percent exercising that fundamental right. That is why those who do insist on a trial will get a harsher sentence if convicted. It is another practice that seems fundamentally unjust.

Imprisonment

In the end, nearly two years after my arrest, I pled guilty and received a three-year sentence. I spent well over a year locked up, which included several weeks in segregation in a provincial jail, several months in a federal prison Assessment Unit, about a year in a federal minimum-security prison, and then close to two years on parole, the first 4 months of that in a halfway house. In what follows I can only skim parts of that experience.

Each of these settings was very different from the others. In segregation or solitary, the key was to survive another day without giving in to despair. In my case, this was mostly possible because of the support I had outside and knowing that my stay there would be relatively short.

In the Assessment Unit, we were locked in our small, dilapidated cells (usually two to a cell) for at least sixteen hours a day. I was just trying to figure out how the system works and desperately trying to keep myself out of trouble, which could arise suddenly and for no apparent reason. I was fortunate in my time there because the prisoners who were effectively in charge of the range I was on were decent people who kept it calm and peaceful. That was certainly not always the case.

Once I got to the minimum-security prison it was possible to focus on more than just surviving; there were possibilities there to have at least some positive aspects to one's life even if the overall situation was bleak. What struck me most in that setting was how badly managed everything was. I have worked in quite a few large organizations; I have never seen one as incompetently managed as this prison. Not one single thing about it worked well. Only the prisoners seemed to care. At best, minimum security is a huge waste of public money that could be used to so much better effect.

Getting out on parole was a hugely disappointing experience. The parole system seemed much more about controlling me than about helping me reintegrate and live crime-free. Like bail, the focus is on compliance with unreasonable conditions, not on those things that might help you live properly.

More importantly, after yearning for release and the chance to rebuild my life, I soon realized that my sentence would never be over. A criminal conviction has a lifelong effect on jobs, housing, social services, friendships, and many aspects of the way we live. There is little real support for rehabilitation despite all the talk and many ways in which ex-prisoners are prevented from living positively. As the slogan goes, 'Every prison sentence is for life.' For many people, once you are convicted it will be a huge struggle against heavy odds to create a positive and satisfying life for yourself. This hardly seems the way to keep people away from crime.

Some essential features of imprisonment

Whatever one's individual experience of prison, there are some things common to everyone. I have picked just a few, and illustrated these points primarily through my own experience, though they are also born out by many conversations with others going through the experience, and by a substantial amount of writing both by prisoners and researchers.

Taken as a whole, these contentions suggest that Imprisonment works strongly against rehabilitation and therefore impairs public safety rather than improving it. Canadians would collectively be better off if we organized things so that these were not dominant aspects of the experience.

('Imprisonment' here refers both to people held in provincial jails, which is ordinarily about fifteen thousand people who are being imprisoned as they await trial and about eight thousand with sentences of less than two years, as well as some fourteen thousand in federal prisons with sentences of more than two years.)

In prison, there are few ways to use time productively.

Most of the time you are imprisoned you are doing nothing. You are locked in a cell, waiting for the next event such as a meal, yard time, or a visit. The biggest challenge facing many prisoners is how to make the hours pass in the least unpleasant way possible. There may be nothing to read. There are few productive activities. If you have some kind of job in prison it will usually occupy only a few hours and make few demands on your skills. You are unlikely to get any training or learn anything that you can use after release. If you are going to school in prison, you will usually experience schooling that is far below the level one would find in the community, and it will be very difficult to earn any meaningful credentials.

In my time in assessment, there was no schooling at all. The only work was cleaning the range, an activity that was available only for two or three out of twenty prisoners. It was no surprise that many prisoners took sleeping pills, easily available from prison doctors, to help the time pass. Or they may have watched huge amounts of TV, either in the cells if one of the prisoners was able to buy a TV or in the common room when we were let out of our cells.

In minimum security, everyone supposedly had a job, but most of these were cleaning jobs that took at most one or two hours a day; there were hardly any jobs that were meaningful or interesting. The school, where I worked as a prisoner tutor, was a farce. It was closed as much as it was open. It offered only computer-based, do-it-yourself adult basic education and limited high school courses with little or no instruction and no provision for anyone with learning difficulties. There were no choices about what you might want to study and no post-secondary options. No meaningful job training was offered despite the needs of prisoners to learn some job skills - and this in a prison that had the prisoners judged lowest risk!

Most people in prison, though certainly not all, have low levels of education and weak employment skills. Prisoners with more skill are often interested in teaching others but there is no way to do that in the system. Very few people will leave with significantly more skill or education than they had when they entered; many years in prison can only cause deterioration of skills and knowledge because of no way to apply them.

In minimum, prisoners can get some meaning from participating in various groups or associations. For example, some prisoners were very involved in music and would meet with others to play together. Some were involved in groups like AA that met regularly. But as the adage goes, 'You aren't in prison to make friends,' and most prisoners are quite cautious about how they interact with others. In one instance, I found that being generous to other prisoners, for example offering to share food, was treated with suspicion. The system makes everyone distrustful of everyone else; generosity is, sadly, regarded as an attempt to gain leverage to exploit. Prison rules actually forbid prisoners from sharing food or any possessions.

No ability to make recompense

Many prisoners desperately want to do something to make up in some way for the damage they have caused. But prison provides no opportunity to do this. Despite rhetoric from the federal government about restorative justice, there is virtually no practice of it for those locked up. There are many other ways in which prisoners might make contributions, such as through community service work. Again, though, almost none of these are permitted by prison rules, and even prisoners' desire to do something positive may be viewed with skepticism by prison staff. Yet opportunities for prisoners to demonstrate good faith and positive intentions would help them feel better and help them prepare for parole or release.

Loss of connection to people

One of the worst aspects of being imprisoned is separation from friends and families, including children. At a time when you most need the comfort of those you care about, you have the least access to them.

When considering this separation from loved ones, it should be remembered that most people in provincial jails are on remand, and have not been convicted of any crime. But even if you have been convicted, what about your spouse, children, parents – all of whom are suffering despite not having done anything wrong? Quite a bit of research has shown that children with a jailed parent typically do not do well.

Many common forms of communication, such as texting, are not available to prisoners at all, as they are not allowed phones or internet access. Phone calls can be difficult to make due to restricted access to phones and high costs; prisoners pay twenty or more times as much for phone calls as anyone else, yet there are never enough phones available so there are often long lines to use them. I spent well over a hundred dollars a month on telephone costs while in prison, an amount far beyond the reach of most prisoners.

Letters are allowed, but they may be censored, both outgoing and incoming. More than once I received a note saying that some contents of a letter had been censored. For example, letters were returned for having crayon drawings or glue, or for having press clippings included.

Visits, if they occur at all, are highly restricted in frequency and in nature. In some prisons, they only occur through glass. Many federal prisons are in out-of-the-way places that require visitors to have private transportation. One fellow prisoner told me that his eighty-five-year-old mother took the bus four hours each way, followed by a taxi ride she could ill afford, once a month in order to visit him. My observation was that about two-thirds of prisoners received no visits at all, and more than one prisoner told me that he had discouraged family from visiting because he did not want them to see him in prison. And that was in minimum security, where visiting is relatively easy. Of course, during COVID visits were cancelled entirely for long periods of time.

No privacy

Another difficult aspect of being imprisoned is the complete lack of privacy. If you are in a cell, guards can and do look in at any time. In most cells, even toilets are not private. Even in minimum security, where you may have your own room, there is a window that allows guards to look in when they wish. Most prisons also have multiple security cameras so you may be watched almost all the time. Your mail will be opened. Your phone calls may be overheard or recorded; signs to that effect are posted beside the telephones. At one point I went to see a psychologist in the prison, and the first thing she told me was that she could not promise that she would be able to keep as confidential anything I told her. You may be required to participate in a therapy group where anything you say may be reported to prison authorities.

No rights

According to the Supreme Court of Canada and under the law that governs Canada's prisons, prisoners retain all their rights as citizens except those specifically related to their imprisonment – such as freedom of movement. The reality is quite different. As a prisoner, you have no rights at all. If you complain about something you may face retaliation, and at best grievances are not taken seriously, as detailed by the Correctional Investigator. One of my housemates was the prisoner grievance officer; he told me that the prison automatically turned down every level 1 grievance without even reading them!

In prison you do not have free speech rights; what you say can and will be censored and may be used against you. You do not have assembly rights; you can only meet with others in ways approved by the prison. You do not have property rights; you can only obtain and have those things expressly approved by the prison. You do not have any right to free movement; you can only go where and when you are told or allowed.

Even legal rights are not honoured in practice. Supposedly you have a right to access your lawyer but just try reaching one by phone! Any prisoner who is seen as too demanding of his rights is likely to be ill-treated by the system. For example, a prisoner may be transferred to another institution.

As another example, I was required to take a therapeutic program, even though the official prison rating system did not indicate that I should. This was overridden by a Correctional Service of Canada official, likely because my case was high profile. I was given a choice; I could decline to take the program, but the result would be that I would not be considered for parole. In theory, my right to choose was respected, but in practice, it was not. Nor was there any hearing or way of appealing this decision.

Judges seem to think that they can include in their sentences provisions about what should happen to someone in terms of, for example, treatment or therapy. But once you are sentenced, CSC has total control over what happens to you, and they are under no obligation to follow anything a judge has suggested, nor does a judge have any way to enforce her or his wishes for a prisoner. It is sadly mistaken to think that prisoners will get meaningful help for, say, mental health or addiction issues.

Parole, release, and rebuilding your life

I was amazed to find that the prison provided me with no written information on how the parole process works, even though this is so important to prisoners. Another thing I learned early as a new prisoner is that institutional parole officers may mislead or even lie to you about the process. For example, parole officers tell you that you cannot apply without their support, when in fact I saw many cases where parole was granted even when the internal parole officer did not support it. One prisoner I knew well told me that when he asked his parole officer about applying for parole, he was told she would not support his application because in her opinion he had not yet spent enough time in prison, even though he was eligible to apply. Many prisoners I knew were encouraged if not told by their parole officers that they should defer applying for a hearing.

At that time, and still now, almost all parole grants are for day parole, which meant you had to live in a halfway house, officially called a CRF (community residential facility). Living in a halfway house made sense for prisoners who were released with no home to go to. It did not make sense for prisoners who had a stable home situation to which they could return. Instead of living at home with my family, I had to spend 4 months sleeping (because I did not need to be there at all during the day) in an uncomfortable facility, taking up a bed that could have been used by another prisoner who was spending weeks or months extra in prison after parole was granted waiting for a space.

Parole comes with many problematic restrictions and requirements. For example, you must phone in several times a day as to your whereabouts, but you can only phone from a landline, not a cell phone. Yet landlines are no longer easy to find; people do not have them in their homes, and pay phones hardly exist. This meant that I sometimes had to find a subway station because they have payphones, or to go into a restaurant and ask if I could use their phone.

Another example is travel. I live in Toronto and my parole condition, as is standard, was that I could not leave the city limits without written permission from my parole officer. This might have made sense at one time in the past, but in my case, it meant that if I wanted to drive my wife to the airport or pick up one of my children who was visiting, I needed written permission from my parole officer because the airport is not in Toronto proper.

I had three community parole officers in my twenty-one months of parole, each of whom had different rules, which they did not always bother to tell me about. I once got a written reprimand because the procedure I used, approved by my former parole officer, was not accepted by my new one. No warning, just a written reprimand, which could be a prelude to being rearrested and returned to prison. Another person I knew had some conflict with his parole officer. He was sent back to prison, only to have the Parole Board release him again saying there were no legitimate grounds for his being re-imprisoned. Meanwhile, he had 4 more months of imprisonment, lost another job, and had more family issues and other difficulties all because a parole officer acted arbitrarily.

For these reasons released prisoners do not generally see their parole officers as helpful. You try to tell your parole officer as little as possible because, as in prison, anything you say may be used against you. By the time you are on parole, you are well aware that the system continues to see you as a criminal, someone to be treated with suspicion rather than support.

One of the biggest problems most parolees and ex-prisoners have is finding employment. It is very hard to find any kind of decent job with a criminal record. I was lucky enough to be able to retire, but the experience of those I met was really quite dreadful, with little or no support available. And it was worse for anyone who already had some kind of labour market credential such as a professional qualification since they were often stripped of these. How do we expect people to rebuild their lives if they cannot find decent work?

We are conditioned to see imprisonment as the appropriate penalty for many kinds of wrongdoing, without giving much thought to why or how the punishment fits the crime. A great deal of coverage of crime talks about harsh sentences as a way of giving 'justice' or 'closure' to victims. Of course, people can be genuinely angered by the harm done by some criminal actions; the lives of victims can be permanently damaged by criminal action.

Yet if the only thing we offer victims is harsh punishment of those who harmed them, what does that make us? Canada does not do a good job of supporting victims of crime financially or socially. We do not do enough to help people cope with damage to their lives, whether that damage is caused by crime or by accidents. But making someone else miserable is not an effective or justifiable way to help anyone feel or live better. The desire for revenge is understandable but cannot bring long-term satisfaction and should not be a purpose of social policy. Instead, our goal should always be to minimize harm - to all parties.

Conclusion

An essay like this can only scratch the surface of the experience of being imprisoned, let alone all the ancillary issues it raises around how a society understands and tries to practice justice around wrongful behaviour. I have omitted entirely some key areas, such as the terrible (and insufficient) food in many prisons, the lack of access to programs even when required for parole, or the sense of impotence and humiliation that prisoners experience much of the time. What I hope I have shown is how our existing system actually creates more harm, at a fearful cost both in its financial impact and in its degradation and destruction of the human spirit. We could do so much better.

CHAPTER 16

BOTH SIDES NOW

Michael Crowley, Senior Parole Board
Member and His Experience on Arrest

By Michael Crowley

M y perspective on parole primarily comes from my experiences of spending three years as a member of the Ontario Board of Parole and then the Parole Board of Canada for another twenty-one years.

Not bad for a convicted (and recipient of a Presidential Pardon) felon in the United States, I suppose. And my opinion is that my experience of having left the US because of my opposition to the war in Vietnam, and the legal consequences that I went through, shaped my eventual career, and the way I tried to treat others who were involved in the criminal justice system in Canada.

The Origin Story

I was born in 1945 and grew up in Central New York in a typically Republican family. I pretty much played by the rules, obeyed the law, went to church weekly, and was a Boy Scout. When I first attended Siena College, a Roman Catholic school, I had to participate in the Reserve Officer Training Corps (ROTC) and seriously considered continuing in it for four years so that I would graduate as a Second Lieutenant in the air force. I also thought about becoming a priest but I don't know if I was ever serious about that. Nonetheless, I was pretty white bread and square.

But then in the mid-sixties, the U.S. found itself being drawn into a war in Southeast Asia. By 1966 I had transferred to Syracuse University and majored in political science with a minor in religion. The notion of a war that seemed to continue growing; one without a declaration of war from Congress, gnawed at me, and so I researched and wrote about the concept of a 'just war' in Constitutional Law class as well as one in Comparative Religions. The result of these studies led me to conclude that the war was not justifiable, either legally or on religious grounds.

While Syracuse tended to be a fairly liberal campus in some respects, there were few anti-war outlets. While I did participate in some demonstrations, usually on campus, I did my best to be assured that none would lead to violence or any illegal activity. During a summer semester, I met up with a young female student that I knew, and she asked if I would like to join her in their planned demonstration that morning. I asked what they were planning to do, and her reply was that they were going to do a sit-in in the Dean's office. That didn't sound promising, so I politely declined. The demonstration went ahead and all of the students were expelled as a consequence. Clearly, I made the right choice.

Campus Demonstrations

I did demonstrate against DOW Chemicals recruiting students on campus. I did so because I thought the use of napalm, which DOW apparently invented, was a heinous weapon to use as it clearly did more than defoliate trees; it clung to and horribly burned anyone with whom it came into contact. This included civilians and there were photographs, some famous, of children who had been burned. So, I spent one morning with about 12 other students picketing the building where DOW recruiters were interviewing students. It was also my last demonstration because it felt that no matter what we (or I) did, it would have no impact on the war. In fact, the majority of students either ignored us and the moral questions we raised or became aggressive toward us. I guess I also was tired of having my photograph taken by whatever police forces were nearby.

Off-campus, I also participated in a weekly, Quaker-sponsored, silent, and non-violent demonstration that took place at noon in downtown Syracuse, directly in front of a well-known jewelry store. Similar demonstrations took place across the country. There were never more than 14 of us, both young men and women, and the males always dressed in sports coats and ties, in order to show our respect for the community. We were taunted on occasion but there were never any real threats to our safety.

Although I had been against the war for a while before I graduated, most of my family was unaware of my stance. I was very circumspect and cautious about revealing my feelings. I told my brother (who was in the Army at the time) and a couple of my cousins. I didn't really trust anyone else.

I think I always had a strong sense of right and wrong, or of some things being fair or unfair. I respected rules and feared consequences, but at the same time understood that rules should be fair and not capricious.

I had registered for the draft when I turned eighteen because the law required it, and carried that card with me, again because it was required. Through my four years in university I received a deferment, which meant that as long as I remained a student, I would not be drafted. I don't believe that I gave much thought to the draft, and during my first two years in college, had given serious thought to becoming a member of the army at graduation. But then that changed, as I matured, grew distant from the church, and researched what was actually happening in Vietnam.

After I completed my education at Syracuse my draft status changed, and I was now considered to be quite draft eligible. Still, I had not given a lot of thought to my options, primarily because I had undergone back problems from high school, and had been advised by doctors that there was an issue with my vertebrae. In other words, I thought I would fail the physical.

However, that was not the case and I learned that my back had been misdiagnosed. I passed the physical and the early Fall of 1968 and then was sent a letter telling me to report to the draft Board in January for induction.

At the time I was working as a civil servant in Albany, the State capitol, and for the first time, I really had to consider what to do. Failing to report for the draft was a federal crime and one that could lead to a fine of fifty-thousand dollars and/or a prison term of five years. To give myself more time to decide what to do, I had my draft Board changed from Syracuse to Albany because I had moved, and I knew that doing so would delay the process for a few months. Hopefully, that would allow me sufficient time to figure out my next moves.

My choices were limited. I could have avoided going into the army by claiming status as a Conscientious Objector. This would have led to my doing some other, alternative service, such as working as an orderly in a hospital (for instance). But to obtain that status one had to be against all war at all times. And that was not how I felt. I believed some wars were justified. I also realized that it was difficult for a Roman Catholic to successfully make that claim as the church was not opposed to war.

Dodging the Draft

In addition, one of my older cousins had married a guy named Peter, who was in the Marines as a helicopter pilot. I didn't really know him all that well, because he was about five years older than me, and wasn't around much after he had become a Marine and was posted to various locations during training.

Then, in the summer of 1965, Peter was wounded while leading a patrol in the jungle. The wounds were serious, damaging his leg sufficiently that he had to be hospitalized and undergo operations, leading to a permanent disability. Peter returned to Syracuse and also decided to return to school, Syracuse University. We became very close friends during the two years that we spent together, both majoring in political science.

I revealed to him my opposition to the war, and my tentative plans, after graduation, to leave the country. He was totally supportive, and in my mind, Peter's support was crucial in making up my mind about what to do or where to go.

I knew that some guys were leaving the country and going to Sweden, which seemed to be happy to welcome them. But that (for me) was just too much of a stretch. I also knew that others were going to Canada and that if accepted as an immigrant, could not be extradited back to the U.S. to be arrested.

I had been to Canada a few times as a teenager but really knew nothing about it. I knew that there was a province that mostly spoke French, and knew that there were some big cities, like Montreal, Toronto, and Vancouver. But that really was about it.

Still, I did not want to go to prison, and I certainly didn't want to fight in a war that was, in my view, illegal and immoral. So going to Canada became my choice.

In the days and weeks that came and went, I received a booklet provided by a Quaker organization that helped draft-age immigrants to Canada understand the process by which Canada agreed to accept someone as a "Landed Immigrant." This status allowed the individual to work or attend school while waiting five years in order to become a citizen.

Lucky for me, my girlfriend, who was still in her last year of college, agreed to marry me, in spite of having to leave the U.S. and forego her plan to attend graduate school in California.

I conducted research on the three largest cities, and finally settled on Toronto as the place to go to, at least initially. It seemed to be large, English-speaking, and one with a good economy. Plus, it had the advantage of being relatively close to Syracuse, in the event some family members or friends ever chose to visit.

As my planning continued, I obtained a copy of the application form to be used when asking for immigrant status in Canada. So, I filled that in and attached a photograph. I decided to shave the beard I had grown while working in Albany so that I would appear to be a clean-shaven, eager applicant, and then decided not to re-grow it until I had acquired a job.

A few days before the date I had picked to leave the U.S., I telephoned the Anti-Draft program in Toronto. They asked where I was intending to go, and after I said it was Toronto, they told me which bridge to cross, which day of the week, and what time frame to use. So I was told to cross at the Queenston-Lewiston Bridge, on a weekday morning, between 10 and 11 am. I assumed that they knew which Immigration officers would be on duty who would be most receptive to people like me.

Arrival in Canada

After a sleepless night at a motel in Niagara Falls, New York, I crossed into Canada on March 24th, 1969. The interview went smoothly, though I thought I had blown it at the end, when they asked for my address in Toronto, as I had never been there. But individuals applying for immigrant status were apparently supposed to have spent time in Canada, decided to stay, and to ask for official status. The Anti-Draft people told me that they believed the Immigration officers were onto their office address, so advised me to use a different address; that of 44 St. George Street. When I gave that address the officer who had been conducting the interview asked me if that was near the University of Toronto. I had no idea, of course, but he seemed pretty positive, so I said that it was. But he then said to his colleague that he doubted the validity of that address. It didn't sound like a residence but rather an office. Then he turned to me and said that once I got an address, I should send it to them, and they would send my Landed Immigrant card to me. And that it was happened. Indeed 44 St. George Street was on the University of Toronto campus and was an alternative office for the Anti-Draft program. When I did find a room (and kitchen/shared bathroom) to rent, it was at 300 St. George Street. True to my conservative nature, I thought if I had the street name right, I could tell the Immigration Officer that I had simply gotten the number wrong.

Finding employment was not easy. I had been a junior level personnel administrator previously and I believed my best chances at obtaining a job would be at a similar position at a larger company. But I was unsuccessful, mostly (I think) because the companies were American-owned, or because they had mandatory training located in the U.S.

Eventually I gave up and decided to apply to the Metropolitan Toronto government. After a nice discussion with the person responsible for hiring, he told me that the single job that I was qualified for was that of a Welfare Worker. Nothing in my background would have prepared me for such a job, but I asked when I would start. Only to be told that there was a waiting list, and that they would keep in touch.

Working Inside the System

A few months later I was contacted, accepted the job, and began a lengthy career in positions dealing with people who were either in need of social assistance, or had become part of the criminal justice system. I remained a Welfare Worker for three years; it was a job that allowed me to experience things that I had never considered previously. I found people who had little but were happy to share what they had, and people who (like me) had to start their lives over, in a new city or new province, knowing no one but possessing a spirit of hope. I also found people who were doing their best to defraud the system, and to receive welfare when they did not qualify.

After three years I had learned all that I could and hoped for something different in my future. As it turned out, there was a

Provincial Probation Officer who used our offices for interviewing his clients once or twice a month. I discovered he was a draft dodger from Nebraska and that his pay was significantly higher than mine, even though he was at the bottom of the pay scale and I was at the top, for roughly equivalent jobs.

Good fortune smiled on me at that point, because my first Canadian friend, who had prepared the resume I used, had become a personnel officer for the Ontario government's Ministry of Corrections. He managed to get me into an interview for a position as a Probation and Aftercare officer. But I knew nothing about probation and did not prepare for the interview. Nonetheless, I did well enough that (he told me) I would be in the next competition and was virtually assured of a job offer.

He was right, as it turned out, though I still didn't know anything about probation. Nonetheless, in 1973 I became a newly minted Probation and Parole Officer for the Province of Ontario; a job I held for six years. More importantly, it led to a love for the field of criminal justice; one that remains with me until today.

Of course, I knew very little about the causes of crime, or the desistance of crime when I started. The training was excellent, but still mostly theoretical. In doing the job, I had to learn how to develop an interest in people, in the factors that likely led them to commit crimes and what they needed to do in order to not reoffend.

I wrote Pre-Sentence Reports (PSRs) for Courts, Pre-Parole Reports for the Ontario Parole Board, supervised a caseload of up to a hundred and forty probationers and gave evidence in Court if a probationer violated the terms of their probation. It was a slow learning curve because I started at zero. I had taken one criminology course in university, and while it was interesting, it was a course that only scratched the surface of understanding criminal behaviour.

Nonetheless, I gradually became fascinated by the job, though not the paperwork. But exploring what I thought were the reasons why people committed crime and why they eventually desisted from continuing intrigued me.

The majority of the offenders on my caseload were young, mostly between ages sixteen to twenty-six. I thought, based on my gut instinct or popular literature, that kids likely turned to crime as a result of cruel or insensitive parenting practices; or because of single-parenting. I thought kids with such parents would rebel at school, perhaps to get attention or to form friendships with others who had similar backgrounds.

What I actually found was different. I learned that many of these teenagers came from intact and often middle-class families. They were not neglected nor were they abused. Instead, I realized that they experienced inconsistent parenting. Where rules changed daily, or where punishments were delayed or never enforced. And teenagers tend to push boundaries; to see what they could get away with. At home that may have worked, but in society the law was different; it was codified and breaking the law led to arrests (often) rather than indifference.

I realized that my experiences were different from many of my colleagues who worked in urban areas, similar to the places where I had been a Welfare Worker. I also learned that younger offenders could be motivated to change their behaviour if they believed that continuing would lead to the loss of something they cared about. In some cases, it was a job, or a car, or a girlfriend. My goal was to learn what was important to each person, and to lead them to conclude that the potential for losing that object was real. In those cases, I could then help.

During that time, I learned how to interview and the importance of being transparent and truthful. If I promised that I would help someone find or keep a job, I made sure that I followed through. It was also during this time that I went through an experience that was difficult, but had an enormous impact on my life.

Getting Arrested

I left the United States in March, 1969 fully intending on becoming a Canadian citizen as soon as I was able, while acknowledging that my actions meant I could not return to reside there. I committed what I considered to be a very serious crime, and knew that there was a significant price to pay.

While I felt that my cousins who were close to me in age would accept my actions, I also felt that the majority of my older relatives

THE REST OF THE STORY | 335

would not. My mother was angry with me and would not accept my rationale for leaving. My fiancée and I were married in Toronto in June, 1969 and we invited very few people to come, mostly because I didn't think others would attend. My wife's family did not come nor did my brother but he was in Europe after finishing his time in the US Army.

Over the next few years, we had a few relatives come to visit us in Toronto but these were scarce. The exception was my cousin Lynn and her husband Peter who had been a Marine in Vietnam. They came for a visit, with their young children, every year, in spite of the distance they lived from Toronto and having limited vacation time. One year they were in Syracuse and tried to borrow a car so they could come to see us. None of my relatives agreed to lend a car, so they took a bus to Niagara Falls; my wife drove across the border to pick them up while I waited on the Canadian side.

Nonetheless, as various family events occurred and I could not attend, it began to bother me, as I grew up in a close-knit Italian family (though I am also half Irish). There were weddings and funerals, and some cousins were becoming involved in show business as actors or directors.

I knew I would be arrested if I tried to sneak across the border to see them. But I also knew that the only way possible for me to be able to see my family would be to clear my case. That meant I would have to go through the court process. I felt that while I would never return to reside there, that it would be nice to have permission to visit, perhaps for brief periods of time.

So, in 1974 I began the process of doing whatever was necessary to be able to return for visits. My family obtained a lawyer in Syracuse, a man who was a former assistant Federal prosecutor and through him, initiated a discussion with the Justice Department. Eventually we agreed that I would return at Christmas of that year. The Justice Department would provide a letter that I would take with me to the border, so that I would not be arrested, but assured the Border authorities that I would be turning myself in the following morning.

Although I did not receive that letter prior to setting out for the border, I decided to try anyway, and to explain to the officers there what I was doing. Gerald Ford was President at the time, and had started an Amnesty program for people like me (draft dodgers) as the war had ended.

The process at the border took approximately five hours to complete; due at least in part to my not having that letter. But the first officer I spoke with was kind; he sent a Telex to the FBI office nearest Syracuse, letting them know I was returning and that I was turning myself in, so that they were not to arrest me. The border services were divided between Customs and Immigration and so once he cleared me, I had to go down the hall, and go through the same questions with the other department. Then they had to Telex the FBI with the same message.

It was mentally draining but also somewhat exhilarating. We spent the night at my mother's apartment, and then the next morning I went to the office of my lawyer and had a brief conversation. Then he and I left his building, entered a different office building, and met with another lawyer. But this person was also a Magistrate and at the end of our rather brief discussion, we left the building. I remember turning to my lawyer once outside and asked him what had just happened, as it was not clear to me. So, he explained that I had, indeed, turned myself in, and that I was released on my own recognizance! I had no idea!

A few months later I received a letter from the Federal Court or the Justice Department ordering me to report to the Federal Court in Albany, New York for my first appearance. My lawyer explained procedures. My intention was to plead guilty but he advised that I should plead not guilty instead. I was told the court would not be prepared to accept a guilty plea at this early stage.

I flew from Toronto to Albany; this was my first time flying to the U.S. of course, and I didn't know that I had to go through U.S. Customs at the Toronto airport before being allowed to board the plane. The officer I spoke to asked me for the purpose of my visit, so, I asked what my choices were, and he said it was either business or pleasure. Well, it certainly wasn't pleasure, so I said, "Business" to which he asked what was the nature of my business. I didn't want to go through a whole battery of questions so after a moment's hesitation, I replied that I was a Probation Officer (showing him my ID) and that I was a attending a trial in Albany. He waved me through! I figured I didn't lie.... but perhaps didn't tell the entire truth.

Appearing in Court

That first court appearance was interesting. The courtroom was filled with people, not because of me, but apparently the press was in attendance for some reason. That led to the story of a Probation Officer in Canada being charged with draft evasion being prominent in both local newspapers. The judge didn't know what to make of me, because he knew that President Ford had proposed an amnesty program and the judge wanted to know why I was in court, rather than taking advantage of the amnesty. I didn't speak but my lawyer said that I was a Canadian and that I wanted to remain in Canada. Again, I was remanded in my own custody, but first I had to be fingerprinted and have my photos taken by the U.S. Marshals.

Many more months went by before anything happened and I was getting tired of the wait. I knew that I had to have a Pre-Sentence Investigation completed before I could be sentenced, so I called my lawyer and suggested I would be prepared to have the PSI completed voluntarily before my plea, so that I could plead guilty in the morning and be sentenced in the afternoon of the same day.

And that is what happened.

The Sentencing

When I stood up to be sentenced, I felt totally helpless. In most cases both the Federal Probation Department and the Prosecutor make sentencing recommendations to the presiding judge. Neither did in my case. I believe that was because of the unusual nature of my case there were no precedents for either office to use as examples.

So there I stood. The judge really knew nothing about me, other than the information contained in the PSI; but that was mostly factual information and could not possibly describe why I chose to defy the law, or explain my motivation for returning to be arrested. I could still be sentenced to up to five years in prison, and fined up to fifty-thousand dollars.

The judge said that he didn't really care that I had chosen a career in criminal justice or that I had apparently lived a pro-social life and then he sentenced me to two years! Then, he said the sentence would be suspended and I would be placed on probation for those two years. I sighed with relief.

In the U.S. system it is the Chief Probation Officer that sets the conditions of probation, rather than the judge, as it happens in Canada. So I had to go downstairs to the probation office. That was when it hit me. I would be going into a probation office as a client, and not an officer. I sagged before I opened the door and saw a waiting room filled with convicted offenders (like me). But I didn't have to wait as the receptionist was waiting for me and ushered me directly into the Chief's office. The Chief, Frank Waterson, was quite welcoming and only required that I send him a form every month, which I did by registered mail. And each month, in the box which asked if I had any contact with known criminals in the past period, I always said "yes, it's my job."

Being Pardoned

Less than two years later I received a Presidential Pardon from President Carter. It was not specific to me, but to anyone else who had been convicted of draft evasion. But that experience, of going through the court process, stayed with me. And to a great degree informed how I would try to treat people when I was a parole Board member.

After spending six years in the field as a probation officer, I was promoted to becoming the Executive Assistant to the Director of Probation and then to being the Director of the branch of the Ministry of Correctional Services for its halfway houses. Following that I left government and worked for a non-profit Therapeutic Community that provided substance treatment in a residential program for Young Offenders. My responsibilities were varied but most often was tasked with interviewing young offenders (under eighteen) to determine if they would be accepted into the program, rather than going into secure custody. I know that the three years I spent with this agency honed my skills at interviewing individuals in stressful situations.

After doing this for six years, I returned to work for the Provincial Government in Ontario in 1992. The New Democratic Party had won the recent election in Ontario and decided to fill government appointments through an open process. So when I saw that the

Parole Board was advertising for people to apply for Regional Vice Chair (RVC) positions, I applied and was successful. There was an interview, by telephone, probably the first time that procedure was used. I was asked for recommendations from anyone in government. I did know any such person and had no letters of support; frankly I didn't know that this was unusual.

I was the RVC for the Western Region of the Board with an office in what had been the Superintendent's house on the grounds of Guelph Correctional Centre. This was a medium security institution located in a small city west of Toronto. The region stretched from there all the way down to Windsor, across the river from Detroit, and contained a number of small jails, large detention centres and one correctional centre. My role was to oversee the Members, both part-time and full-time as well as the staff in the office. I participated in conducting hearings as often as I could, partly as a quality check on the other members, but also because I appreciated the experience.

Oddly, while I had written a number of Pre-Parole Reports for the Ontario Board and was the liaison with the probation service, I had never observed a parole hearing. In fact, although I asked permission to do so, the Chair of the Board refused. This meant that I really had no idea what a parole hearing would be like.

Serving on the Parole Board

Provincial inmates serve a maximum sentence of two years less one day, then are released with no supervision. But Provincial offenders also had the option of applying for parole and when they did, a hearing would be conducted and even though a sentence of a year (for example) may not seem very long, it is. Especially for someone who has not been in jail before.

I still remember the first hearing I participated in. The offender was a young man who was serving a sentence for robbery. At the time there were always three Board members, and a full-time member was always the lead Board member. So that was me, even though I was new to the process. I don't remember the facts of the case, just that he was a first-time offender who had been led into his role by more mature and more criminally-minded friends. After we were done with our questions the young man left the room while we discussed what decision to make. It was a fairly straight-forward decision to grant the release. I wrote the decision, which was then read out to the inmate after he came back in. The normal practice was to go through the negatives of a case, then comment on his progress while incarcerated and finally the decision.

When he came back, he was quite on edge. And as I started reading, he started crying, convinced he was going to be denied. I saw the tears and didn't know what to do. I started reading faster, but that didn't help. So I finally just cut to the final sentence, and told him we were granting parole.

I thought about my experiences of being in court and how I felt when this stranger had my life, or at least my future, in his hands, and decided that in future, I would always just give the decision first, and then provide the reasons. Those three years allowed me to learn a great deal about how the system works; the importance of professional reports and programs, and the value of halfway houses. The Board had had little contact with Probation and Parole Officers, even though they provided fairly brief reports about an inmate's release plan. In general, our only meaningful contact took place when an officer wanted to have a warrant issued in order to have a person on parole returned to custody because of an alleged breach of a condition, or because they had committed new offences. A parole officer required the approval of a full-time member of the Board before a warrant could be issued, unless the incident took place after normal working hours or on a weekend. Although the legislation that governed parole in Canada applied both to Provincial parole authorities and to the Parole Board of Canada, there were some important differences. In Ontario, offenders were not provided with copies of the information that the Board used in its decision-making. The opposite was true with the National Parole Board. While victims could contact the Board there were no staff assigned to assist them, and no uniform policy regarding how to handle any information they provided. Again, the offenders would not be permitted to read any correspondence, such as victim impact statements that were sent to the Board. In addition, the federal legislation (the *Corrections and Conditional Release Act*) defined parole as being both day parole and full parole. Day parole was for a maximum of six months, and required an offender to reside at a community correctional centre or halfway house during that time with restricted access to the community. Provincially, Ontario only had full parole. This meant that if we believed an offender would benefit from residing in a halfway house, we had to impose that as a special condition. In fact, an offender had to agree to the condition, otherwise it was not likely that the halfway house would agree to accept them.

I served as a Vice Chair for the three years of my appointment, and anticipated being re-appointed once, as that was the norm. However, the government changed during my final year, and the new government chose not to reappoint anyone who had been appointed by the New Democratic Party and was at the end of their appointments. This was pretty devastating to me personally, as I was fifty years-old and out of work without any sense of what I would do for income. For about ten years I had been on the Board of the International Halfway House Association (IHHA). The other Board members and most of the regular members, both individuals and agencies, were located in the United States. I had developed close friendships with a few of these others, some of whom were responsible for operating large, non-profit organizations, and they reassured me that they would help in some way.

This led to my creating my own consulting company (Criminal Justice International) and allowed me to spend the next two years assisting organizations learn how to improve the quality of what they were doing with offenders. I became an "expert qualified trainer" in the use of a risk assessment instrument called the Level of Service Inventory (LSI), and trained staff in halfway houses in

New Jersey (for example) and in a prison in Texas. I trained staff over a period of two days, and then required that they video-tape a few of their interviews with their clients, then I would review the tapes for quality assurance. The training that I went through to become a trainer was intense; but I was fortunate that one of the two psychologists who created the LSI was a close friend and I was able to ask him countless questions that helped me to clarify or better understand the factors that were generally responsible for criminal behaviour.

In 1995 I learned that the National Parole Board of Canada (later changed to the Parole Board of Canada or the PBC) was advertising for openings for both full-time and part-time members. I applied and was successful at being selected as a part-time member. This is a complicated process but essentially it meant that I received an Order in Council from Parliament for a three-year appointment. Because it was not full-time, I continued operating my consulting company, and for many months either flew to the United States on a Monday morning, or drove to Kingston, Ontario (the headquarters of the Ontario Region of the PBC) on a Sunday night. Working part-time generally entailed one or two weeks per month.

In 1998 I was appointed to a full-time position for five years. This required that I had to live within commuting distance of the office in Kingston. This city of 130,000 is the regional headquarters for both the Board and the Correctional Service of Canada, a separate organization that is responsible for operating prisons and for the staff who work in those prisons or supervise individuals who have been released into the community. Normally anyone who is appointed to the Board can anticipate being reappointed, though that is never a guarantee, something I had already learned with my Provincial experience. One generally required some level of political support from the party that was in power at the time an appointment was due. And everyone is told that the maximum anyone can be appointed for is ten to twelve years. I was fortunate in that I spent the next twenty-one years as a member, and was appointed by both Liberal and Conservative governments, something that was apparently quite unusual.

Being a Board Member carries (and should carry) a great deal of weight and responsibility. The Board's mandate is primarily to ensure public safety through the timely release of offenders. If an offender is assessed as posing an undue risk to the community by reoffending, they should not be granted a discretionary (day or full parole) release. In the federal system an offender (generally) is released, nonetheless, after serving two-thirds of their sentence on what is called "Statutory Release." In those cases, the Board's responsibility is to impose special conditions that are intended to assist the individual in reintegration but also to reduce the risk they would otherwise pose. The majority of decisions made by the Board are based solely on file information, rather than through the conduct of hearings, unlike public perception.

Parole hearings (normally) are held inside federal prisons. Sometimes the hearing rooms are in separate buildings but mostly they are found in the administrative section of a particular institution, rather than being near the living units or cells of the inmates. The rooms that are used generally have other purposes, and are often set up in boardroom style, with seating on three sides and a table in the middle that is used by the inmate and his or her assistant. Usually, the only participants in the hearing are the Board members and Hearing Officer) the staff member who manages the hearing process), the offender (and assistant) and the institutional parole officer. On occasion members of the inmate's family or friends are present, but that is more the exception than the norm.

Additionally, registered victims of the offender's index offence (the crime that led to their federal sentence) attend hearings, and often they provide written impact statements in advance of the hearing, and then may read their statements before the hearing starts. Board members are usually given one day of preparation for each day of hearings. Some inmate files are relatively small, containing two or three hundred pages of material. Much of it is related to the inmate's criminal history, police reports and judges' reasons regarding the index offence. There are also classification reports or other documents that assess the relative dangerousness of the inmate as well as a projection as to the likelihood that the inmate will reoffend prior to the end of their sentence. More complex cases; particularly for offenders serving lengthy or life sentences, may contain thousands of pages of documents.

Every member prepares differently for hearings. I always went through each document, highlighting those sections that I thought might be relevant in assessing risk, and took many pages of notes.

Following my review, I would focus on what I thought were the most critical aspects that we needed to bring out during the hearing, and then create an outline of those areas. I never wrote questions out ahead of time. Normally I would just jot down a few words that reminded me of the particular concern that I wanted to follow up on. When I started conducting hearings, I was fairly nervous. After all, although I had supervised offenders, interviewed many hundreds more, had worked with drug addicts and trained people to do risk assessments, the enormity of the decisions I was making was not lost on me. I still remember the first hearing I was a part of. As a new member I really wasn't expected to take the lead by being the first Board member to ask questions of the person up for parole consideration. It is usually an experienced member was expected to take the lead and to make the decision. My first case was a post suspension hearing; an offender had been suspended for violating one of the conditions he was required to follow. I don't remember any of the details of the case, but what startled me was that he was a lifer, a man serving a life sentence for murder. The informality of the process struck me along with the rather gentle probing of my colleague. I recall thinking "But he killed someone! How can we give him a second chance?" But we did; we cancelled the suspension and allowed him to return to the community. In theory, I realized this was the right decision; but the harsh reality of who we were dealing with was made very real on that day. Knowing what it was like when I was in court some years earlier, I tried my best to develop rapport with each person who appeared before us. I knew that most inmates, especially the ones

THE REST OF THE STORY | 349

who were new to the process were going to be nervous. After all, we were either going to grant a release, or require that they remain in custody.

At the outset of a hearing, the Board's staff person, known as a Hearing Officer (HO) goes through a number of procedural steps and safeguards, so that the offender will know what to expect. This is a requirement, even though the offender has likely been given that information and advice by their parole officer, fellow inmates and other staff. Nonetheless, I always listened carefully to the inmate's responses to the questions put to them; partly to be able to see how nervous they might actually be or what level of language or tone I should use when questioning them. If they seemed ill-at-ease or bewildered by something the HO had said, I would stop the proceeding and ask if they needed clarification or more information.

I remember a young man from Newfoundland who had never been in trouble and had committed a non-violent offence. His father had flown in from Newfoundland to support his son, but still he was so nervous that his knuckles were literally white gripping the papers he had. I knew that I had to ease into the hearing, rather than having it be quite as formal as it usually was. So, I just pointed out his white knuckles, and said we would talk about his release plan first, and then work backwards to his history and the offence. He breathed a huge sigh and I knew we were going to be OK.

A Good Hearing

A good hearing, in my view, was more like a conversation than an inquisition, even though that was how the Board did its job. That is, the members ask questions in order to elicit or confirm information. This process is unlike that of court, where the Crown and defence attorneys elicit information from witnesses so that a third party, either the judge or jury, makes a decision as to guilt or innocence. If I thought someone was deliberately lying to me, I would try to point out the discrepancy, based on file information, and then challenge the inmate to explain.

There was more than one occasion when I believed, again based on file information including witness statements from court, that the offender was minimizing their role in the index offence.

But at the same time, I was less concerned than some of my colleagues about some of those details. I was more interested in knowing whether the inmate understood the reasons why the offence occurred, rather having them recite what had taken place. I knew recollections could be faulty, and I tested that theory out from time to time. In preparing for certain hearings of inmates I had previously seen, I sometimes would listen to the tape recording of that prior hearings, primarily to refresh my memory about what had been said. And I realized, more often than not, that my 'faultless' memory was generally wrong! Although my recall of the gist of the conversation was generally accurate, I was wrong about what both I and the inmate had actually said, or what had transpired during the hearing.

For me that was an important lesson. It meant that while individuals might have firm 'recollections' about what they said or did at a particular point in time – that did not mean those memories were accurate and I started putting less emphasis on trying to have their recollections about historic events match file information.

Listening to Victims of Crime

During my time on the Board, victims of crimes had always been able to send letters or other submissions in advance of parole hearings. They could also attend hearings, but were not able to make any statements. But that changed in 2001 and after a training period, I chaired the first hearing in Ontario in which victims read their statements.

These Victim Impact Statements (VIS) must be shared with offenders, as they always had been the case. But the emotional impact of a victim reading their statement changed the nature of hearings. In 1976 Jon Rallo killed his wife and two young children in Hamilton, Ontario. He was convicted of first-degree Murder (times three) and his parole eligibility was set automatically at twenty-five years. His wife's parents wrote numerous, lengthy and detailed letters regularly to the Board, in their attempts to keep him from being paroled. Rallo applied for and received Escorted Temporary Absences (ETAs) for a number of years prior to his parole eligibility. The first time I did a hearing with him was for a continuation of those ETAs. His in-laws attended the hearing and had written the Board but were unable to speak.

Although I was familiar both with the details of the case (Rallo has never admitted the murders) and the views of the victims, I acutely remember the first time I was involved in a hearing in which they read their statements. It was riveting and so emotional that I had to find a way to not weep as I listened to this older couple describe the pain of the losses they had suffered. There were other observers in the hearing room that year and everyone was affected the same way; or almost everyone as Rallo remained stoic.

I've often been asked whether the Victim Impact Statements delivered at hearings have a bearing on the Board's decisions. The reality is that the information contained in those statements is not new, but when you can easily feel the impact, it changes the nature of the hearing. But it is the information itself, as it relates to the potential harm that might occur if the inmate is released, that is the factor the Board should consider. As noted, parole hearings are conducted in an inquisitorial manner. That is, the Board asks questions that the inmate answers. Although an inmate may have an assistant, often a lawyer, that individual cannot answer for the inmate, nor should they provide prompts prior to the inmate's answering the question. A hearing should be seen as an opportunity to elicit information that may help to clarify file information, aid the Board in understanding what level of insight or understanding the inmate has regarding their crime cycle and help the Board to assess the level and type of risk that the offender may pose if released. A good, useful hearing should sound more like a conversation, rather than a cross-examination that one might observe in a courtroom, or a police interrogation. But that also means that the Board members know the details contained in file information without having to ask questions that are already clarified in the file. This also allows members to confront inmates when the information they are providing is contradicted in file information.

I recall a hearing that involved a very high-profile case, one with about a hundred and twenty observers, including victims, media and supporters of the inmate. In response to a question that I asked, the inmate responded in a way that seemed deceitful to me and I wanted to confront him, But I could not immediately recall the location in file information that would confirm my observation. I asked my two colleagues to go through the file while I continued to ask questions. Then I recalled the issue and reminded him why his initial answer could not have been accurate. His reply was that he misunderstood the question, even though it was quite straight-forward.

Lessons Learned

When I think of the hearings that I conducted, a handful of thoughts reoccur. The first is the importance of developing a rapport or a connection to the inmate. I always tried to be attentive to their moods or emotions and to demonstrate that I was listening carefully to what they were saying. After all, I wanted them to explain the 'why' something had occurred, rather than the 'what'. To me, that meant that I sometimes had to help them understand and verbalize their thought process from an event or series of events. I believed that being able to engage them in a non-confrontational way would aid in that process.

Another factor that I often think of is that conducting a hearing must be similar to staging a play. Before anyone enters the empty hearing room, it is quiet. Board members are reviewing notes and mentally preparing their lines of inquiry. When the members are ready, they advise the Hearing Officer, who opens the door and lets the other participants into the room. Things then get quiet after a few minutes as people settle into their seats. But nothing really happens until the lead member directs that the hearing is ready to get started. Finally, I was always mindful when there were observers, whether they were victims or family (or friends) of the inmate we were seeing, to try to make certain that they would understand what the purpose of the hearing was, and the factors the Board would be focusing on. In doing so I tried to be respectful of everyone who had made the effort of attending, and to be as sure as I could be that they would understand the process. I don't know that I was always successful in those efforts but I know that I tried hard to be as open and transparent as I could be about the process, so that everyone involved would believe that they had been heard. I think it would be true to say that most (if not all) Board members are acutely aware of the impact of their decisions. I was constantly aware that the inmates that I was seeing had committed serious crimes, and that they were capable of doing so again. My job was to release individuals whose risk for re-offending was relatively low; individuals I believed were likely to conform with the conditions of their releases, as well as the rules and strictures imposed by their supervising parole officers.

Even after all the years that I spent in the criminal justice system in Canada, I still firmly believe that parole is an effective way of reintegrating individuals back into their communities.

EPILOGUE

Although the stories set out here may appear as criticisms of Canada's criminal and correctional systems, they are really a plea to the reader to become more involved in the process. We follow news coverage of horrendous crimes but it is far more important that we focus not solely on the "what" has happened but on the "why" things transpired as they did. It is important for the understanding of our criminal justice system that we know what went on before the newspaper headline was written and what goes on after the media move on to other sensational stories.

When psychiatric hospitals were being dismantled in the 1960s through to the 1980s, there was the promise that comprehensive community care could be an acceptable alternative. Unfortunately, we have not demanded that the supports needed have been provided. Our penitentiaries have become the dumping ground for people that might have been given humane treatment in the past.

There is a current movement to deal with drug crises by providing safe injection sites. That is all well and good if we are to do the important job of determining why people have become addicted to substances and we are willing to provide the supports necessary to deal with the underlying factors that caused their addiction.

We have a tendency to ignore an individual's problem until that person gets caught up in the criminal justice system. What if we were to devote some of the resources we spent in criminal apprehension and incarceration on supports for troubled youth before they got caught up in an underworld from which it is impossible to escape. We say that in jailing an offender, that person is paying a debt to society. All too often that debt bears an enormous interest rate that means it can never be repaid. We still think of prisons as place to punish rather than place to rehabilitate.

Crime is more than a singular infraction. It is the result of many factors that led to the infraction. If we are to address crime and root out its causes, we must look to the criminal and see the "why" and not just the "what" behind the action. We need to know the rest of the story.

ACKNOWLEDGEMENTS

The writer gratefully acknowledges the support and encouragement received from my friends and colleagues: Kris Babcock, the Vancouver-based Ashley Meier, his brother Shane Meier, and Evan Pitt-Payne. Their extensive experience in the film industry has caused me to reflect on the importance of story-telling.

Fellow authors, Greg Barnsdale, Patrick Tomey, and Barry Siskind have also kept up my drive to understand the publishing industry during our monthly Authors Zoom meetings. Their supportive emails are not only kind but helpful.

I am also appreciative of the support and guidance of Michael Occhionero and the editors at AOS Publishing in Montreal. Their comments and corrections have been invaluable.

I was absolutely delighted that Justin Ling read my manuscript and volunteered to write a Foreword. Justin Ling has made major contributions in explaining the criminal and corrections systems in his many newspaper and magazine articles and in his prize-winning book, *Missing from the Village*. It is indeed an honour to have his name appearing on the cover of this book.

The contributions to this book from Michael Crowley and David Dorson deserve to be noted. Michael is well-respected and was a long-serving Parole Board member. David was a former inmate. Even though on seemingly opposite sides, they share insight into our criminal and correctional systems that the public needs to know.

I am tremendously appreciative of my former clients, many of whom have their stories told here. My hope in recounting their stories is that the public will see them as human beings and not just criminal statistics. Kurt Suss, a former Correctional Service of Canada officer and expert dog-handler has been an invaluable resource in correcting any misperceptions I may have had on CSC policies and procedures.

Thanks also to Peter Carter, the Analysis Editor at Law 360 Canada. He has always stood behind me even when the subject matter of my published columns tended to be on the controversial side.

I extend my great admiration to Jeffrey Hartman, an Ontario lawyer who has taken up the cause of prisoner rights. Jeff is just one of a handful of lawyers from across Canada who continues to fight to ensure that justice is not overlooked after a conviction has been entered. To my friends, Jeff, his wife Katie and their dog, Bruno, thank you for doing what you do.

Most of all, my heartfelt thanks to my wife, Roxann and our English cocker spaniel, Hedy who have given me the time and encouragement to take up writing after retiring from my legal career. Even so, I am still required to load the dish washer and go for walks outside.